REPRESENTATIVE
PERFORMANCE OBJECTIVES
FOR HIGH SCHOOL ENGLISH

A GUIDE FOR TEACHING, EVALUATING, AND CURRICULUM PLANNING

THE TRI-UNIVERSITY PROJECT
ON BEHAVIORAL OBJECTIVES IN ENGLISH,
under the direction of:

J. N. HOOK, *University of Illinois at Urbana*
PAUL H. JACOBS, *University of Illinois at Urbana*
EDWARD B. JENKINSON, *Indiana University*
ARNOLD LAZARUS, *Purdue University*
THOMAS PIETRAS, *Purdue University*
DONALD A. SEYBOLD, *Indiana University*
ADRIAN P. VAN MONDFRANS, *Purdue University*

THE RONALD PRESS COMPANY • NEW YORK

Preface

This book of representative performance objectives for secondary school English is intended for use by high school teachers in planning units and lessons, for consideration by departments that are revising or rewriting an existing curriculum, and for discussion by pre-service teachers in college methods classes and by groups of in-service teachers.

In early 1969 the Research Branch of the United States Office of Education sent out requests for proposals for the preparation of a catalog of behavioral objectives for English in grades 9–12, specifying that the objectives should "serve as guides for the selection of curriculum content and as criteria for appraisal of students' progress." These objectives "should represent *desirable* attainments of high school students of a wide range of backgrounds, interests, and abilities."

Representatives of the University of Illinois, Indiana University, and Purdue University submitted a joint proposal, which was accepted by the United States Office of Education. The proposal was for a two-year project, with the first year devoted to the drafting of the catalog with the aid of a number of consultants from high schools and colleges, and the second year devoted to field-testing and rewriting.

We as co-directors shared equally in the development of this book, and are solely responsible for its content. We wish to thank sincerely the consultants listed in the Acknowledgments, but want to emphasize that the consultants were by no means uniform in their recommendations and that not all of them would endorse every objective and every statement in this book.

We also wish to thank the English teachers and administrators in twenty-three of the twenty-four field-testing schools. (The twenty-fourth took part only at the beginning.) Eight of these schools at the time of selection were participating in the experimental ES '70 program of the United States Office of Education, eight others were from the same general areas as the first eight, and the remainder were schools in Indiana and Illinois with which we hoped to keep in close contact. Teachers and students in these schools tested in their classes large numbers of the objectives presented in a preliminary catalog, reacted to them, and arranged for us to visit classes and meet with students, teachers, and administrators for discussion of the catalog content. Substantial revisions were effected in all sections of the catalog as a result of this field-testing, and we are grateful for the splendid assistance provided by the English teachers in these schools, as well as the liaison persons and principals named in the Acknowledgments.

J. N. HOOK
PAUL H. JACOBS
EDWARD B. JENKINSON
ARNOLD LAZARUS
THOMAS PIETRAS
DONALD A. SAYBOLD
ADRIAN P. VAN MONDFRANS

Urbana, Illinois
Bloomington, Indiana
Lafayette, Indiana
May, 1972

Acknowledgments

We wish to thank the following consultants, liaison persons, and principals for their generous assistance and counsel in helping to develop this project:

Senior consultant for the project was DAVID KRATHWOHL of Syracuse University, chief author of *Taxonomy of Educational Objectives, Handbook II: Affective Domain*.

ROBERT MAGER of Palo Alto, author of *Preparing Instructional Objectives* and *Developing Attitudes for Learning*, gave a critical reading to an early draft of the handbook.

Consultants:

J. JEFFERY AUER, Indiana University; JOAN D. BERBERICH, Mineola High School, Garden City Park, New York; OSCAR BOUISE, Xavier University of Louisiana; CHARLOTTE K. BROOKS, Supervisor of English, Washington, D.C.; FRANCIS CHRISTENSEN (deceased), Northern Illinois University; STEPHEN DUNNING, University of Michigan; MARGARET J. EARLY, Syracuse University; MARJORIE FARMER, Board of Education, Philadelphia, Pennsylvania; JEANNE FAY, Quincy Public Schools, Quincy, Massachusetts; JAMES GAITHER, Crispus Attuck High School, Indianapolis, Indiana; RICHARD GRAY, Indiana University; THE REVEREND ASHLEY HARRINGTON, Mt. Carmel High School, Chicago, Illinois; J. THOMAS HASTINGS, University of Illinois at Urbana; ARTHUR S. HEALEY, Broward County Public Schools, Fort Lauderdale, Florida; HARWOOD HESS, Purdue University; WARREN HUBBARD, School No. 570, Baltimore, Maryland; BARNET KOTTLER, Purdue University; ROBERT S. LAWSON, Breathitt County Board of Education, Jackson, Kentucky; ANDREW MACLEISH, University of Minnesota; ELINOR McLENDON, John Adams High School, Portland,

v

Oregon; JAMES POPOVICH, University of South Florida; ALAN PURVES, University of Illinois; KENNETH SMITH, The Nova Schools, Fort Lauderdale, Florida; ANTHONY TOVATT, Ball State University; PRISCILLA TYLER, University of Missouri at Kansas City; F. D. WESLEY, Booker T. Washington Junior-Senior High School, Houston, Texas.

Liaison Persons and Principals:

FLORIDA:
Nova High School, Fort Lauderdale, Florida. *Liaison Person:* EDDIE PEARL DEGRAFFENREIDT. *Principal:* HILTON C. LEWIS.
Plantation High School, Plantation, Florida. *Liaison Person:* PATRICIA BRADLEY. *Principal:* WILLIAM HANES.

ILLINOIS:
Edison Junior High School, Champaign, Illinois. *Liaison Person:* ELIZABETH HAMILTON. *Principal:* ODELL MOSELEY.
Champaign Central High School, Champaign, Illinois. *Liaison Person:* MARION STUART. *Principal:* BERNARD FLEENER.
Urbana Junior High School, Urbana, Illinois. *Liaison Person:* JANICE BENGTSON. *Principal:* ROGER MARCUM.
Urbana High School, Urbana, Illinois. *Liaison Person:* CAROL LeSEURE. *Principal:* WILLIAM FROMM.
Mt. Carmel High School, Chicago, Illinois. *Liaison Person:* REVEREND ASHLEY HARRINGTON. *Principal:* REVEREND DANIEL McFADDEN, O. CARM.

INDIANA:
West Lafayette High School, West Lafayette, Indiana. *Liaison Person:* BERNARR FOLTA. *Principal:* ERIC CASSON.
West Side High School, Gary, Indiana. *Liaison Person:* SHIRLEY SPEILMAN. *Principal:* QUENTIN P. SMITH.
Benjamin Bosse High School, Evansville, Indiana. *Liaison Person:* EDMUND SULLIVAN. *Principal:* PAUL JENNINGS.
North Central High School, Indianapolis, Indiana. *Liaison Persons:* THOMAS TAYLOR, RUTH BERTSCH. *Principal:* EUGENE CLOUCS.
Lebanon Junior High School, Lebanon, Indiana. *Liaison Person:* MARY BROWN. *Principal:* WILLIAM D. HAMILTON.

KENTUCKY:
Breathitt County High School, Jackson, Kentucky. *Liaison Person:* RUTH SPICER. *Principal:* MILLARD TOLLIVER.

MARYLAND:

Dunbar Senior High School, Baltimore, Maryland. *Liaison Persons:* WARREN HUBBARD, RITA JONES. *Principal:* CLARENCE BLOUNT.

Southern High School, Baltimore, Maryland. *Liaison Person:* JAMES LAMAR. *Principal:* OSCAR HELM.

NEW YORK:

Mineola High School, Garden City Park, New York. *Liaison Person:* ANTHONY VALERI. *Principal:* JOHN L. SULLIVAN.

Northport Senior High School, Northport, New York. *Liaison Person:* MICHAEL GLENNON. *Principal:* DAVID ALLARDICE.

OREGON:

John Adams High School, Portland, Oregon. *Liaison Person:* MARJORIE E. GEORGE. *Principal:* ROBERT SCHWARTZ.

Jackson High School, Portland, Oregon. *Liaison Person:* MICHAEL KELLY. *Principal:* ROY CARLSON.

PENNSYLVANIA:

West Philadelphia High School, Philadelphia, Pennsylvania. *Liaison Person:* PHILIP DEHNICK. *Principal:* WALTER SCHOTT.

John Bartram High School, Philadelphia, Pennsylvania. *Liaison Person:* RICHARD CACCHIONE. *Principal:* LOUIS D'ANTONIO.

TEXAS:

Booker T. Washington Junior-Senior High School, Houston, Texas. *Liaison Person:* ROBERTA DEASON. *Principal:* F. D. WESLEY.

M. C. William Junior-Senior High School, Houston, Texas. *Liaison Person:* BETTY JOHNSON. *Principal:* EMERSON NORRIS.

Contents

REPRESENTATIVE PERFORMANCE OBJECTIVES FOR HIGH SCHOOL ENGLISH

1

Caution:
Read Before Using

An old tale tells of various kinds of birds that went to the magpie for a lesson in nest-building. Some birds observed that the magpie used twigs; they flew away, and to this day their descendants use twigs. Others noticed the grass, so now their descendants build their nests of grass. Still other birds took note of the mud or the rootlets or the shape or the method of anchoring; their descendants' nests are today made with those characteristics. But none of the birds observed and made use of all that the magpie did in constructing his nest. As a result, magpies alone still build remarkably sturdy nests.

The ornithology in this tale may be shaky, but the principle nevertheless holds that superior work of almost any sort depends upon an understanding of all the steps involved and at least some awareness of underlying theory.

To use this book most intelligently, a teacher should read this chapter carefully, in order to be aware of the principles involved in the creation and use of performance objectives in English. It is *possible* to dip into any of the following chapters and find something that can be used in a lesson or a unit. But our experience with the twenty-four schools that field-tested the preliminary edition of this handbook showed clearly that teachers who were not aware of the basic theory and the varied array of potential uses (as well as mis-

This project director in charge of this section, J. N. Hook, Professor of English, University of Illinois, was assisted by several consultants and all the other directors.

3

uses) of performance objectives were considerably less successful than others.

Therefore, the title of this chapter: PLEASE READ THIS CHAPTER CAREFULLY BEFORE USING ANY OF THE OBJECTIVES IN THE OTHER CHAPTERS.

PERFORMANCE OBJECTIVES: WHAT AND WHY

The Need for Specific Destinations

When we are traveling, if we know our precise destination we will probably be able to find a way to get there. When we are teaching, if we know our precise objective we will probably be able to find a way to reach it.

But too often in teaching we are vague about objectives. We know in English that we would like our students to improve their reading, for instance, and to learn to appreciate literature, and to become more proficient in communicating orally and in writing. Such objectives, though, are big, indefinite blobs; they are not precise destinations. They are like saying "The destination is Europe" rather than "Stockholm" or "London" or "Rome" or "Vienna." With such an unspecific destination our students often flutter uncertainly onward, with aimless butterfly dashes to the right or left or even backward, and many of them, their energies spent, sink quietly into the waves.

The Antiquity of Performance Objectives

Ever since man existed, though, good teachers—with or without the title of teacher—have had in mind specific objectives for their teaching. It is doubtful that cavemen thought in terms of teaching children the appreciation of fire. Rather, they must have thought of enabling the children to *do* things with fire: select wood, start the fire, keep it burning, and use it to frighten away animals and (later) to cook food. Long afterward, Socrates did not attempt to teach the Greek slave "to understand mathematical principles"; rather, he drew upon the slave's observation and common sense as the slave learned inductively to solve a specific mathematical problem.

In other words, performance objectives are not twentieth-century inventions. They are extensively used, however, by effective modern teachers who have never heard of them or their alternative name, behavioral objectives. Whenever a teacher and his class think in terms of what specific things the students should be able to *do* as a result of learning activities, they are thinking in terms of performance objectives. Thus, the first-grade teacher who wants his pupils to distinguish *pop* from *mop* is using a performance objective, which fits into a larger performance objective concerning distinctions among shapes and sounds of letters. So is the high school English teacher using performance objectives when he wants his students to distinguish figurative from non-figurative language in a short story, to point out similarities between Macbeth and Hitler, or to speak or write persuasively on behalf of a candidate in a forthcoming school election.

Why Call Them "Performance Objectives"?

The term "behavioral objective" is more widely used than "performance objective." It is based upon the assumption that all education is intended to effect changes in the learner's behavior—that the learner will in some way act differently or be capable of acting differently as a result of the instruction. We prefer the term "performance objective," however, for three reasons:

1. In many people's minds "behavior" has the limited meaning of "behaving"—of "being good," of "not misbehaving."
2. "Behavioral" is associated in many minds with behaviorist psychology, with a primitive stimulus–response bond, with pigeons learning to peck in a certain place in order to get their reward. B. F. Skinner's stimulus–response–reinforcement model is far too narrow and mechanical for what we are attempting.
3. "Performance" has the for-us desirable connotation of *doing*. We are interested in establishing objectives that will stress what the student should be able to perform, to do, as a result of instruction.

Characteristics of Performance Objectives

Performance objectives, then, as the authors of this handbook define them, are statements about desirable outcomes of educational interaction and are phrased in terms of what learners should be able to do as a result of the interaction. The components of the interaction may be three: the learner, the materials (broadly defined), and the teacher (the term *teacher* may include classmates and anyone else from whom the student may learn); in some instances only the learner and the materials may be involved.

Performance objectives are always expressed in terms of the learner, or student: the student will do thus and so. They are not expressed in terms of what the teacher will do, and ordinarily not in terms of what explicit content coverage is expected. The important thing in education is what happens to the student as a result of his interaction with the materials and with the "teacher"; what can the student do that he could not do before or could do less well?

Since performance objectives stress doing, the choice of verb in each statement is important. The verb is transitive and active, and is semantically on a low level of generalization. Verbs like *appreciate* and *understand* are too general, too abstract. The acts of appreciation and comprehension cannot themselves be seen or heard, even though their reflections or shadows sometimes can: chuckling, reading absorbedly, sharing a story or poem with others, explaining a concept to someone else, etc. Performance objectives often use verbs that are descriptive as indicators of something larger: *describe, identify, compare, make* (e.g., a collage), *give examples of, write, explain, pantomime, list*, and many more that are illustrated throughout this handbook-catalog.

A performance objective must, however, be placed within a context. The context is partly that of the student's level of maturity, ability, and past experience. Distinguishing between *pop* and *mop* is obviously an elementary skill suitable for young children with little experience in reading. Distinguishing between figurative language ("The fog comes/ on little cat feet") and non-figurative language ("The fog appears without being noticed at first") is a more sophisticated skill. It is wasteful and frustrating to work toward performance objectives that are either too elementary or too advanced for a given student or class.

Another part of the context is the broad goal of which the performance objective represents but one part. Some educational goals are very broad indeed: learning to get along with others, learning to be a good citizen, learning to practice good health habits, learning to communicate, etc. Call them Level 1. From these very broad Level 1 goals the teachers in specific subject matters extract those to which their subjects have something to offer: the *general goals* of English, mathematics, music, history, and the like. These are Level 2. When Level 2 objectives are stated in terms of students' actions, we have Level 3, which are *performance objectives*. Often a Level 3 objective can be further divided—for example, in English, to very specific objectives in the study of a certain piece of literature or in the practice of a particular non-verbal, oral, or writing activity. These Level 4 objectives are called *representative enabling objectives* in this handbook.

A final characteristic of performance objectives is that criteria for some kind of measurement and evaluation are implicit in the objectives themselves. For example, in the language section of this book, in the context of history of the language, this objective appears: "The student lists a number of English nouns that have plurals other than the customary *s* or *es* and explains why these differences exist." That objective, like hundreds of others that could be cited, has evaluation built in. The student either formulates his list with *teeth, men, criteria, cherubim,* etc., or he does not. He either explains why such plurals exist or he does not. His list and his explanation are either accurate or they are not. He has been given a clear objective at which to aim, and both he and his teacher will know whether or not he has reached it.

Summary

As was implied at the beginning of this section, performance objectives clarify the destination of a class and of individual students. Through their emphasis upon what specific things students are to do, they enable a class to move with greater sureness toward each destination. When properly geared to students' maturity, ability, and past experiences, and when selected with regard to worthy larger goals, they offer a chance to accelerate students' progress and to measure that progress step by step.

THE DANGERS IN PERFORMANCE OBJECTIVES

Performance Objectives Can Be Used or Abused

The past several years have witnessed tremendous amounts of discussion of behavioral objectives. A national objectives exchange has been established in California. Almost every issue of every educational journal has featured or at least mentioned behavioral objectives. They have been the topic of endless explication and argument at educational conventions and in college courses in Education. Statements of objectives in performance terms are required in some states and in many school districts. Behavioral objectives have been tied in—often in an unwise fashion, we believe—with demands for greater educational accountability.

Like almost any other educational concept or tool, performance objectives can be both used and abused. Their use can help children learn; their abuse can be harmful to children. Some performance objectives are good; some are poor. Some represent educationally worthwhile goals; some represent trivia. We shall take a quick look at a few genuine dangers, keeping in mind that no less serious dangers may reside in other types of objectives and even graver dangers in no objectives at all.

The Danger of Trivialization

If teachers lose sight of their larger goals, they may state their objectives in trivial terms. Similarly, if they think only in terms of what learnings are easily measurable, the objectives may be trivial. For example, if the objective is "The student identifies similes," the student may learn to pounce upon sentences containing *like* or *as* and, in a test, to pick out successfully all the similes in a poem. But that is an essentially empty, mechanical exercise. It leaves out of consideration such questions as why people use comparisons or other figurative language, what types of communication figurative language makes possible, and what the esthetic values of imaginative comparisons may be.

Note, though, that the fault lies not in performance objectives but in the narrowness and triviality of this particular one. In the chapter on Reading and Literature in this handbook, a number of the objectives are related to figurative language, but can hardly be called trivial. Here is one example: "In any literary work the student shows (orally or in writing) the relationship(s) between the metaphor(s) and the main idea(s) of the work as a whole."

In the past, much of what went on in English classes was indeed trivial, focusing far too often on memorizing authors' dates, conjugating verbs, diagraming sentences, filling blanks, and telling what happened next. It is small wonder that countless students have considered English largely a waste of time. Their English classes did little to help them to communicate better or to learn about the human condition. Performance objectives are subject to the same perils. With them, too, teachers can stress the petty, can fail to see the meaningful. A mere rephrasing of old objectives cannot make those objectives valid.

But rephrasing in performance terms nevertheless may be useful, because it sometimes may point to the need for substantive change or even the need for deletion. Expressed in terms of what the student is expected to do, an objective may be revealed to be of little worth. To return to our earlier example, if the teacher writes "The student identifies similes" and then asks himself why he thinks the student should do so, his pondering may cause him to substitute something more significant. "Why," he wonders, "should the student learn to pick out similes? Will doing so really contribute to literary appreciation? Will it make him a better man? Can he serve mankind better because he passes a test on picking out similes? Is there, perhaps, something more valuable to do with figurative comparisons than just to identify them?"

The Danger of Overemphasizing Measurement

Early writers on behavioral objectives put much stress on their usefulness in measurement or evaluation, and as has already been said, objectives phrased in terms of performance can indeed be of value in measuring student attainment. But some of these writers appeared to be saying that measurement rather than child development is what is most important in education. Their examples tended to consist of objectives very easy to measure mathematically: "The student solves 9 out of 10 quadratic equations correctly," "The student spells correctly 23 words in a list of 25," and so on. Teachers who followed the lead of these writers tended to choose as objectives those elements that were relatively easy to measure. In doing so, they often omitted some of the most important learnings, because they could not devise any numerical system of measurement for them. The response to a piece of literature may be a gleam in a student's eye, a quickening of his pulse. How can you measure a gleam? Can you ask a student to report on his heartbeat or his respiration?

Today's English teachers are a little more sophisticated, in a way, than were the early writers on behavioral objectives. They regard as specious the argument "If you can't measure it, how do you know it's there?" (Man could see the stars long before he could measure their diameters.) They say that exact measurements often are not possible, especially in the affective domain, which necessarily occupies a large share of the attention in English and the arts. But even though one cannot count or use a micrometer or a yardstick or an odometer to register students' gains in literary response, for instance, indirect measurements are possible. Alan C. Purves, in the NCTE's *On Writing Behavioral Objectives* (1970) likens the process to measurement of shadows to determine the height of a flagpole and the shape of the ornament at the top. The measurement of shadows can tell teachers what they most need to know about a child's development in the affective domain.

The point, though, is that the importance of measurement should not be exaggerated, regardless of the type of objective used. A measurement is only a symbol of an accomplishment. What is vital is the accomplishment itself. Through their emphasis upon what students do, performance objectives inevitably stress accomplishment. When the accomplishment is observable, as it usually but not always is, measurement is relatively simple, although not always mathematically precise.

The Danger of No Time for Fishing

Robert F. Hogan, in "On Hunting and Fishing and Behaviorism," a beautiful and sentimental article in the March, 1970, *Media & Methods,* expressed worry that the current emphasis on behavioral objectives may result in the loss of something very important in English and in life. We need time, Hogan says, for fishing—not so much to catch fish as to enjoy "the good sea air, some sunshine, and a few other fishermen." In English class we shouldn't always be stalking a quarry; we should have fun with literature, should enjoy serendipity, and should allow for the possibility that today Jennie just doesn't want to write a five-sentence outline because Jennie yesterday discovered "Annabel Lee" and "would really prefer to write poems about star-crossed lovers."

Hogan's caution is appropriate. Certainly an inexorable march from objective to objective to final destination can be tiring and dull. Certainly everyone, even a student, needs time for fishing. And certainly not everyone need be doing the same thing at the same time: Jennie should have a chance to write her dreamy poems about star-crossed lovers. There should be plenty of opportunity, too, for the excited discussion that spills over into the next day, for the individual project of the boy who becomes fascinated by Ray Bradbury or Ernest Hemingway, or for occasionally following a tangent that leads no one knows where.

Not everything in life can be planned. Not everything in school should be. But much ought to be. Even English teachers like James Moffett and Geoffrey Summerfield, who have written and spoken extensively in favor of free-wheeling classes with much individual student initiative and few teacher-made-plans—even such teachers have objectives in mind, descriptions of the kinds of things they hope that students will be able to feel and do before they leave the schoolhouse forever.

The Danger of Too Strict Tie-ins with Accountability

The word "accountability" recurs frequently in modern educational discussions. Worried by the constantly increasing costs of education, taxpayers and public officials ask whether they are getting their money's worth from the schools. Schools, they claim, should be accountable for their products. Teachers who don't get results should be fired.

To determine whether schools and teachers are successful or not, the argument runs, one needs to know what the objectives are and the extent to which those objectives have been reached. When accomplishments appear meager, someone should be held accountable and told to shape up or ship out.

It is hard to argue on the other side—against the concept of accountability. No one likes to be considered unaccountable for his actions. Everyone hopes to get a high-quality product or service at his grocery store, hardware store, theater, doctor's office, city hall, or school, and he would like to be able to hold someone accountable when he does not.

The danger in education, though, is that a rigid scale of accountability is impossible to apply fairly. Teachers in an area of poor homes and illiterate parents cannot be expected to bring all their students to the usual levels of those from physically and intellectually well-nourished suburbs. Teachers of below-average students cannot bring those students to as high a degree of accomplishment as teachers of superior students can bring theirs. Teachers in a poorly equipped school with an inadequate library may accomplish less than teachers in other schools. Teachers in schools with very large English classes cannot engage their classes in many worthwhile learning activities possible in schools with relatively small classes. Teachers badly prepared by their colleges will probably do less well than adequately prepared teachers. Who then should be held accountable—the teachers or the institutions that prepared them? Potential abuses and misapplications of the concept of accountability are numerous.

If the current emphasis on accountability continues, as it probably will at least for financial reasons, teachers will need to clarify for the administration and for the public what it is that they are trying to accomplish, show that those goals are worthwhile, and demonstrate the degree to which they are succeeding, given the limitations imposed upon them. Well-conceived and clearly stated performance objectives can assist in such clarification and demonstration. Most parents want to understand what the schools are attempting to do, but are sometimes baffled by the vague objectives that they find in many current descriptions. When, however, a teacher can explain clearly and specifically what he is attempting, he can go far to answer criticism, assuming that the goals and objectives he has selected have genuine social value.

The Danger of Unwise Administrative Pressures

In at least one state in 1969, the state department of public instruction issued an ultimatum that by 1970 all objectives for every course offered by any public school in the state would have to be stated in behavioral terms. The officials brandished a powerful club: Schools that failed to comply might lose their state aid. Although the ultimatum was later modified, teachers were understandably in an uproar. Many of them did not clearly understand what behavioral objectives are; some thought that complete curriculum revision was called for; some realized that translation of objectives into behavioral terms requires time and thought; nearly all were offended by the high-handed, dictatorial stance of the state department.

Such unconscionable tactics, whether on the state or the local level, can only be condemned. The authors of this handbook believe that the use of performance objectives can enrich learning experiences and can result in higher levels of student attainment than are presently reached. But we believe that the preparation of such objectives must not be hasty, for hastily prepared objectives are likely to be trivial, will fail to consider adequately the depth and breadth of the subject, and will short-change students by failure to explore sufficiently what worthy present objectives should be retained in a rephrased form, which ones should be modified, and which should be deleted. We believe that teachers need information about what performance objectives are, what their merits are, what their dangers are, how they can be written, how they can be used, and how student accomplishment can be measured through their use. Above all, we believe that teachers and departments should enter upon the construction of performance objectives because they believe in them, not because they are forced to write them by a command from a higher authority.

Summary

Performance objectives, like other ends and means in teaching, can be abused as well as used. Among possible abuses of performance objectives in English are the choice of trivial objectives, failure to relate objectives to larger goals, over-insistence upon mathematical measurement, failure to allow for individual exploration, poorly thought-out use of the objectives in attempts to determine accountability, and administrative pressures to convert schools and teachers too hurriedly to a complete translation of objectives into behavioral terms. All of these dangers, or comparable ones, however, exist no less in conventional objectives than in performance objectives.

HOW TO USE THIS HANDBOOK

The Purpose of the Handbook

This is a book listing *representative* performance objectives in English for the secondary schools. The word *representative* is important. The book does not include *all* objectives for English; if the authors and their consultants were close enough to omniscience that they could include all possible objectives (and they assuredly are not), such a listing would have to be printed in many volumes, for the number of defensible objectives could rise into the thousands.

As a catalog of representative objectives, this book is intended first of all to inform English teachers about what performance objectives are, and about typical shapes that they may take. Thus it may serve as a sourcebook for teachers and departments who embark on the task of revising their present objectives and translating them into terms of performance.

The book is not intended for use by students. Not only is its terminology too esoteric for most students, but also only a person with the teacher's broad view of the subject can understand the relationship of individual parts to the whole. However, the objectives that a teacher has selected or created can and should be made known to the students so that they too can have a sense of destination. Much of students' unhappiness with school is rooted in their unawareness of where a unit or a lesson is taking them, and why.

Despite what has just been said, teachers in some of the field-testing schools did put sections of the catalog into the hands of students. Less able students could make little sense of these sections without help. Highly able students, however, found ideas for individual or group projects and sometimes modified objectives or formulated new ones for themselves.

Secondly, the authors hope that this handbook will suggest, to many teachers, ways to obtain greater student involvement in classroom activities. Such involvement is intrinsic in performance objectives, simply because they stress what students should do. However, the numerous representative enabling objectives scattered through the catalog provide many specific suggestions for engagement of individual students and the entire class. Many of these objectives suggest the possibility of individual and group projects, tailored to the needs and interests of particular students. Not every student in a class has to be working toward exactly the same objectives at the same time, nor is it necessary that all students follow the same path to an objective. There is usually more than a single way to reach any destination. If the concept of the "open classroom" becomes widely accepted, destinations will not lose their importance, but increased freedom in choice of routes will be inevitable. This handbook gives many examples of routes with different scenery, different obstacles, different but related and perhaps equally valuable rewards.

Thirdly, the handbook is intended to call to teachers' attention some facets that seem desirable in a secondary school English program but are often omitted. The sections on Non-verbal Communication and on the Mass Media are the outstanding examples here. (These sections were, incidentally, very popular in the twenty-four schools that field-tested the preliminary version of the catalog.) Among other somewhat innovative facets are the parts of the Language section dealing with history of the language, dialect, words and dictionaries, and syntax. Still other innovations may be found in the sections on Speaking and Listening, Reading and Literature, and Writing, in which often the innovative features are less in content than in purpose and point of view. Wherever innovations occur, they are included not for the sake of novelty but because the authors and consultants sincerely believe that they represent facets of English that can greatly enrich students' experiences within the classroom and in their later lives.

The authors want to emphasize, though, that much in this handbook will not seem new to experienced teachers. "I've been using that objective for years," a number of the field-testing teachers reported, sometimes in a surprised or aggrieved tone. "Fine!" we replied. "We anticipated that the book would reflect much that effective teachers already do. True, we have attempted to go beyond what the majority of teachers do, but we did not set out to create a set of objectives all or most of which would be so new and frighteningly strange that teachers would not use them. Our function is to support and strengthen, not to disrupt."

Fourthly, when a department is engaged in curriculum revision—which in some schools is only occasional but in others is almost constant—the handbook may serve as a resource book. It may suggest types of content that are sometimes overlooked, and it may also suggest for consideration curricular emphases and ways of approaching a portion of the subject. It can be a catalyst in curricular change, but it does not pretend to be a curriculum.

Finally, the handbook may have value because of its many hints concerning methods of evaluation. This does not necessarily mean formal tests. Students' oral reactions, changes in their attitudes toward reading or writing, changes in their responses to literature, evidence of their growth in understanding of non-verbal communication and the resources of the language and the strengths and limitations of the mass media—such things, and not just formal examinations, are revelatory not only of the students' own growth but also of the success of the curriculum and the methods and materials employed by the teachers. Sometimes the most revealing answers come from asking one simple question: "What have you learned in this unit (or this week, etc.)?"

Grade Levels

The original grade-level designation of this handbook was Grades 9 through 12. In the field-testing, though, it was found that many of the simpler objectives were quite suitable for many classes in Grades 7 and 8.

Elementary material, however, such as objectives for basic reading skills, are not included, even though some secondary school students still need such basic work. To have included such elementary objectives would have necessitated more consultants, more time, and a larger and more expensive field-testing program, and would have resulted in a much larger and less manageable catalog.

The catalog does contain, however, objectives for various levels of ability, amounts of experience, and types of background. Teachers will find that some objectives are too simple for some of their students, too advanced for others, just right for still others. Frequently it may prove desirable to modify an objective to make it more suitable for a given class.

No grade-level labels are given, largely because of the likelihood of abuse. For example, a teacher of seniors might choose only "twelfth-grade" objectives for his students, even though his class might not be ready for objectives with that label; only frustration could result.

Similarly, there are no labels like "For slow students." Categories like "slow" cannot be adequately defined. However, as often as possible the objectives under each goal are arranged according to difficulty, and "entering objectives" are sometimes specified. Therefore, a teacher whose students are performing below average may choose the more readily attainable objectives, particularly those for which the students possess the requisite entering behaviors.

Sequence

The order of objectives within each chapter is that of a cookbook, in which meat dishes are together, salads together, and so on, but the recipes are not arranged in order of difficulty or in order of appeal to different tastes. In using a cookbook one does not start with the first recipe and then move on to the second, third, and fourth. Rather, one is selective, choosing from anywhere in the book the recipes that appear appealing and suitable to one's family, that taken together will provide a balanced menu, and for which the ingredients are available. Also, a cook frequently makes substitutions, using for example chicken instead of turkey or cinnamon instead of nutmeg.

Similarly, in using this book the teacher–cook should be selective (and at least on occasion should consult her "family" of students). It is ordinarily inadvisable to start with Goal 1, Performance Objective 1.A., and move straight ahead through a chapter. (Some exceptions may be apparent; e.g., in the chapter on Non-verbal Communication or possibly that on Writing.) And just as the cook makes substitutions, so should the user of this book; in the Reading and Literature chapter, for instance, many works (not just those mentioned as examples) may be studied with the same objective in mind.

Point of View

The authors of this handbook have avoided following any party line. The catalog, therefore, does not reflect either the rigidity of the early Robert Mager and the later James Popham or the almost complete planlessness apparently advocated by some participants in the Dartmouth Conference.

We have found that the cognitive and affective domains are not really separable in English, nor should they be. We applaud the work done by Bloom, Krathwohl, and their colleagues, and that work has been influential in our thinking, but repeatedly in our objectives we have found it best to combine the two domains, which are often inextricably related parts of a single whole, as Piaget realized: "Affective life, like intellectual life, is a continual adaptation, and the two are not only parallel but interdependent, since feelings express the interest and values given to actions of which intelligence provides the structure." [1]

[1] John H. Flavell, *The Developmental Psychology of Jean Piaget.* Princeton, N. J.: D. Van Nostrand Co., Inc., n.d., p. 80.

Three ingredients, however, are present in almost all recent thinking about objectives, about curriculum, and about learning of English, and these we have adopted:

1. English is a process, not a thing.
2. The process can usually best be learned inductively.
3. Learning must be centered on the student—on what the student does, not what the teacher does or what the content "means."

As an example of English as a process, consider writing. The act of writing does not consist of a set of skills and isolated bits of knowledge; it is not just an awareness of sentence patterns or a knowledge of rhetorical theory. Rather, it consists of things that a writer does. These things are not necessarily identical for every writer, and not every writer proceeds in exactly the same way. To learn the parts of the process, a student must perform the parts and practice putting them together. He must find out what steps work best for him. He must learn not just *about* writing, but how to *do* writing.

Learning a process can generally best be accomplished inductively, by active participation. In a botany class, a student will learn much more about a twig if he holds the twig in his hands, examines it carefully, describes what he sees, cuts the twig apart and again describes and draws conclusions about what he sees, smells the twig and perhaps tastes it, looks at parts of it under a microscope, observes twigs on trees, and once more draws conclusions; he will not learn nearly as much if the botany teacher holds the twig and names its characteristics.

Implied in what has just been said is that learning must be centered on the student. An educational psychologist has testified that he obtained poor results when he lectured to graduate students about how to prepare a proposal for educational research. Only when these students—graduate students, remember—actually tried their own hands at drafting a proposal did they really understand what was involved.

As a consequence of these three interrelated items of agreement in the profession, we have attempted to draw up objectives that will enable the student to learn the process that is English and to learn that process inductively; these objectives, always phrased in terms of "the student *does* something," are constantly focused upon the student. This focus is already present in the thinking of many teachers—probably of most good teachers. But for others it presents a revolutionary change: a change in their way of looking at their own roles, a change to regarding themselves as facilitators of learning rather than as dispensers of information, "the cynosure of all eyes," lecturers, presenters, the only critic in the room. The new role is not easier; it may be more difficult.

But we have never been very successful in *teaching* English. Through the change of focus that has just been described, maybe we can be more successful in *helping students to learn English*—in helping them *do* English.

A Suggested Description of the Learning Process[2]

A theoretical description of the learning process may help in clarifying what seems to happen within a human being as experiences are translated into behavior, even though psychologists cannot yet with assurance delineate the precise steps.

In the diagram on page 19, the large arrow at the lower left depicts input, which comes in the form of some sort of experience and necessarily involves one or more of the senses. The input may be something simple and quick like a flash of light or a sonic boom, or complex, like the reading of a novel.

The base line in this model represents the barrier that exists between the subconscious and the conscious. Until a stimulus penetrates this barrier, which is called the LEVEL OF AWARENESS, the conscious mind is not involved with the stimulus (e.g., a person may see leaves on a tree, or words on a page, without anything 'registering'). Once this barrier is breached and the mind becomes conscious of the stimulus, cognitive activity occurs during which the individual decides whether or not the stimulus is of interest. In the learning process, this represents a very critical period. If the individual decides that he is not interested in further exploration of the stimulus, he 'turns it off,' and his conscious mind turns to other, more interesting matters.[3]

Assuming that interest is generated (and in the classroom such generation may be the most important role of the teacher), a process of association and differentiation occurs. This process is the essence of thought. The stimulus is related to any other experiences the person has had and is differentiated from them. But such interrelationship is not necessarily only cognitive. Earlier-learned feelings (affective reactions) are often involved, as when a reader reacts emotionally to a word like *mother* or *Communist*. Or the interrelationship may be psychomotor, as when a boy reading about a basket-

---

[2] This section has been influenced by Albert F. Eiss and Mary Blatt Harbeck, *Behavioral Objectives in the Affective Domain,* Natural Science Supervisors Association, Washington, D. C., 1969, pp. 4–5. The diagram is modified from Albert F. Eiss, *Instructional Systems,* Experimental Edition, 1968, p. 15, as printed in the Eiss-Harbeck monograph.

[3] *Ibid.,* p. 5.

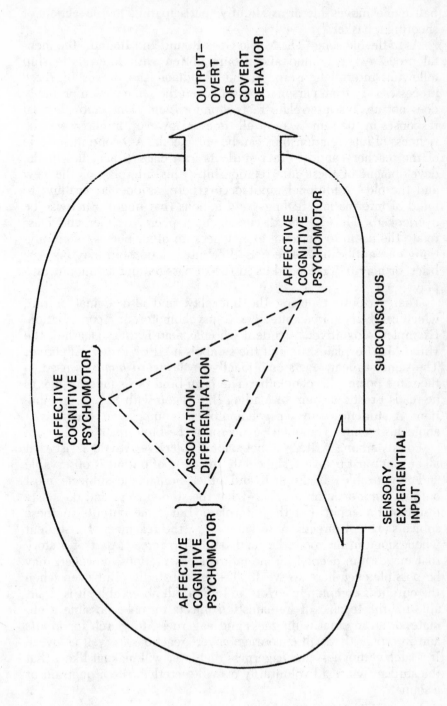

ball game moves his arms slightly, participating in the action of shooting a basket.

As in the old song "The Music Goes Round and Round," the mental processes go around and around, often with interrelationship following interrelationship. In all likelihood the details of these processes vary from person to person; even the same person probably does not always interrelate facts, opinions, emotions, and physical responses in the same way at all times. However, in classwork the richness of interrelationships can be enhanced. A second major role of the teacher (and of other students in a class), then, lies in the development of these interrelationships, this interplay of the new and the old. Additional input occurs here, as does a recalling to mind of information, feelings, and actions that might otherwise be overlooked. Thus in the discussion of a poem, teacher and class relate the poem to personal experiences, to other poems, or to anything else applicable. The period of interrelationship may be very brief, or may be prolonged as in the discussion and acting-out of a play.

There is output during the interplay, and also a final output, which can be cognitive, affective, or psychomotor, or a combination. Examples: Cognitive: A student who has read Frost's "Death of the Hired Man" explains some of the symbols used by Frost. Affective: The same student reacts emotionally to the word *home* as used in the same poem. Psychomotor: The farm-bred boy's muscles flex as he reads Frost's account of loading the wagon with hay. Combination: A student writes (psychomotor) a composition (cognitive) about his feelings (emotive) concerning the hired man.

Purists among writers of behavioral objectives would insist that all output must be overt, since only this kind of output is observable and measurable. In English and other humanistic subjects most outputs are indeed observable—what the student says and does as a result of the input and the interplay. But some outputs in these subjects are not directly observable—e.g., the reactions of a student when, alone in his room, he reads and then rereads part of a story that moves him deeply. Some indirect observations, however, may be possible even here, as we shall note repeatedly. But even when the output is completely covert and not at all observable, it is desirable for the teacher of humanistic subjects to make possible a climate, or an internal willingness and eagerness, to search for inputs and interplay that will encourage covert reactions as well as overt. It is such willingness and eagerness that later will make it likely that the student will read voluntarily or will secretly write a quatrain or a sonnet.

The Organization of Each Chapter

Each of the following chapters begins with a brief rationale. These statements are intended to present a modern view of why one large segment of the English curriculum is important today. Just why, for example, is the teaching of writing included in the curriculum? What potential benefits does writing have for students? How does the modern viewpoint differ from that of the past?

The remainder of each chapter is ordinarily divided into sections. Thus the chapter on Reading and Literature, which emphasizes student responses to literature, has sections on Valuing, Describing, Discovering Relationships, Discriminating, Inferring, and Evaluating.

Under each of these sections are a number of goals, numbered with arabic numerals. These goals are relatively broad; they are the Level 2 objectives referred to on page 6. They are usually not phrased in strict behavioral terms, but rather in the more familiar general terminology used in the past. For example, Goal 3 under Reading and Literature is "The student values reading as a humanizing experience, as an act that adds zest and meaning to his life, a habit that offers him not only wider access to what people are saying (wider access than is ordinarily available through television and cinema) but also more private opportunity for thought about what to accept and reject."

Under a few of the goals are Representative Entering Performance Objectives. With most classes these can usually be skipped, but with some classes these very elementary objectives need to be worked on first.

The goals are divided into Performance Objectives. Under Goal 10, for example, there may be Performance Objectives 10.A, 10.B, and 10.C. They are stated in terms like "Given so and so, the student does so and so." Obviously not all Performance Objectives possible under each goal are presented, but the authors have attempted to select those that are most representative and useful.

Many of the Performance Objectives are further divided into Representative Enabling Objectives, identified as a., b., c., etc. These are more specific versions of the Performance Objective. They may refer, for instance, to specific literary works, to specific speech activities, or to specific characteristics of a news story. Once more, these are representative, not exhaustive. They indicate some of the smaller objectives that a class may work on while moving toward realization of the Performance Objectives and the still larger goal. Often they are the right size for a single class period or even part of a class period.

In summary, each section of a chapter follows an outline like this:

Goal 1
   (Representative Entering Performance Objectives A, B, etc.)
   Performance Objectives 1.A, 1.B, etc.
      Representative Enabling Objectives a, b, etc.

Goal 2
   etc.

Goals are numbered consecutively through a chapter. There are occasional cross-references to other objectives in the same chapter or in other chapters.

Using Performance Objectives in the Classroom

It cannot be repeated too often that performance objectives focus on things to be done by the student. The activities of the teacher are not the focus. As indicated earlier, a significant change in student–teacher relationship should take place because of the adoption of performance objectives. Instead of teacher activities determining what a student will learn, student activities determine what the student will learn.

One implication of the change in focus is that students become more active agents in the student–teacher relationship than is the case in the classrooms with conventional, teacher-centered or content-centered objectives. The teacher still provides appropriate conditions and assistance to involve the student in the activity named in the objective. But both teacher and student are working toward the student's performance of a specified task.

This task and its purpose should not be concealed from the student. Quite the opposite. Just as in a music lesson the student should realize that what is expected of him is a smooth rendition of the "Moonlight Sonata," so in English the student should know at all times specifically where he is going—and not just toward a distant and rather undefinable "appreciation" or "understanding." In a botany class at Purdue, the performance objectives for each week are posted on the bulletin board for the students to read. Listed with each performance objective are the lecture materials, lab experiences, movies, etc., which are available to help students reach each objective. Such a listing is quite appropriate for English, too, under some such heading as "Where Are We Going?"

In addition to keeping students informed, it is of course the teacher's responsibility to make sure that needed materials are available. Sometimes the materials needed for performance objectives are the same as for others, but sometimes more or different materials are needed because of the possibly greater variation in student activity. Often, however, many of these extra materials can be found by students themselves.

Practice in performance is obviously essential. The amount of practice varies with the activity. In general, performances should be actual, not simulated. A person who practices all his swimming strokes only on dry land may drown when he jumps (or is pushed) into the pool. If in English an objective has to do with writing, the student must write. If it has to do with listening, he must listen. If it has to do with reading a sonnet, he must read a sonnet (not read about reading a sonnet, or read what somebody else has said about sonnets).

A teacher who lectures a great deal may need to modify his tactics. Not that lectures can't lead to performance, because they can. But the student needs to know what performance is expected of him as a result of listening to the lecture, and then he needs opportunity to practice doing that thing. If a five-minute lecture, for example, gives instructions for writing a series that builds to a climax, the student must have the opportunity to try to write such a series and to try again and again until he succeeds.

A class in which performance objectives are used may often show much more variety of activities than may sometimes be true in other classes. This is simply because more students will be doing things—small group work, consulting a dictionary or other reference book, going to the library, interviewing someone, preparing for a pantomime or improvisation or dramatization, making a collage, drawing a sketch for a stage setting, cutting stories from a newspaper, and so on. Sometimes a student may even be actively at work when he appears only to be staring into space.

The word *succeeds* is important (whether or not performance objectives are used). If tasks have been selected that most students can do, the tasks may sometimes be modified for the others so that every student can experience a degree of success. Appropriately chosen performance objectives may diminish the numbers of defeated students, students who hate school because for them it represents failure after failure.

If the change of focus from teacher-at-the-center to student-at-the-center is accomplished, if students know where they are going, and if opportunity to succeed is constantly present, there is no special "trick" in using performance objectives. A good teacher is a good teacher, but many good teachers can become even better teachers if they stop teaching so much and give more attention to helping students learn, to helping students do.

Examples of the Catalog in Use

The following examples are based in part upon ways that the preliminary version of the catalog was used in various field-testing schools.

A. In-Service Teacher Education

In some schools, teachers may be completely unfamiliar with performance objectives. As time permits, they may study portions of the catalog and devote some departmental meetings to discussing them. Thus they may familiarize themselves with the theory and have a chance to compare performance objectives with those in their existing course of study. In one or two departmental meetings they may practice rewriting some of their present objectives in terms of student performance. Individual teachers may adopt or adapt some of the handbook objectives for their own classes, and later report to their colleagues on the results.

B. Curricular Enrichment

Some portions of the handbook describe English content not commonly taught. One teacher in a field-testing school developed a unit on American dialects, employing suggestions in the Language chapter. Another found his students fascinated by non-verbal communication, and still another introduced study of the mass media. Some of the objectives in the other chapters, such as those on inferring in Reading and Literature and on listening in Speaking and Listening, led some teachers to instructional emphases they had formerly used sparingly if at all.

C. Student Participation in Planning (1)

In one new and innovative field-testing school, students participate extensively in decision-making about almost all facets of school life, including curricular matters such as what courses should be offered and what the goals of each course should be. They asked for and got, for example, courses in film-making, Black writers, and short story writing, and in all their courses they and their teachers

discuss what students want to be able to do by the end of the course
and by the end of individual segments. Some students, as well as
teachers, examined the preliminary version of this catalog and drew
or adapted some of their objectives from it. (As indicated earlier,
although the handbook is intended for teacher use, able students
can sometimes get workable ideas from it.)

The spirit in this school, when some of the authors visited it, was
unbelievably good. Although there were some abuses of the great
freedom that the students had, for the most part the students were
engaging much more wholeheartedly in their learning activities than
most teenagers do. Questioned by visitors they said, "School is the
most fun it has ever been. We know where we're going in each
class, because we've helped to make the decisions about where we're
going. We aren't kept in the dark about the purposes of a course
or what is expected of us. And there's a lot of room for individual
initiative. We can do special projects if we like; we don't all have to
do the same things. In some classes we establish minimum things
to achieve, but we can follow different paths to get there. We have
plenty of opportunity to share, to talk about what we're doing.
Often we work in groups, too. The teacher is a helper, a resource
person—not a dictator who every day stands up in the front of the
room and tells us to open our books to page 231. Some of us are
doing more reading and writing and stuff like that than we've ever
done, but we don't mind doing it, because we've, like, you know,
assigned the work to ourselves."

D. STUDENT PARTICIPATION IN PLANNING (2)

English teachers in much more conservative schools may also give
students some voice in course planning, although a smaller voice
than in the school just described. The teachers in one such school
decided the goals for each course, choosing many of them from the
preliminary version of this book. Then, in class, each teacher in
effect said this: "The purposes of this course are such and such.
There are a number of smaller purposes, or objectives, that can help
in reaching the course goals. Let's talk about some of these possible
objectives; you may choose the ones you believe you would like
most." Then the teacher presented in simple language a number
of the performance objectives under the goal, added his own suggestions to them, and solicited still others from the class. Such democracy was so unfamiliar in this school that at first the students
seemed a bit dazed, but in a short time, convinced of the teacher's
sincerity, they began contributing. Thus, within the boundaries of

the goals prescribed by the teacher, they selected the specific objectives and decided upon enabling objectives or activities that would lead them toward the performance objectives and the goals.

E. Teacher Choice of Objectives

In a still more conservative field-testing school, which appeared highly fearful of democracy, teachers selected course goals and used the catalog as a source of performance and enabling objectives. They then went before their classes and said, "This is what we are going to do in this course, and this is how we are going to do it." Even this procedure was better than the one followed previously there, since earlier students had never really been informed about their destinations. But it worked less well than the procedures described in Sections C and D above.

F. Determining the Value of an Objective

In an increasing number of schools, English teachers are assigned the responsibility of rewriting existing objectives in behavioral terms. Often, using the phrasing of objectives in this handbook as a model, this task is easy to do; teachers learn rather quickly the knack of writing "Given so and so, the student does such and such," although sometimes the choice of the *do*-verb may require considerable thought.

A more serious problem, though, may arise in connection with certain of the objectives in the old course of study. We shall use as an example an incident in one school, where a committee had been assigned the rewriting task. One of the objectives in the existing language section was "conjugation of the verb *to be*." This was rewritten by a committee member, "Given instruction in the forms of the verb *be*, the student writes a complete conjugation in all the tenses, moods, and voices." This is unquestionably a performance objective, for the student is required to do something that is observable. But, quite rightly, there was dissent among the committee members about the *value* of the objective.

"I don't like it," said one teacher. "It's trivial; it's busywork."

"I agree," said another. "Suppose that a kid memorizes the whole conjugation and writes it down and gets everything right. What good will it do him?"

"Well," said the teacher who had written the objective, "we all know that students have trouble with *be*. They use *is* when they should use *are*, they say 'if he was' instead of 'if he were,' and some of them leave out the form of *be* entirely. They need this."

"Yes, they need help with *be*," the first teacher responded, "but will they use the forms in the standard ways just because they've memorized the conjugation? I don't think that such abstract learning will carry over at all to their usage."

"I think," said still another teacher, "that what our students do in school should approximate reality as much as possible. In real life people don't go around reciting the conjugation of *to be*."

The argument went on. Finally the objective was rephrased in this way: "Given practice in the use of *be* in formal contexts where the forms are sometimes confused, the student constructs original sentences using the forms now considered standard, and in subsequent formal writing employs those forms consistently."

Similar discussions may occur in connection with many other objectives, such as some on memorizing poetry, indicating rhyme schemes, preparing formal outlines, and analyzing a speech. In each instance the point at issue is whether the specified objective is a worthy one and whether the action specified will indeed contribute substantially to reaching the goal. Some objectives may be thrown out entirely; others may be rephrased so that the activities involved can lead to solid achievement. One of the strong points of performance objectives is that, thoughtfully considered, they can help teachers to evaluate the real, lasting worth of anything they propose to have students do.

G. CURRICULUM REVISION

The English teachers in one field-testing school were in the throes of curriculum revision. They were questioning everything they had been doing; they had examined the reports from Dartmouth, the reports of the Squire-Applebee studies of selected American and British schools, the Moffett materials, the volumes on taxonomy by Bloom and others, and the books and articles emanating from the curriculum study centers of the 1960's. They determined early that they wanted more student freedom, more attention to individual needs, more relevance to life, less attention to the picayune, less lockstep instruction. They also decided early that they wanted to state objectives in terms of what students should be able to do as a result of instruction.

They used the preliminary catalog to find significant areas needed for curricular enrichment. (See Section B above.) In addition, they selected objectives that would lead to a maximum of student participation and that would allow much student initiative, permitting students often to pursue individual interests that were in keeping with the overall goals. Not all students, they decided, would have to read the same literary works, although they agreed that some commonality was desirable. Not all students would have to be writing the same kind of thing at the same time. Not all students would adhere to the same emphases in language study. In work involving skills, students who had already mastered a particular skill (e.g., in spelling or punctuation) could skip work being done by others and move immediately into projects that would have enriching values for them. They found that the catalog called attention to neglected areas of instruction, helped in eliminating deadwood, and suggested emphases that may be especially rewarding. It is not a curriculum, but as previously stated it can serve a catalytic function in curricular revision.

H. Measurement

One of the field-testing schools had a principal who was pretty dogmatic in his insistence upon what he called "pure behavioral objectives." An ingredient of this "purity," he believed, was the requirement of a mathematically precise statement of measurement such as early writers on behavioral objectives tended to recommend. Such an objective is very closely parodied by Robert Hogan in his previously mentioned article. As the result of a six-week unit in expository writing, Hogan says, such an objective might read, "90 percent of the students will be able 90 percent of the time to write an acceptable five-sentence running outline for an expository composition of approximately 250 words."

The English teachers in the school tried to go along with what their principal wanted. They encountered difficulties, though. How could they determine whether a percentage should be 90 or 100 or 85 or 70? and given the differences in students and in classes, was 90 or some other percentage appropriate for all? More important, many significant learnings in English cannot be measured in terms of percentage. Maybe in mathematics, but not in English. Should the response of a student who is enthusiastic about a Cummings poem be said to be worth 100 percent, and that of a student who doesn't like it be worth 0 percent? Does everybody have to like Cummings? Can the quality of writing be accurately judged on a mathematical scale? (Educational Testing Service has invested millions of dollars in unsuccessful attempts.) How does one judge mathematically the appropriateness of language in a given situation?

Faced with such questions, the teachers resorted to the Purves analogy of the flagpole and its shadow. They told the principal that performance objectives in English are useful in evaluating degrees of student success, but that attempts to convert such evaluations into strict percentage terms were futile. They could describe what students should be able to do, and they could observe the shadows or indications that revealed rather closely how well the students were doing, but they could not assert positively and honestly that 90 percent of the students were doing something or other or should be doing something or other 90 percent of the time; it might well be 85 percent or 95 percent or some different percentage. In a spelling test they could say that 95 percent of the students spelled at least 95 percent of the words in accordance with present practice, but in something not countable they could not be so precise. They could, however, estimate students' gains on how frequently they used the library, how much and how well they contributed to class discussions, how regularly they turned in written work, how much initiative they showed in undertaking individual projects—on a multitude of things that revealed growth and enthusiasm.

I. COMBINATION OF MATERIALS FROM DIFFERENT CHAPTERS

English teachers in many fine schools do not teach just literature at one time, or just composition at another time, or just language at still another. They interweave the various components of English in each unit: their students read, talk about what they have read, write about it or write something inspired by their reading, discuss the author's use of language and their own use of language, and work on various individual projects related to the topic of the unit. To these teachers the organization of this handbook into chapters on various components of English may seem artificial.

In a way these teachers are right. Actually any arrangement is artificial, because items in print must be presented one at a time, whereas in class they may be interwoven in countless patterns.

Close scrutiny of the handbook, however, will reveal that a considerable amount of interweaving is present. In the objectives for the Reading and Literature chapter, for example, much writing of many different kinds is involved, and much oral work—including discussion, role-playing, dramatization, and other speaking and listening activities; authors' use of language is also often a focus, and so sometimes is the relationship between printed materials and other media. Similarly, the Speaking and Listening chapter includes work involving reading, writing, non-verbal communication, the use of language, and the mass media. Other chapters likewise reach toward each other through the pages. Use of the index and of the cross-references will assist teachers in finding a number of possible additional interrelationships.

Teachers in field-testing schools found that, once familiar with the catalog, they themselves could readily effect combinations of objectives from different chapters. Thus, when their juniors were reading Mark Twain, they found it appropriate to include some of the dialect objectives from the chapter on language. In the reading of Orwell in another class, work on semantics and on the mass media was incorporated. Other teachers effected still other combinations.

J. SELECTIVITY

As an example of selective use of objectives from this handbook, we'll look at an inexperienced teacher in a small school, who on her own was using the preliminary catalog, and did not know how to begin. She was teaching freshmen. At first she thought that she would start with Goal 1 in Reading and Literature, work on the objectives under Goal 1, then move on to Goal 2, and so on through the year. But she found that some of the objectives were beyond the ability of her freshmen, and that some seemed inappropriate for her classes for other reasons.

She sought advice from the department head. "We do have some goals set up for our freshman classes," the head reminded the teacher, "although they're pretty vague. As you know, you can do pretty much as you like in this school. I think, though, that you ought to examine our goals, then pick out roughly corresponding goals from the catalog, and see which of the performance objectives seem most suitable for your classes. You no doubt will also want to develop some of your own, since the catalog does not pretend to be exhaustive."

So the teacher compared the established goals with those in the preliminary catalog. A few of the school's goals she did not like, and given the freedom that she had, she threw them out and replaced them with others from the catalog. Other goals she modified. She found that many of the suggested performance objectives seemed suitable for her students, but that others were not; she crossed off those which appeared inappropriate, took over some of the others intact, modified others, and added some of her own.

This teacher's use of the catalog may represent that which will become most common. This handbook–catalog is a resource book. It is not a bible. Not everything in it is suitable for all classes. Not all of it fits everybody's individual teaching style. Much of it needs supplementation in light of the peculiar circumstances of each school, each class, each teacher. Selectivity is the key.

K. TEACHER PREPARATION

The preliminary version of this handbook was used for discussion purposes in methods classes in the three sponsoring universities. The college students in these universities take the usual array of Education courses, in some of which they are introduced to general goals of education and to the more specific goals of their subject matter. In methods courses for the past few years they have been considering objectives phrased in behavioral terms.

Students in one English methods course, while discussing the preliminary catalog, found themselves facing the difficult-to-answer question of why we teach English, what we are really trying to accomplish in year-after-year exposure of students to this thing labeled "English." Answers from these teachers-to-be were varied, ranging from conservative statements about "correctness" to radical ideas about "learning to live life." The students by no means accepted as valid all the goals in the catalog; some, they said, are not "relevant" to the world the high school youngster will soon face. Others they applauded.

They looked with care at the performance objectives, accepting many, casting out others. They liked the idea of phrasing objectives in terms of what students should do, and especially the idea of not keeping objectives hidden from students. "When I was in high school," one prospective teacher said, "I never knew where we were going. I did what the teacher said I should (most of us did), but I generally didn't know why I was doing it or what good I was expected to get out of it. I didn't see relationships. I'd read something, write something, give a talk, fill in some blanks, and it all seemed a hodgepodge that was supposed to add up to something called 'English.' When I teach, I want to make sure that the kids will know what we're doing and why. In fact, I want them to have some share in deciding what we're going to do."

"I feel that way, too," said another prospective teacher. "But what I like best about performance objectives is that they're more specific than a lot of the objectives I've read about in other Education courses. Most of them avoid high-level abstractions like 'appreciation' and 'ideals of citizenship.' I think that appreciation and ideals of citizenship may be fine things, but I never had much notion of how to get at them or what they mean in actual behavior.

The performance objectives help me to break such big goals down to manageable size."

Following their student teaching, these same young people were reflecting on their experiences. One said, and others echoed, "What I like best about performance objectives is that they give every student a good chance for *success*. For some of my students school has meant a long series of failures. They haven't been able to reach or even to comprehend the often ill-defined objectives of their teachers. But with performance objectives, sensibly and sensitively selected and made clear to the class, each student knows precisely what he is expected to do, and he can work toward that, and again and again he succeeds. It's a marvelous, unfamiliar experience to him. School becomes meaningful—maybe for the first time. I'll swear that some of my kids' eyes became brighter every day."

Summary

This handbook is intended to be a flexible instrument for use by teachers, and indirectly by their students, in English classes in secondary schools. For its intelligent use, it should be examined *in toto* and whenever possible be made a topic for discussion in departmental meetings and a tool for experimentation in various classes. It can be examined for suggestions for curricular enrichment, provide ideas for greater student involvement, be of assistance in choosing and evaluating objectives in relation to overall goals, be a tool in curriculum revision, and help in measurement of the worth of a course and the extent of individual students' gains, and it should prove valuable in college courses in which future English teachers are being prepared.

II

Sending and Receiving Non-Verbal Messages

RATIONALE

Few verbal messages are sent without accompanying non-verbal messages. Yet, even though most people know the meanings of many non-verbal symbols, relatively few are aware of the many non-verbal messages they send daily without intending to. Most people are also not aware of the many messages they do not receive because they do not know the particular non-verbal symbols used in a specific situation, or they do not realize that non-verbal symbols, like words, can change meaning in time and context.

To be an intelligent communicator, a student must be as effective in sending and receiving non-verbal messages as verbal ones. He needs to understand how non-verbal messages such as gestures and facial expressions can change the meaning of verbal messages. He also needs to be aware of the significant cultural and social contexts in which non-verbal symbols are frequently not understood by an outsider, but are extremely significant for members of a particular group. He further needs to understand how individuals, as well as the mass media, can combine pictures, signs, symbols, and sounds

The project director in charge of this section, Edward B. Jenkinson, Director of the English Curriculum Study Center and Associate Professor of Education, Indiana University, was assisted by several consultants.

with spoken and written messages to inform, persuade, or entertain an audience. Thus, it is imperative that instruction in non-verbal communication become a part of the secondary school English curriculum if teachers plan to help students learn how to communicate effectively, especially in a pluralistic society. This unit can be used early in high school, or even in junior high, and augmented as the need arises.

To prepare to teach a unit on non-verbal communication, a teacher will want to read these books:

Fast, Julius, *Body Language*. New York: M. Evans and Company, 1970.
Hall, Edward T., *The Hidden Dimension*. Garden City, New York: Doubleday, 1966.
————, *The Silent Language*. Garden City, New York: Doubleday, 1959.

Goal 1

The student can send and receive a variety of non-verbal messages.

Performance Objective 1.A

Given a variety of situations, the student demonstrates his ability to send and receive non-verbal messages. *See also* IV 20.A;* V 36.A; VI 2 and 9.

Representative Enabling Objectives

a. Having examined a set of signs and symbols, the student identifies, orally or in writing, the meaning(s) he attaches to each sign or symbol.
   (Here are some examples the teacher might use: traffic signs, +, =, U.S. flag, cross, Star of David, red cross, peace symbol, skull and crossbones, treble clef, donkey and elephant.)
b. After seeing a demonstration of signals referees use in football and basketball games or umpires use in baseball, the student identifies the meanings of the signals. He also identifies those signals that have different meanings in different contexts.
c. The student lists as many signs and symbols as he can, orally describing the situations in which each sign or symbol is normally used and telling what meaning(s) he attaches to each sign or symbol on his list.

---

* Roman numerals refer to chapters, Arabic numerals to goals, capital letters to performance objectives, and lower-case letters to enabling objectives.

d. The student conveys to his classmates a non-verbal message using signs and symbols. The meaning of the message described by the receivers should match the meaning intended by the sender.

e. After considering some scents that are specifically designed as forms of non-verbal communication (e.g., perfume, after-shave lotion, new-car smell), the student lists other such scents.

f. After listing several communicative odors, the student asks several classmates what each specific odor communicates and records the responses of his classmates. The student explains, orally or in writing, why he received different responses from different students if they did not agree on the meanings of the odors.

g. Given an example of a non-verbal act of communication that uses the sense of touch (e.g., a father puts his hand firmly on his son's shoulder to keep him from doing something), the student lists as many acts as he can and identifies, orally or in writing, the meaning(s) of each act.

h. The student uses gestures that depend on the sense of touch (e.g., a pat on the back, a restraining grip on the arm) to communicate a pre-specified message. The meaning of the message as described by the receiver should match the meaning specified by the sender. He also explains how the meaning of the gesture depends on the context. (For example, the meaning of a mother's patting an infant's back differs from the meaning of a principal's patting a student on the back after the latter has accomplished something.)

i. The student explains, orally or in writing, how a single facial expression can be used to send different messages. (For example, a frown can indicate worry, concentration, sadness, disapproval, unhappiness, discomfort, etc. A smile can indicate happiness, friendliness, contempt, cynicism, nervousness, etc.) He explains, orally or in writing, how the situation can change the meaning of the expression.

j. Given various situations to dramatize, the student uses facial expressions in front of classmates to send different messages.

k. The student examines several pictures of people of all ages in various kinds of dress, telling how he reacts to the person because of the clothing.

l. The student explains, orally or in writing, why his reactions to clothing might differ from those of one or more of his classmates.

m. The student uses clothing to send a non-verbal message. The meaning of the message as described by the receiver should match the meaning intended by the sender.

n. The student records the facts that he can determine simply by looking closely at a person. (For example, he might be able to tell if the person is married or engaged, a member of a social organization or religious group, etc. The person's clothing and posture might also give the observer some facts about the person.)

Goal 2

The student uses other forms of non-verbal communication in addition to those discussed in class.

Performance Objective 2.A

The student lists, orally or in writing, a number of forms of non-verbal communication. *See also* II 6.A, 7.A, and 8.A; V 25; VI 1.A, 2.A and B.

(Here the student might consider the uses of colors, sounds, music, lights, and so forth for sending non-verbal messages.)

Goal 3

The student considers the elements in acts of non-verbal communication.

Performance Objective 3.A

The student identifies and defines, orally or in writing, these four elements present in every act of non-verbal communication: sender, receiver, medium, and message. *See also* VI 3; VII 1.A.

Representative Enabling Objective

Given a representation of a non-verbal act of communication (e.g., two persons shaking hands), the student identifies the four elements of communication present in the act.

Goal 4

The student tells what different non-verbal messages communicate in various contexts.

Performance Objective 4.A

Given a description of different contexts in which people are communicating non-verbally, the student explains what the act communicates in each instance.

Representative Enabling Objectives

a. The student explains what is communicated by shaking hands in situations such as these:

1. Two persons meeting for the first time shake hands.
2. Two men who have known each other for years shake hands when they meet on the street.

3. A guest at a wedding reception shakes hands with the bridegroom immediately after the wedding ceremony.
4. After fighting one another, two men shake hands.
5. After two men agree to launch a business together, they shake hands.
6. An athlete, congratulating a teammate upon scoring a touchdown, slaps his hand in a "Give me some skin" gesture.

b. Given a non-verbal symbol (e.g., the raised index finger and middle finger on one hand to form a V or both arms raised over the head), the student describes situations in which the non-verbal symbol might be used and identifies the meaning of the symbol in each situation.

Goal 5

The student analyzes various aspects of different acts of non-verbal communication, such as repetition and movement, and tells what they mean.

Performance Objective 5.A

Having analyzed a variety of messages conveyed through repetition and movement, or even variations in pitch or intensity, similar to the message in examples such as those below, the student tells what each message means to him and what he thinks is the purpose of the sender of each message.

Suggested example groups—

1. a flashing red light on a highway barricade
a red traffic light at an intersection
a flashing red light on an ambulance
a red light on the front of a TV camera in a studio
2. A person knocks on a closed door.
A person knocks on the closest available wood after telling us he hasn't had a cold in a year.
A carpenter knocks on a wall with his knuckles.
A man punches a door with his fist after losing $10.00 at a race track.
3. A baby cries while his mother is preparing his breakfast.
A baby cries after he falls.
A baby cries when he discovers that he is alone in a room.
A baby cries when his mother takes away a toy with which he has been playing.

Goal 6

The student considers how a setting can influence a verbal message.

Performance Objective 6.A

Given an explanation of how a background specifically designed as a means of non-verbal communication can enhance or detract from a verbal message, the student explains the effect(s) that such backgrounds can have on a verbal message in situations such as these:

1. a backdrop of psychedelic colors and designs behind a speaker's platform for a political candidate who is appealing to the young;
2. a large picture of police clubbing "hippies" as a backdrop behind a speaker whose topic is the generation gap;
3. a burning cross at a Ku Klux Klan rally.

Goal 7

The student uses color to send messages.

Performance Objective 7.A

The student recognizes that color can be used to establish and/or convey mood and that it can also be used as a sign or symbol. He demonstrates this recognition by giving examples of how color can be used to establish mood or to symbolize something. *See also* V 25.Aa; VI 1.A.

Representative Enabling Objectives

a. Given a scene from a play, the student demonstrates how color can be used to establish mood by explaining, orally or in writing, why he would select certain colors for the set and for the lighting.
b. The student explains, orally or in writing, how people use colors such as red, yellow, black, and white symbolically in different contexts.

Goal 8

The student uses music to send messages. *See also* V 25.B; VI 2.Ab and 14.A.

Performance Objective 8.A

The student uses music to convey a specific non-verbal message or to supplement other forms of non-verbal communication or verbal communication.

Representative Enabling Objectives

a. The student demonstrates his ability to send a non-verbal message transmitted by a combination of non-verbal forms of communication by presenting a pantomime with background music in which the message he intends to convey (as specified only to the teacher before the presentation) is identified by the members of the audience. The student then explains, orally or in writing, his selection of background music.

b. The student selects background music that will convey a mood he deems appropriate for a non-verbal photo, cartoon, or film essay. The student defends his selection of specific music.

c. The student uses various musical compositions as a background for a story, poem, or play and explains how the choice of music affects the verbal message.

Goal 9

The student explores different ways that a person's point of view affects both the sending and receiving of non-verbal messages. *See also* III 7.C; IV 22.A and 23.A; V 12; VI 13.

Performance Objective 9.A

After class exploration and discussion of the factors that influence point of view, such as physical, emotional, experiential, educational, and cultural, the student explains, orally or in writing, how a sender's point of view would be likely to affect both the selection and use of the medium. The student will also describe how point of view affects the response a person or group might make to a message.

Representative Enabling Objectives

a. Given that point of view affects the selection and use of the medium, the student explains how he might expect persons such as the following to make use of a symbol (e.g., the U. S. flag) as a means of non-verbal communication.
1. an average, middle-class homeowner
2. a member of the John Birch Society
3. a member of the Students for a Democratic Society
The student then explains why his expected generalizations might not apply to every member of a group.

b. Given that the receiver also has a point of view, the student explains how he, as a receiver, interprets non-verbal messages such as the following:

1. A homeowner displays the U. S. flag on Memorial Day, Flag Day, and the Fourth of July.

2. A homeowner whose son is in Vietnam displays the U. S. flag daily.
3. A homeowner displays the U. S. flag day and night all year long, and, in addition, bathes the flag in a powerful spotlight at night.

c. Given two photographs or two cartoons of the same public figure, the student demonstrates his ability to analyze ways in which point of view affects a message by giving reasons why the photographer's or cartoonist's point of view changed the message.

Suggested examples—

1. Having been shown photographs, TV films, or news clips of a public demonstration, the student demonstrates his ability to analyze how the mass media sometimes focus on the more violent and sensational aspects of the event rather than on the entire event.
2. After reading selected passages from a book like Edward T. Hall's *The Silent Language,* in which the author explains how cultural differences change the meaning of non-verbal messages, the student lists non-verbal messages that change meaning from group to group and culture to culture. (Example: In the Middle East, the showing of the sole of the foot to any person is a supreme insult; yet, in the United States, the news picture of the sole of Adlai Stevenson's shoe with a hole in it made him a more popular figure.)

Goal 10

The student recognizes the necessity of common experiences for both the sender and receiver of non-verbal messages for effective communication.

Performance Objective 10.A

After discussing the necessity of common experiences for the sender and receiver to communicate successfully with non-verbal forms, the student demonstrates his knowledge of the concept by describing situations in which non-verbal communication failed because the sender and the receiver did not have common experiences or had attached totally different meanings to the same non-verbal symbols.

Goal 11

The student recognizes that the message sometimes determines the medium. *See also* V 37, 40.B, and 41.C; and VI 2.

Performance Objective 11.A

After a discussion or demonstration exemplifying the statement, "The message sometimes determines the non-verbal medium," the student identifies the form of non-verbal communication appropriate for sending messages such as these:

1. A boy sees a pretty girl walking down the street and wants to convey his appreciation of her beauty. (wolf whistle)
2. Two boys who are close friends meet in the hall as they come into school early in the morning. One wants to show his friendship toward the other. (He punches the other on the upper arm.)
3. A person finds that he cannot express himself adequately in verbal terms in his attempt to show another person how to put a gadget together. (He might first try to explain how the parts go together by making gestures. If he fails, he might make a drawing.)

Goal 12

The student uses several non-verbal media to convey a single impression.

Performance Objective 12.A

The student produces a film, drawing, collage, poster, cartoon, or series of pictures in which he conveys one dominant impression through colors, shades, sounds, movements, gestures and so forth. *See also* V 25; VI 1.A.

Goal 13

The student recognizes how writers describe non-verbal acts of communication to give a better picture of their characters, to develop the plot, or to describe the setting more effectively. *See also* IV 19; V 9; VI 9.A.

Performance Objective 13.A

Given a variety of written materials in which writers have embedded descriptions of non-verbal modes of communication, the student demonstrates his ability not only to recognize these non-verbal modes but also to interpret their meanings in particular contexts.

Representative Enabling Objective

a. After reading passages like the following, the student explains, orally or in writing, the non-verbal modes of communication embedded in these passages and the meanings of these particular modes in the larger contexts of the entire works.

1. "That was six points for Duncan, but only four for Terry. The next time the ball came his way, he was up the floor and Suds was near the free throw line. Terry hesitated, sighted the basket and shot. The ball hit the backboard and bounced out.

   Suds' eyebrows traveled up. Terry said 'darn it' under his breath . . ." (from "Kid Brother" by B. J. Chute)

2. *Martine* (Her arms akimbo, speaks to M. Robert, and makes him draw back; at last she gives him a slap on the face.) And I like him to beat me, I do. (from *The Physician In Spite of Himself* by Moliere)

3. "The pony talked with his ears. You could tell exactly how he felt about everything by the way his ears pointed. Sometimes they were stiff and upright and sometimes lax and sagging. They went back when he was angry and fearful, and forward when he was anxious and curious and pleased; and their exact position indicated which emotion he had." (from "The Red Pony" by John Steinbeck)

4. "Wing Biddlebaum, forever frightened and beset by a ghostly band of doubts, did not think of himself as in any way a part of the life of the town where he had lived for twenty years. Among all the people of Winesburg but one had come close to him. With George Willard, son of Tom Willard, the proprietor of the New Willard House, he had formed something like a friendship. George Willard was the reporter on the *Winesburg Eagle* and sometimes in the evenings he walked out along the highway to Wing Biddlebaum's house. Now as the old man walked up and down on the veranda, his hands moving nervously about, he was hoping that George Willard would come and spend the evening with him. After the wagon containing the berry pickers had passed, he went across the field through the tall mustard weeds and climbing a rail fence peered anxiously along the road to the town. For a moment he stood thus, rubbing his hands together and looking up and down the road, and then, fear overcoming him, ran back to walk again upon the porch on his own house." (from "Hands" in Sherwood Anderson's *Winesburg, Ohio*)

Performance Objective 13.B

The student analyzes a novelist's use of an object described to send the reader messages that foreshadow events to come.

Representative Enabling Objectives

a. Given a passage such as the following one from *Jude the Obscure* by Thomas Hardy, the student identifies the medium (non-verbal), sender, receiver, and the message foreshadowing events to come.

Arabella said she would like some tea, and they entered an inn of an inferior class, and gave their order. As it was not for beer they had a long time to wait. The maid-servant recognized Jude, and whispered her surprise to her mistress in the background, that he, the student, 'who kept hisself up so particular,' should have suddenly descended so low to keep company with Arabella. The latter guessed what was being said, and laughed as she met the serious and tender gaze of her lover—the low and triumphant laugh of a careless woman who sees she is winning her game.

They sat and looked round the room, and at the picture of Samson and Delilah which hung on the wall, and at the circular beer-stains on the table, and at the spittoons underfoot filled with sawdust. The whole aspect of the scene had that depressing effect on Jude which few places can produce like a tap-room on Sunday evening when the setting sun is slanting in, and no liquor is going, and the unfortunate wayfarer finds himself with no other haven of rest.

b. After a discussion of a novel such as *The Scarlet Letter*, the student writes his conception of the message sent from the non-verbal medium found in a passage like the following. He then relates it to one of the following elements of the novel: development of plot, characterization, or a subtle comment by Hawthorne.

The new abode of the two friends was with a pious widow, of good social rank, who dwelt in a house covering pretty nearly the site on which the venerable structure of King's Chapel has since been built. It had the graveyard, originally Isaac Johnson's homefield, on one side, and so well adapted to call up serious reflections, suited to their respective employments, in both minister and man of physic. The motherly care of the good widow assigned to Mr. Dimmesdale a front apartment with a sunny exposure, and heavy window curtains to create a noontide shadow when desirable. The walls were hung round with tapestry, said to be from the Gobelin looms, and, at all events, representing the Scriptural story of David and Bathsheba, and Nathan the Prophet, in colors faded, but which made the fair woman of the scene almost as firmly picturesque as the woe-denouncing seer. . . . On the other side of the house, old Roger Chillingworth arranged his study and laboratory.

III

Speaking and Listening

RATIONALE

Twentieth-century man lives in an age of communication; radio and television now reach into even the remotest areas of the world. With the increasing frequency of both domestic and overseas telephoning, more and more people in all parts of the world talk and listen to one another in the course of a typical day. Telephone conferences of people in different countries are now arranged and conducted almost routinely. Countless business executives, facing the rising costs of secretarial service and the often lower costs of telephone service, are rapidly supplanting the letter with the telephone call. By means of the communications satellites floating in outer space, man can now see and hear news events at the very time they occur in virtually any part of the world. But the height of man's efforts thus far to communicate with his fellow man is his recently proven ability to maintain both oral and visual communication with men on the moon. And, yet, the end of man's efforts and potential is nowhere in sight.

Speaking and listening have traditionally been given short shrift in secondary school English programs. Most English teachers evidently have forgotten that professional people, not to mention skilled and unskilled workers, spend approximately 75 percent of

The project director in charge of this section, Paul H. Jacobs, Associate Professor, Department of English, University of Illinois, Urbana, was assisted by several consultants and directors.

their time in communicating orally, i.e., in situations calling for use of speaking and listening skills. Further, teachers evidently assume that students learn on their own the speaking and listening skills they need to know, and that, therefore, no need exists for direct teaching of those skills. Research reveals, however, that this assumption is totally unfounded; as a matter of fact, it shows that many adults, even when communicating orally in their daily work, function at an efficiency level of approximately 20 percent.

Speaking and listening are complex, learned communication behaviors. Together they constitute man's primary means of communication, his conveying of his ideas to other men and his receiving of their ideas in return. The processes of speaking and listening enable man to discover what he already thinks and knows about a particular topic and, through various experiences, to learn still more. Further, they enable him to examine, integrate, and synthesize his knowledge and experiences and to come to an understanding of himself and his world. Speaking and listening are social processes involving interactions among people whose purposes are to find a common ground of understanding. Speaking and listening are basic to the functioning of society. Without these vital forms of communication, men could only with great difficulty carry on their daily affairs. Man's ability to communicate effectively and successfully through speaking and listening has never been so crucial to his survival as at this very moment.

Effective interpersonal speech communication does not "just happen"—it occurs when individuals are adequately sensitized to communicative situations and when they have been exposed to carefully planned learning experiences in oral communication. Secondary school students must have, therefore, many and varied oral experiences with language if they are to speak and listen effectively.

There is no single method of exhibiting competence in speaking and listening. The goals and objectives that follow are therefore quite varied, but all are intended to teach students to appreciate both the universality of oral expression and the qualities unique to individuals, and to give students substantial amounts of practice in different kinds of speaking–listening situations.

These goals and objectives were written expressly for use in the teaching of speaking and listening skills within the context of the English classroom. While some of the objectives may well be used for an elective course in speech (quite a few were so used during the field-testing of the preliminary version of this catalog), they were not designed for that purpose. The oral communication skills outlined here are much too important to students' daily lives to be relegated to the chance that students might elect a speech course sometime during their years in secondary school.

Goal 1

The student feels comfortable and finds pleasure in various types of speaking–listening situations.

Performance Objective 1.A

After self-analysis and observation of others, the student describes the kinds of satisfaction that can be derived from speaking and listening.

Representative Enabling Objectives

a. After listening to and observing a series of several speakers, or after watching a variety of TV programs (news, commercials, Flip Wilson, Carol Burnett, for instance), the student identifies the kinds of pleasure that each apparently was gaining through his speaking (for example, stimulation by the group, pleasure in arousing controversy, pleasure in arousing emotion).
b. After observing audience response during several speeches, the student lists the kinds of enjoyment an audience could receive from a good public speaker.
c. After giving a speech before his class, or any other group, the student analyzes and describes the satisfaction he felt at the time he was speaking.
d. Given a series of options, such as reading a humorous poem aloud, making a speech to inform, relating an interesting anecdote, or playing a role in a play, the student ranks the options in order of the pleasure he anticipates they would give him, and then he explains his ranking.
e. Confronted by a classmate who is reluctant to make an assigned speech (or participate in a panel discussion, etc.) the student lists for his classmate the psychological rewards, such as poise and equanimity, to be derived from the speaking experience. (Role-playing also works well here.) *See also* IV 12.D *; VI 10; V 17.Ca.
f. After listening to a recording of a short story, or after reading one, the student retells the basic plot of the story, and then comments on the satisfaction he received. *See also* V 9.D.

Goal 2

The student understands the nature of speaking and listening and their roles in the communication process. *See also* VI 2.B.

* Roman numerals refer to chapters, Arabic numerals to goals, capital letters to performance objectives, and lower-case letters to enabling objectives.

Representative Entering Performance Objective

The student has identified the elements necessary for communication to occur: speaker, speech, audience, or sender, message, receiver. *See also* II 3.A; VI 3; VII 1.A.

Performance Objective 2.A

The student discusses the importance of speaking and listening in the shaping of man's thoughts and opinions.

Representative Enabling Objective

After a discussion of the roles of speaking and listening in the shaping of ideas, the student does the following: (1) lists several of his strong convictions about current controversial issues, and then identifies the speakers who, he believes, helped to shape his convictions; (2) recalls occasions when he himself, using speech, helped to change the convictions of a friend or relative. *See also* IV 22.A; V 44.A.

Performance Objective 2.B

The student reports on ways most people give a great deal more time to speaking and listening than to reading and writing.

Representative Enabling Objective

Following a discussion of the varying percentages of time that people in different situations spend in speaking, listening, writing, and reading, the student develops and administers a questionnaire for finding out the approximate amount of time that at least two of the following persons spend in a typical day using each of the four communication modes; then he analyzes the results and gives an oral report to his class.

(1) himself
(2) his mother or father
(3) one of his teachers
(4) a business executive
(5) a child 6 to 9 years of age
(6) a retired man or woman

Performance Objective 2.C

Given a variety of situations demanding communication either through the speaking–listening process or through the writing–reading process, the student demonstrates an awareness of the nature of each process and of the advantages and disadvantages inherent in each process. (Some teachers find recordings of such situations quite useful.) *See also* VI 2.B.

Representative Enabling Objectives

a. Given an assignment to rouse his classmates to immediate action on an urgent issue, the student indicates speaking *or* writing as the preferred medium and lists the reasons for his choice.

b. Given a situation in which he is to retain lengthy detailed instructions for a projected motor trip, for example, the student indicates listening *or* reading as the preferred medium and gives, orally or in writing, the reasons for his choice.

c. Given an assignment, for example, to cheer up a hospitalized friend, the student indicates speaking *or* writing as the preferred medium and lists the reasons for his choice.

d. Given a task such as helping five people choose a common vacation resort, the student indicates speaking *or* writing as the preferred medium and lists the reasons for his choice.

Goal 3

The student understands that various non-verbal elements contribute to verbal communication. *See also* Ch. II.

Performance Objective 3.A

After participating in several oral communication situations, the student explains the paralinguistic elements, including kinesics (non-verbal body motion), present in the communications, and further explains, where possible, the relationship of such elements of speech to the social and cultural experiences of the speakers, as well as to their attitudes and states of mind.

Representative Enabling Objectives

a. Having heard a talk by an effective or ineffective public speaker, the student identifies and describes the effects of specific paralinguistic elements (tone, pace, stress, pause, and such vocal sounds as laughing, snorting, and humming; or gesture, facial expression, stance, movement) in shaping and conveying the speaker's message.

b. After seeing a silent videotape of a classmate's speech, for example, the student, on the basis of kinesic elements in the speech, describes what he believes to be the emotional stance of the speaker and the audience to which the talk was addressed, and then assesses the likelihood that the speech will have achieved the speaker's goals.

c. After choosing a specific role to create (culturally, socially, or temperamentally defined), or after choosing a specific literary or TV role, the student pantomimes (or expresses through dramatic improvisation, etc.) elements of character appropriate to his particular role. *See also* V 35.I; VI 2.Ba.

d. After viewing a short film of a pantomime artist (Marcel Marceau), or watching one on TV (Red Skelton), or after attending a performance by a mime group, the student reports, either orally or in writing, what the artist(s) has (have) communicated. (The films "The Parable" and "The Stringbean" might be used here.)

e. After watching a pantomime by some of his classmates, the student explains, orally or in writing, what has been related. *See also* VI 2.Ba.

f. After participating in role-playing situations or after viewing films or tapes, the student discusses, orally or in writing, those non-verbal factors (facial expressions, bodily gestures and attitudes, etc.) which add significant dimensions to oral communication.

g. Given an opportunity to view short films (including some on TV) of interchanges between persons from different cultures, the student makes a record of the number of times that they communicate even when the sound is cut off, and then he checks the record for accuracy when the sound is turned on. (In some instances, he determines *what* the persons are communicating when the sound is off.) (Foreign-language films might be used successfully here.)

h. After seeing a stage or screen production of a play using non-verbal characteristics of a culture other than his own (*Playboy of the Western World, Raisin in the Sun, The Cherry Orchard,* Kabuki or No [also Noh] dramas, for example), the student lists those non-verbal characteristics, and assesses their effect upon his effort to understand the meaning of the dramatic statement. (*Lilies of the Field* and the television version of *Jane Eyre* might also be used here.)

i. After observing a simulated job interview between the personnel manager of a local bank and a high school senior, the student describes any paralinguistic behaviors that seem to have influenced the participants in the interview.

j. Given an opportunity to role-play an interview, a conversation, or an excerpt from a literary work, for example, involving a person whose cultural background is different from his own, the student sympathetically assumes the character and manifests the physical behaviors of that person.

k. Given a chance to explore different neighborhoods (for example, Chinese, Italian, Spanish) in his city, the student reports on the non-verbal language behavior he observes.

l. Given a filmed or videotaped spoken presentation, the student observes facial expressions, gestures, movements, or other non-verbal factors which explain more fully what is being said, and then he identifies the non-verbal factors and tells how they complement, detract from, or in some other way modify, the verbal message itself.

m. Given an opportunity to see himself giving a speech on film or on videotape, the student makes an objective analysis of his own non-verbal behavior.

n. After observing and listening to the oral reading of a poem such as "My Last Duchess" (perhaps it should be read two or three times), the student lists the observable behaviors of the reader that seemed to communicate something other than (different from, more than, etc.) the words of the poem. (A prose dramatic monolog also works well here.)

o. After observing a two- or three-person dialog in a confrontation scene from a play (performed in the classroom as a demonstration, on a stage in full production, on film, or on television), the student describes the paralinguistic behaviors of the characters and explains the apparent effects of these behaviors upon the other character(s). (The funeral scene from *Julius Caesar* works well here.)

p. Without explaining their purposes to the rest of the class, two students agree upon a specific assignment to be made to the class, write out a text that both will use, and then memorize it. Next, one of them presents the assignment to the class orally and with paralinguistic elements he believes will arouse interest and enthusiasm for the assignment. At the same time the other student uses paralinguistic elements he believes will result in indifference or resentment toward the assignment. Having observed this enactment, the other class members list and evaluate the effects of the specific paralinguistic elements employed upon the shaping of their attitudes toward the assignment made.

q. Given the assignment to write several sentences reflecting their individual views toward a common problem, two students, representing different cultural, economic, or social backgrounds, do so, and then they portray before the class, as they speak the sentences, the non-verbal elements that reflect their different backgrounds. Following this, the class identifies the background-related communications behaviors in both of the students.

r. After listening to a tape recording of a conversation, the student identifies apparently culture-related vocal intonations that are different from his own. (A recording of regional dialects can be useful here.) (*See also* 4.Bb below.)

s. After listening to a tape recording of a conversation between another student and himself, the student examines his own vocal intonations, and decides whether any of them are related to his particular cultural background.

t. After viewing a videotape of a conversation (but with the sound turned off), the student identifies apparently culture-related postural and gestural patterns that are different from his own.

u. After observing a role-played interview between a well-educated public opinion interviewer and a differently educated person of a different ethnic group, the student identifies the physical behaviors that reveal the participants' different cultural backgrounds, and describes any adjustments that the interviewer makes in an effort to communicate more clearly with the interviewee. (The interviewee might also be a well-educated person.)

v. After viewing a television "talk" show (David Frost or Dick Cavett, for example), the student identifies the interviewer's verbal and non-verbal characteristics that remain constant for all interviewees, and those that vary from one interviewee to another. The student then evaluates the variations on the basis of the sex, age, profession, etc., of each interviewee.

Goal 4

The student recognizes, appreciates, and respects idiosyncratic and dialectal speech differences. *See also* IV 11; V 14.Eb.

Performance Objective 4.A

Given appropriate listening situations, the student demonstrates respect for and appreciation of diversity in speech, and demonstrates the ability to cope with language that may seem obscene, rude, stilted, or old-fashioned.

Representative Enabling Objectives

a. Given taped or recited passages including words considered irreverent in some places (like "bloody" in England), the student concentrates upon *what* is being said rather than *how* it is being said and accurately restates the meaning of or paraphrases the passages. The student then examines *how* and weighs the relationship between the *how* and the *what*, pointing out whether the language emphasizes, contradicts, distracts from, or is unrelated to the content.

b. Given the same set of passages, the student concentrates upon the words only, and then lists those expressions which might once have kept him from hearing the major message, or may still keep others from doing so.

c. After listening to a recording of a conversation among three young children (approximately 3 years of age) from different social and cultural backgrounds, the student interprets the conversation and explains how the varying backgrounds of the children figured in his arriving at his interpretation. (The student would of course have to be provided with the background information.)

d. After listening to recordings or viewing segments of conversations or meetings between various groups of people, such as American Indians, natives of Vermont, men and women in their 80's, people who know each other well and don't need to speak much (like some husbands and wives), the student discusses and accurately interprets the communication that has taken place. (Television ["The Honeymooners," etc.] may be useful here.)

e. After listening to an oral reading of three different translations of the same Biblical passage, the student states that he has heard the same passage three times and, further, identifies the significant similarities and differences of the three translations. (Different translations of selected classical literature might also be used.)

f. Given a recording of literary selections, some written by Chaucer, some by Shakespeare, and some by Burns, for example, the student analyzes and points out how the language changed over the years represented. See also IV 8.B.

g. After listening to recorded passages selected from Dickens' novels in which certain characters use stilted language, the student identifies and analyzes those passages and, further, discusses the tendency of some present-day governmental officials to use similarly stilted language. See also IV 8.B.

Performance Objective 4.B

Given appropriate listening situations, the student demonstrates respect for and appreciation of dialectal differences, and demonstrates the ability to understand the differences.

Representative Enabling Objectives

a. Given his own and his classmates' individual recordings of a selected passage, the student compares the various recordings and indicates, orally or in writing, the ways in which his idiolect and dialect differ from those of his classmates. He might show acceptance of, and perhaps delight with, the variations from his own speech.

b. After listening to tapes or records of selected passages read or spoken by persons from various dialect regions of this country, or from other English-speaking countries, the student analyzes and discusses the differences in the dialects. (*Americans Speaking*, a recording of regional standard dialects, is available from the National Council of Teachers of English.)

c. Given a tape recording of a discussion in which he was a participant, the student listens to the recording and points out the significant differences between his speech and that of his classmates. (The same tape could be used for other instructional goals involving group interaction, group dynamics, discussion techniques, etc.). See also IV 12.E.

d. Given a tape recording or a phonetic transcription of his own speech, and given one of the "standard" speeches on his "home ground," the student compares and contrasts the two. (Discussion of speech nuances should follow such an experience.) *See also* IV 12.E.

e. Given a recording of selections by Paul Laurence Dunbar, Langston Hughes, Robert Frost, and John F. Kennedy, for example, the student points out their dialectal differences.

f. Given recorded speech samples of the major regional standard American dialects (including the dialect of his own region) and given a recorded sample of his own speech, the student compares and contrasts his own speech with the regional samples, one at a time, and he identifies basic differences between the two and, further, determines whether or not his own dialect is standard for his region.

Goal 5

The student realizes that one of the primary purposes of speaking and listening is the communication of ideas, and he recognizes that the value of what is communicated is the first criterion for evaluating the success of most oral presentations.

Performance Objective 5.A

Given a speaking–listening situation, the student identifies, as one of the primary concerns, the ideas that are being communicated.

Representative Enabling Objectives

a. After listening to a recording of an eloquent speaker of non-standard English who says something worthwhile, or after watching one on TV, the student evaluates the presentation for its ideas and the development of those ideas, on the basis of objective criteria.

b. After listening to several recorded passages from speeches of contemporary Americans (for example, Dick Gregory, Julian Bond, Kate Millett, Margaret Chase Smith, Pauline Frederick, George Wallace, William Buckley, George McGovern, and Spiro Agnew), the student makes and defends such tentative value judgments as "High-flown but insignificant in content," "Eloquent and full of significant ideas," "The presentation is enhanced by the quality of the speech."

c. Given several classroom situations in which he is free to choose his own topic, the student presents a message rated significant in content by most of his classmates. (The speeches may also be taped and played back.)

d. Given a proverb, the student demonstrates his understanding of obfuscation by rewriting the proverb in high-flown, ambiguous language. (E.g., A solitary feathered biped clutched digitally is of infinitely greater worth than a pair of similar bipeds ensconced in the shrubbery.)

e. Given a sample of spare, concise speech, the student demonstrates his understanding of obfuscation by rewriting the prose in elegant, extravagant, ambiguous language.

f. Given a sample of circuitous and imprecise prose, the student tries to abstract the key idea and, if he cannot, explains why he cannot.

Goal 6

The student fully understands the importance and potentialities of his voice as a communication instrument.

Representative Entering Performance Objective

Given exercises on nonsense syllables and sound combinations, the student produces at will all the indicated sounds.

Performance Objective 6.A

Given a variety of speaking situations, the student demonstrates control of his voice in ways such as articulation, intonation, and emotional range.

Representative Enabling Objectives

a. Given instruction in the dynamics of voice production, the student, speaking on successive tape recordings, modifies the quality of nasality (or harshness, shrillness, etc.) in his voice.

b. Given a short sentence (for example, "I thought that you would know"), the student says it in several different ways to convey different meanings. (Some students prefer to make up their own sentences.) (This can also be used to get at various interpretations of characters in literature, as, e.g., in V 35.I.)

c. Given a speech situation, such as a sharply defined role in a one-act play, the student uses his voice effectively to create character, mood, tone, etc., through use of such devices as shifts in pitch, level, rate, intonation, and pause. (Some students can write their own plays, based in some instances on stories they have read.)

d. After silently reading (several times) a story for children, the student tells the story to his classmates, paying particular attention to the elements of speech mentioned above in c.

e. Given a part of the alphabet or a series of nonsense words, the student reads them aloud to an audience, using only his voice to convey successively attitudes of sincerity, sarcasm, and affection. (The list of nonsense words could be made up by members of the class.)

f. Given tongue-twisters (for example, "She sells seashells by the seashore"), the student reads each one rapidly without difficulty. (Students may also create their own tongue-twisters.)

g. Given a large auditorium or the classroom, a mike or a lectern without a mike, the student adjusts the projection of his voice to suit the particular circumstances.

Goal 7

The student knows specific techniques for effective speaking and listening in a variety of situations, including small conversational and large discussion groups, and uses effective oral style in all of his speaking. (*See also* III 16.)

Performance Objective 7.A

As he participates in a variety of speaking–listening situations, the student sometimes concentrates on the structure of the presentation. *See also* V 10; VI.

Representative Enabling Objectives

a. After listening to a well-structured informational speech, the student distinguishes between the main and supporting points and explains the logic of their sequence.
b. After listening (perhaps more than once) to a recording of a speech in which the ideas have been presented in a scrambled order, the student lists the main and supporting points in a reasonable sequence and defends his choice.
c. Asked to prepare five-minute talks on topics of his own choice, the student organizes his thoughts, first, with paper and pencil for an extemporaneous speech, and, then, without paper and pencil for an impromptu speech.
d. When listening to any oral presentation, the student pays attention all the way to the very end, and then points out the relationship between the body of the presentation and the conclusion.
e. After listening to any oral presentation, the student demonstrates in discussion his ability to relate one part of the speech to another, and to relate the various parts to the whole.
f. After listening to a political speech that is clearly effective, the student identifies the structural parts (considering especially the beginning, middle, conclusion, and major transitions) that make the speech effective.
g. After listening to a political speech with worthwhile content but ineffective organization, the student suggests concrete revisions (considering especially the beginning, middle, conclusion, and major transitions) that will make the speech more effective.
h. Given an assignment to plan a five-minute speech on a particular topic, the student outlines a speech and lists specific techniques (for

example, the use of a quotation, a rhetorical question, a joke), for the beginning, middle, conclusion, and major transitions.

Performance Objective 7.B

As he participates in a variety of speaking–listening situations, the student recognizes and uses various speaking styles.

Representative Enabling Objectives

a. Given a speech with a series of statements which might be misinterpreted, the student extracts from the statements several key words with more than one meaning and prepares a list of questions or comments to show which meaning was probably intended in each context. *See also* IV 20.A; VI 6.A.

b. Given a series of oral instructions, the student follows the ones he understands and asks questions about the ones he does not understand. (The person giving the instructions might include, as an example, some such regional expressions as: "Then take a right left," and "Drop the dog out of the window some food"; or he might include instructions phrased in the current slang of teenagers.) *See also* IV 11.A.

c. While giving a prepared speech, the student adjusts his language (without talking down) to his audience, reading as little as possible from a paper, but observing audience reactions as he speaks. He does not assume that everyone is listening, that everyone understands him, that his speaking style is right for every audience, or even that his vocabulary is clear. For example, given a topic, the student will prepare a presentation and give it, making adjustments in vocabulary and tone as needed, to at least two of the following audiences (or others equally disparate and identifiable):

   (1) Illiterate persons
   (2) Navajo Indians
   (3) Persons who have just learned English as a second language
   (4) Children under 10 years of age
   (5) People over 70 years of age
   (6) Teachers of English
   (7) Peer group

   See also VI 11.

d. After preparing a speech on a current topic of interest to most people in his community, the student presents his speech to at least two different audiences—a school assembly, a club meeting, his English class, a group of adult citizens—and in doing so, he makes shifts in his language (his usage, vocabulary, syntax, tone, and speed of delivery) so that it is appropriate for most members of each of his audiences.

e. After silently observing his class in a discussion session for approximately twenty minutes, the student discusses the different speaking styles of his teacher and selected members of his class.

f. After listening to recordings of speeches by men such as Dwight D. Eisenhower, Franklin D. Roosevelt, and John F. Kennedy, the student compares and contrasts the various elements of their speaking styles.

Performance Objective 7.C

As he participates in a variety of speaking–listening situations, the student sometimes focuses on techniques that contribute to point of view. *See also* II 9; V 12; VI 13; VII 14.

Representative Enabling Objectives

a. After listening to a political speaker, the student shows—in writing or in an oral discussion of the speech—that he *heard what was actually being said,* and not his own inner voice or the voices of others which might have prejudiced him against the speaker.

b. Given a choice from a wide range of poems, short stories, or excerpts from longer works, and given instructions to select one for oral presentation to each of several different age-groups (pre-school children, twelve-year-olds, teenagers, adults, for example), the student presents his selections and then gives and defends his reasons for his selection for each group. (Classmates might role-play the various age-groups.)

c. Instructed to pay particular attention in his television viewing one evening to the various age groups to which commercials are aimed, the student outlines, and then orally presents, commercials that appeal to each of the following groups: children, teenagers, and adults. (If necessary for dramatic purposes, he may enlist the help of classmates in the presentation.)

Performance Objective 7.D

The student participates in small conversational and large discussion groups and demonstrates the basic courtesies of oral communication.

Representative Enabling Objectives

a. Given a conversational situation, the student participates appropriately, particularly in terms of the following: the amount of speaking he does, the amount of listening he does, his willingness to communicate, the extent to which he communicates his own ideas, the quality of his questions, the way he uses feedback from other members of the group, the vocabulary he uses, and the way he adjusts his rate, tone, and volume.

b. Given a message to communicate by telephone, the student makes all essential elements of his communication clear and makes effective use of feedback from the person with whom he is talking. (A tele-trainer, which most telephone companies provide free of charge to schools, may be used to great advantage here.)

c. After being assigned to a group of class members with a particular topic to discuss or problem to solve, the student works as an effective member of and contributor to the group by: understanding the task assigned, executing his part of the task, adjusting or modifying his role when necessary, and respecting the personalities, tasks, and contributions of other members of the group.

d. After viewing a videotape of a class discussion, the student analyzes it for the following features: how some students talk too much, some too little; how some students make irrelevant remarks; and how some students ignore, or seem not to hear, what other students say.

Goal 8

The student orally interprets printed materials effectively. *See also* V 14.Da; V 21.Ea, b; V 29.Aa.

Performance Objective 8.A

Given selections from various types of printed material, the student presents them effectively in terms of both linguistic and paralinguistic elements of presentation. Effectiveness will be determined by audience response. *See also* V 35.E.

Representative Enabling Objectives

a. Before presenting a selection, the student prepares a short statement describing his intended effects upon his audience. His effectiveness will be evaluated by comparing actual audience response with his stated intentions.

b. Given a carefully selected poem (perhaps one chosen by the student) to interpret orally before his class, the student presents the poem effectively in terms of clarity of message, of desirable eye contact and bodily movement, and of appropriate use of the voice: rhythm, phrasing, intonation, tempo, articulation, word-coloring, and pause. (A popular song might be substituted for the poem, and a student may be encouraged to interpret it by singing it.) *See also* V 25.Ba and b.

c. Given a selection from a short story, such as Poe's "Tell-Tale Heart," to read orally before his class, the student reads it so as to appropriately convey meaning, character, mood, tone, etc.

d. Assigned a part in the group-reading of a play, or an excerpt from one, the student reads his part effectively according to criteria prepared by the class and, moreover, reveals through his interpretation and reading of his lines an awareness of the interaction desirable among all the members of the group.

e. As a participant in the choral reading of a poem (Rudyard Kipling's "If" or John Masefield's "Sea Fever," for example), the student performs effectively according to the following criteria (among others): reasonable understanding of the meaning, plausible interpretation of the mood, clear articulation, acceptable pronunciation, thorough understanding of the function of the punctuation marks used, full awareness of his voice qualities, control of his voice volume, sense of tempo, and an obvious sense of belonging to a unified choral reading group.

f. Reading from the text of a recent speech by a public official, the student conveys an accurate understanding of the purpose, the tone, and the movement of the speech. (The *New York Times* often prints the complete text of important speeches.)

Goal 9

The student understands and follows the fundamental principles and basic rules of parliamentary procedure.

Performance Objective 9.A

Given a class set up as a business meeting, with an assignment such as the drafting of a request to the Student Council, each student participates according to the prescribed fundamentals of parliamentary procedure.

Representative Enabling Objectives

a. At the beginning of the meeting, a student is designated to take the minutes, the accuracy of which is subsequently checked with all members of the class.

b. During the meeting each student speaks only when recognized by the chair, and addresses his remarks to the chair.

c. In making a motion, the student uses accepted terminology (for example, "I move that . . . .").

d. Given a situation in which the appropriateness of discussion is questionable, the student raises a "point of order."

e. Given a discussion of an amendment to a motion, the student confines his remarks to the amendment only.

f. Given a moderately complicated parliamentary situation, such as may arise from an amendment to an amendment, the student explains, or demonstrates by doing, the steps to be sequentially followed before the main motion is once more in order.

g. After participating in several meetings run according to accepted parliamentary procedure, the student does the following:

(1) lists, or demonstrates, the steps between the introduction and adoption of a motion.

(2) identifies, or demonstrates, the kinds of limitations on individual behavior that can be imposed only by an extraordinary majority (for example, a two-thirds majority to cut off debate).

(3) identifies, or demonstrates, parliamentary procedures that can properly be used to speed up consideration of and action on a motion.

(4) identifies, or demonstrates, parliamentary procedures that can properly be used to delay consideration of or prevent action on a motion.

Goal 10

The student recognizes the fundamental importance of accuracy and objectivity in the reporting of what he hears and sees. *See also* V 42; VI 7; VII 14.Aa and 15.

Performance Objective 10.A

Following his participation in any speaking–listening situation—either through person-to-person encounter or by means of recording or film—the student demonstrates accuracy and objectivity in reporting what he has heard and seen.

Representative Enabling Objectives

a. After listening to the reading of a short factual passage, the student accurately summarizes it, orally or in writing, and his classmates evaluate the accuracy of his summary.

b. Given a one- or two-minute radio public service announcement, the student accurately and objectively identifies the specific action(s) he is urged to take.

c. After seeing a staged scene in the classroom (the staging of which he was uninformed about), the student gives an accurate and objective oral report of what happened, and his classmates evaluate the accuracy and objectivity of his report.

d. Given a recorded series of random segments from a radio or television newscast (for example, on the war in Vietnam), the student identifies those segments containing generalizations which are supported primarily by factual information accessible to any competent observer and, on the other hand, those segments containing generalizations supported primarily by the opinion of the reporter.

e. Given a recording or the script of a radio or television commercial, the student identifies those sentences containing verifiable statements of fact and those containing unsupported assertions or appeals to emotion. *See also* IV 22.A; VII 4.

f. Given a radio public service announcement such as that in *b*, the student lists the evidential data or information used by the broadcaster to support his appeal. *See also* VII 20.

g. Given a recorded or transcribed three-minute speech in which the language has been obviously manipulated, the student rephrases the message with more accurate and more honest use of language.

h. Given a primarily informative short speech for a general audience, the student demonstrates his understanding of the differences between language adaptation and language manipulation by rewriting the speech for a specifically different audience and by rewriting it a second time to change its purpose from information to persuasion. *See also* IV 23.A; VI 11.h.

Goal 11

The student reflects a sense of responsibility for his use of spoken language. *See also* V 39.A; VI 8; VII 15.

Performance Objective 11.A

Given a variety of specific speech situations, the student demonstrates through what he says and through the language he uses those ethical considerations (a list of principles drawn up by the class) that must be taken into account by any responsible speaker.

Representative Enabling Objectives

a. After participating in a class discussion of ethics in communication, and after listening to recorded excerpts from several political speeches, the student draws up a list of ethical considerations appropriate for a responsible speaker. Examples: (1) He supports his opinions with facts. (2) He reports facts fully, accurately, and objectively. (3) He avoids irresponsible euphemisms (*see* V 39.A).

b. During a campaign for a local, state, or national election, the student analyzes one or more actual speeches, listing the arguments he considers ethical and those he considers unethical, and then supports his choices. *See also* V 2.B, 16.B, 39.A, and 43.K.

c. Given the assignment to pretend that he is running for a local, state, or national political office, the student prepares his platform and writes a campaign speech that is ethically responsible according to the list of considerations he has previously prepared.

d. After viewing a number of TV commercials, or listening to some on radio, the student draws up a list of sales appeals which are ethically sound. *See also* VII 20.

e. After viewing and/or listening to a commercial on a given product, along with the usual arguments addressed to potential consumers, the student selects those arguments that seem to be ethical.

f. After experiencing a production of a play (for example, *Oedipus, Hamlet, The Zoo Story,* or *Pygmalion*), the student identifies those characters whose behavior is ethically acceptable by current standards, and distinguishes examples of ethical and unethical behavior by each of the major characters. *See also* V: **Valuing.**

g. Given a fixed position to defend in a debate before his peers, the student prepares a list of supporting arguments he considers ethical and another list of those he considers unethical, and then he explains why he has placed each item on each list.

h. Given a variety of audiences, and given a definite point of view to defend before each, the student lists any arguments that he would not consider ethical for one of his audiences, and explains why.

Goal 12

In certain germane situations of speaking and listening, the student distinguishes between logical and illogical reasoning, can analyze a problem, and develop a logical solution. *See also* V 10 and 30.

Performance Objective 12.A

Given a recording or manuscript of any speech, conversation, or discussion, the student points out both the valid and invalid arguments presented; he identifies conclusions that follow from stated premises; he composes questions that will help in discovering and defining problems and possible solutions.

Representative Enabling Objectives

a. After listening to a speech by a public orator, the student identifies the conclusions that follow logically from stated premises.

b. After listening to a public orator or to a radio or TV commercial, the student identifies the stated and/or implied premises and the allegedly logical inferences or conclusions intended to be drawn from them.

c. After hearing a "one line" advertising appeal (for example: "If it's Gambel's, it's got to be good!" or "You can be *sure* if it's Testinghouse!") the student states the implied premises. (Students should be encouraged to make up their own commercials, for which other students state the implied premises.)

d. Given a broadcast commercial or a speech by a public figure, the student identifies implied premises from which conclusions are apparently drawn.

e. Given a discussion assignment (on the legalizing of marijuana, for example), the student develops a series of questions designed to define and establish the parameters of the problem.

f. Given a discussion assignment (on environmental pollution, for example), the student prepares a series of questions designed to elicit an inventory of possible solutions. (One class took a very different approach: they wrote songs containing possible solutions to environmental pollution, and then sang the songs.)

g. Given a discussion assignment (on U. S. involvement in the Far East, for example), the student develops a series of questions designed to establish the minimum essentials for any acceptable solution.

h. Given a discussion asignment (on nuclear arms control, for example), the student prepares a proposed solution and then develops a series of questions designed to test the logicality of his solution.

i. As he listens to a series of speeches by his classmates, the student, at the conclusion of each speech, does the folowing:

(1) writes down the conclusions he (the listener) was asked by the speaker to accept.

(2) writes down the premises from which the conclusions are drawn.

(3) compares the conclusions and premises he (the listener) has written down with the conclusions and premises in an outline provided by the speaker.

j. While listening to a discussion of any problem of current interest to him and his classmates, the student jots down those questions asked by the active participants in the discussion in an effort *to discover or develop possible alternative solutions.* At the conclusion of the discussion, the student then makes additions to the list of those questions he would have asked had he been a member of the discussion group.

k. While listening to a discussion of any problem of current interest to him and his classmates, the student lists those questions asked *for the purpose of testing the logicality of proposed solutions,* and then, at the conclusion of the discussion, he adds questions that he might have asked had he been an active participant in the discussion.

l. Assigned a clearly defined role in a discussion on a normally debatable topic, the student states his ideas in essentially neutral terms in order to achieve maximum rational discussion of the topic.

m. After listening to a recording of a discussion on a "hot" issue, the student identifies those bits of dialog that seemed to escalate nonobjective analysis of the ideas presented, and then recasts the initial statement in language that will receive maximum rational response.

Goal 13

The student is sensitive to the nuances of language, and understands the roles of denotation and connotation, as well as emotive terms and phrases, in the use of language. *See also* IV 20, 21, and 22; VI 6.C.

Performance Objective 13.A

After listening to a speech, the student identifies subtleties in the speaker's diction, and distinguishes between the essential lexical meaning of the speech and the emotive language in which it was expressed.

Representative Enabling Objectives

a. Given a radio or television interview with a political candidate, the student identifies those statements and questions couched in essentially objective terms and those using affective words.

b. Given a radio or television commercial, the student selects those sentences containing language primarily intended to inform and those using terms primarily intended to arouse or intensify feelings.

c. After viewing a videotaped political talk, the student identifies the prejudices and the linguistic distortions, justifies his choices, and then does the following:

   (1) translates pejorative verbs (*spawn, blast, coddle,* for example) into less emotionally charged verbs.

   (2) translates ambiguous words or phrases (*justice, wrong, fair play,* for example) into operational terms.

   (3) describes the connotative effect of such ambiguous words and phrases.

   (4) translates emotive labels (*Commie, impudent, snob, hippie, yippie, draft dodger, bum, pig, square, chicken, hawk, beatnik,* for example) into neutral terms.

d. After viewing a videotaped talk (one by Spiro Agnew, George Wallace, or Eldridge Cleaver, for example), the student identifies examples of linguistic distortions and suggests the speaker's reason for using pejorative verbs and the probable effect of such use on various types of listeners.

e. Given a tape recording of an argument (from a student demonstration, a courtroom cross-examination, etc., or a simulated situation), the student lists the words and phrases with connotative meanings.

f. Given several taped or read-aloud passages (perhaps editorials and news stories), the student decides which ones are primarily objective, which primarily subjective or opinionated. (Columns by Sidney Harris, John P. Roche, Mike Royko, and Art Buchwald would serve particularly well here.)

g. Having heard a sermon (on radio or television, or at church), the student presents an objective oral report on the speaker's use of denotative and connotative language.

h. After listening to a passage from Jonathan Edwards' "Sinners in the Hands of an Angry God," the student discusses its probable effect on an eighteenth-century Puritan congregation and its probable effect on a twentieth-century audience, and then lists reasons for the disparate reactions. (Different oral interpretations may be tried.)

Goal 14

The student appreciates (reveals ability to identify with, describe, value, and assess) dramatic presentations.

Performance Objective 14.A

While "attending" a dramatic performance (on stage or on a movie or television screen), the student participates intelligently and emotionally in the experience. *See also* V 40 and 41.

Representative Enabling Objectives

a. After attending a three-act musical (for example), the student explains the relationship of such elements as physical behavior, voice production, music, other sounds, movement, form, scenery, and color to the dramatic denouement (or to the delineation of character, the definition of theme, etc.).

b. After viewing a movie or play on television, the student discusses the elements of theme and plot, character portrayal, and visual and sound effects.

c. After attending two different performances of the same scene (or entire play), the student selects the one he considers superior, and then explains his selection as it may have been influenced by contrasts in character portrayal.

d. After attending two different performances of the same scene (or entire play), the student selects the one he considers superior, and then explains his selection as it may have been influenced by contrasts or emphases in visual and sound effects (scenery, properties, lighting, music, etc.).

e. After seeing a play (or a scene from one) which he has previously read, the student discusses the advantages of the dramatization over the reading.

f. After seeing the same movie twice, the student assesses any increase in his understanding and/or appreciation of the movie.

g. After seeing a current "young" movie (as *Easy Rider* was in 1969), the student designs a series of interview questions intended to discover the judgments of his peers about the film and the bases for those judgments.

Goal 15

The student discerns differences between textual and subtextual communication. (*Subtextual* refers to "reading between the lines.")

Performance Objective 15.A

After listening to communications in various forms, the student explains the textual and some of the subtextual meanings. *See also* V 35.

Representative Enabling Objectives

a. After hearing a recording of a conversation from a Hemingway novel or a part of a play with brief conversations, the student paraphrases the conversations, "filling in" with information from the context.
b. After viewing a segment of a film narrative, the student supplies, orally or in writing, an authentic (appropriate) beginning and/or ending to the narrative.
c. After hearing a brief dialog from A. B. Guthrie's "Bargain," Shirley Jackson's *After You, My Dear Alphonse* or Eugene O'Neill's *Strange Interlude*, for example, the student identifies the contrasts between what the characters "say" and what they "think."
d. Given a selection from a speech, the student reads it aloud as though he is endorsing what he says, and then as though he is skeptical about what he says.

Goal 16

The student distinguishes between elements of effective style in oral and written discourse. (One's *style* is his manner or mode of expressing his thoughts in speaking or writing. Elements of style include, among others, such things as punctuation, organization, sentence length, clause complexity, word choice, persona, and tone.) *See also* III 7; VI 10. and 14.

Performance Objective 16.A

Given a recording of a formal speech, along with the manuscript of it, the student identifies those elements of style which give it its effectiveness.

Representative Enabling Objectives

a. After reading the manuscript of a five-minute radio or TV news commentary on a single topic (Eric Sevareid kind of reporting of approximately 1,000 words), the student writes a "letter to the editor" covering the same topic, and then compares and contrasts the stylistic elements in his essay with those in the essay of the other author.

b. Given a series of excerpts from speeches by public orators, the student restates the same ideas in styles suitable for inclusion in essays.

c. Given a persuasive editorial (one written by himself or by someone else), the student recasts the same content into a speech manuscript for audiences such as the following:

   (1) a men's luncheon club
   (2) a high school assembly
   (3) a radio audience
   (4) a television audience
   (5) a teenage Sunday School class

   See also VI 11.

d. Given the same speech as in *c* above, the student rewrites it with a different structure.

e. Given the same speech as in *c* above, the student rewrites it with a different tone.

IV

Language

RATIONALE

Because of the contemporary concern and emphasis on language as a medium of spoken and written communication, enlightened English teachers realize that one of the most interesting parts of the English curriculum to study is the English language. In the process of helping students not only to communicate effectively but also to understand and evaluate the communication of others, these teachers involve students in the many aspects of language: history, usage, dialect, syntax, lexicography, semantics, and modern grammar.

These enlightened English teachers further realize that the language program must equip the student to become an active observer and investigator of the English language, whereby he begins to make and test generalizations about spoken and written language and compares these with the data and opinions of recognized language scholars. With this approach, the student begins to discover the flexibility and life of the language; it frees him from the traditional view that language is exact, correct or incorrect, unchanging.

In keeping with these stated ideas, the language section contains representative objectives that familiarize the student with the following areas of language study: history, dialects, usage, structure, semantics, lexicography, and grammar.

The grammar, however, is not a separate section because it would not be practical nor feasible to write a complete grammar since teachers have various texts available to them to select from for this

The project director in charge of this section, Thomas Pietras, Assistant Professor of Education and English, Purdue University, was assisted by several consultants and directors.

instruction. What the language section does contain is various grammar objectives throughout its subsections which reflect linguistic insights and points of view to help the student in his understanding of some of the basic features and concepts concerning the structure of American English. Furthermore, these grammar objectives are interwoven with the various areas of language study to enable the student to realize that grammar influences and is influenced by these various areas.

Objectives related to mechanics are included in the writing section. Propaganda techniques, although related to semantics, are included in the mass media section because it is felt that their study would be more meaningful in that section. Furthermore, it is here noted that language objectives occur throughout this catalog.

GENERAL KNOWLEDGE

Goal 1

The student becomes aware that his ability to use the English language demonstrates an inherent knowledge of the systematic principles of that language.

Performance Objective 1.A

The student demonstrates an elementary knowledge of the grammar of his language by using the appropriate inflectional endings to signal a change in meaning or function for any given word.

Representative Enabling Objectives

a. Given a list of dictated words that contain a mixture of nouns, adjectives, and adverbs, the student orally responds to each word with as many different inflectional endings as he can (e.g., system: systematic, systematically, systematize).

b. Given a list of words and various acceptable inflectional endings for each, the student explains, orally or in writing, how each ending affects the meaning and/or function of each word (e.g., employ: employer, employee).

Performance Objective 1.B

The student demonstrates his inherent knowledge of the grammar of English by recognizing that the position of a word in an utterance usually signals the word's form class (noun, verb, adjective, adverb) in that particular utterance.

Representative Enabling Objectives

a. Given a series of utterances (such as those that follow) which substitute nonsense words for actual words, the student explains what form class each nonsense word is and why.

> The cold *niss* is quite delicious.
> The boy *glings* whenever he is angry.
> Mary is *wuggier* than John.
> The car is running *ostily*.

b. Given a discussion of several utterances substituting nonsense words for actual words, the student explains how he was able to infer what form class the nonsense words were.

Performance Objective 1.C

The student shows his knowledge of the predictability of language as measured by his ability to insert appropriate form class words in appropriate positions within sentences. (E.g., The _____ was happy. My father was _____. The boy _____ the ball. Children _____.)

Performance Objective 1.D

The student recognizes that the English language consists of a predictable arrangement of letters representing sounds specific to English when he distinguishes between English and non-English combinations of letters.

Representative Enabling Objective

Given a list of combined letters (such as those that follow), the student distinguishes the English combinations from the non-English combinations.

ing	est
tion	ks
gh	er
cz	wl
sz	szk
ly	ml

Performance Objective 1.E

The student demonstrates his operational knowledge of English grammar, in particular syntax and phonology, by constructing an artificial language of nonsense words based on the principles which he has discovered about English.

Representative Enabling Objective

a. The student constructs an artificial language containing at least twenty-five nonsense words that will reflect the basic morphology, sentence patterns, form classes, and letter combinations of English. With these lexical items he will construct declarative, imperative, and interrogative sentences.

Performance Objective 1.F

The student will demonstrate knowledge that language is arbitrary as measured by his ability to formulate "nonsense" words and agree upon arbitrary meanings for them. *See also* IV 19.*

Goal 2

The student develops skills, insights and attitudes about the English language through his analysis of an artificial language. *See also* IV 1.Ea.

Performance Objective 2.A

After the construction of an artificial language and given the problem of analyzing its sound system, the student learns an accepted phonetic alphabet.

Representative Enabling Objectives

a. Hearing a list of words from the artificial language, the student produces an accurate phonetic transcription for each word.
b. Having phonetically transcribed such a list of words accurately, the student pronounces each word.
c. The student discovers that conventional spelling of words does not always correspond to the phonetic spelling by comparing his phonetic transcriptions with his conception of how these words would be spelled conventionally.
d. The student recognizes that often times the conventional spelling for a given word may vary by comparing his spelling with those of other students, e.g., *nurd, nerd, nird.*
e. The student discovers that there are certain regularities in the combinations of letters in conventional spelling that usually represent certain sounds in English (e.g., *ing, or, er, ment, ness, ent, pre, dis*) by his ability to spell words orally dictated to him which have such combinations. (Although a student might substitute the *or* com-

* Roman numerals refer to chapters, Arabic numerals to goals, capital letters to performance objectives, and lower-case letters to enabling objectives.

bination for *er*, he is aware that these are the choices for representing this sound.)

f. The student operationally describes how the grammar of his artificial language signals a change in meaning and/or form class for the nonsense words.

g. The student operationally describes how the syntax of his artificial language produces sentences.

h. The student writes his own working definition of language, which reflects the recognition that language has rules but that the rules are flexible and exist to facilitate clear communication.

GENERAL KNOWLEDGE—SYNTAX

Goal 3

The student becomes aware that the four basic types of English sentences may be expanded and modified by use of various transformations, and that these transformations follow a specific system. (The intention here is to help the student realize that the English sentence is marvelously systematic, and to give him increased confidence in himself because he mastered most of the intricacies of the system at an early age. Additionally, practice with some of the transformations—especially those involving the combining of sentences—may add to the student's syntactic repertory.)

Note: No attempt is made here to explain transformations elaborately, with a wealth of linguistic detail. Such explanations are available in some textbooks and may be necessary for a thorough understanding. The purpose here, however, is to acquaint the student with only a nontechnical, working description upon which he may build later if he wishes. *See also* V 14; VI 4.

Performance Objective 3.A

The student explains and illustrates how sentences of each of the four basic types are transformed into negative statements.

Representative Enabling Objectives

a. Given Type 1 sentences like *Dad is a golfer, The oysters were delicious,* and *Visitors have been here,* the student makes each one negative by inserting *not* in the appropriate place. He observes that in such sentences *not* is always dropped in between the second and third slots. (I.e., We do not say *Dad not is a golfer*. The asterisk indicates an un-English kind of sentence.)

b. Given Type 2 sentences like *The peaches taste sweet, Larry became the victim, Larry remained quiet,* and *Larry remained here,* the student makes each negative by the use of the appropriate form of *do* plus the addition of *not* plus any needed change in the verb. He observes that in such sentences a systematic procedure is used repeatedly. (E.g., *The peaches taste sweet* → *The peaches do not taste sweet,* or *The peach tastes sweet* → *The peach does not taste sweet.* In each instance, the appropriate form of *do* is used, *not* follows *do,* and the simplest form of the verb *taste* is used.)

c. Given sentences of Types 3 and 4, such as *The children cry, I found a penny, Dad gave Jim a penny,* and *They made Henry the leader,* the student makes each one negative by following the same procedures as with Type 2 sentences. (E.g., *The children cry* → *The children do not cry; I found a penny* → *I did not find a penny.*)

d. Given sentences of any type in which the verb consists of two or more words (e.g., *have been, was laughing, has eaten, may have struggled*), the student makes each one negative by inserting *not* between parts of the verb (e.g., *have not been, may not have struggled*).

Performance Objective 3.B

The student explains and illustrates how sentences of each of the four basic types are transformed into questions.

Representative Enabling Objectives

a. Given sentences of Type 1 (e.g., *Joe is the quarterback, Susie is beautiful, Helen was there*), the student transforms each into a yes–no question by interchanging the slot 1 and slot 2 words. (E.g., *Joe is the quarterback* → *Is Joe the quarterback?*)

b. Given sentences of Types 2, 3 and 4 (e.g., *Roe looks tired, The coin vanished, She bought a skirt*), the student transforms each into a yes–no question by starting with the appropriate form of *do* and using the simplest form of the verb. (E.g., *Roe looks tired* → *Does Roe look tired?*)

c. Given sentences of any type, the student transforms each into one or more *wh-* questions. (These questions generally start with words like *what, when, where,* and *how.* Possible transformations may be created and examined by the student. For example, the statement *Friday Joe sold three colorful seashells* may be transformed into such questions as *When did Joe sell . . . , Who sold . . . , What did Joe do? How many seashells . . . , What kind of seashells . . . , What did Joe sell?* The student may observe and describe the system followed in each of these transformations.)

Performance Objective 3.C

The student illustrates how the voice creates the emphatic transformation by placing special stress on one part of a sentence.

Representative Enabling Objective

a. Given a sentence like *Three students heard his answer*, the student repeats the sentence several times, stressing a different part each time. He explains the slight differences in meaning that arise, and may also state an imaginary context in which each variation might be especially suitable.

Performance Objective 3.D

The student forms imperative transformations by deleting *you will* from sentences of the four types.

Representative Enabling Objective

a: Given sentences like *You will be ready, You will remain there, You will hurry,* and *You will give him his instructions,* the student transforms each into an imperative by deleting *you will.* (E.g., *You will be ready → Be ready.*)

Performance Objective 3.E

The student transforms sentences of Type 4 into the passive voice.

Representative Enabling Objectives

a. Given a sentence like *Joe answered the question*, the student transforms it to the passive voice. (*The question was answered by Joe.*) He explains in his own words that in this transformation the slot 3 word is moved to the beginning, the verb is changed by the addition of a form of *be*, and *by* is placed before the original slot 1 word.

b. Given a sentence like *Joe gave Bill a bicycle*, the student transforms it to the passive voice in either of two ways. (*Bill was given a bicycle by Joe* or *A bicycle was given Bill by Joe.*) He explains in his own words how these alternative transformations are made.

Performance Objective 3.F

The student transforms certain kinds of sentences into a form beginning with the expletive *there.*

Representative Enabling Objectives

a. Given a sentence like *Ants were in our picnic basket*, the student transforms it by starting the new sentence with *there.* (*There were ants in our picnic basket.*) He explains that this transformation involves not only starting with *there* but also interchanging slots 1 and 2.

b. Given a sentence with a verb consisting of a form of *be* plus another word (e.g., *A boy was cracking his knuckles*), the student changes it by using the *there*-transformation. (*There was a boy cracking his knuckles.*) He explains that this transformation involves the use of *there* plus the front-shifting of the form of *be*.

Performance Objective 3.G

The student transforms various kinds of sentences by altering the usual word order.

Representative Enabling Objective

a. Given sentences like any of these: *The clowns come next. He understood her meaning only hours later. They cannot do this*, the student transforms each by moving a different part into slot 1. He explains what additional changes then may become necessary. ((*Next come the clowns. Only hours later did he understand her meaning. This they cannot do.*)

Performance Objective 3.H

The student uses substitute words in some of the slots in the four basic sentence types.

Representative Enabling Objectives

a. The student substitutes pronouns for nouns in appropriate slots. (E.g., *Helen brought the cake* → *She brought it.*) He discovers inductively and then explains that the personal pronouns that may fit in slot 1 are *I, we, you, he, she, it,* and *they,* and that the usual personal pronouns in slots 3 and 4 are *me, us, you, him, her, it,* and *them.*

b. The student substitutes prepositional phrases for one-word adverbs. (E.g., *It is here* → *It is in the bag.*)

c. The student substitutes clauses for certain nominals. (E.g., *Tell me her reply* → *Tell me what she said. His motive is unknown* → *Why he did it is unknown.*)

d. The student substitutes verb forms (gerunds or infinitives) for certain nominals. (E.g., *I like this sport* → *I like swimming. I tried something* → *I tried to unlock the door.*)

Performance Objective 3.I

The student uses various transformations to combine sentences. Note: This objective is especially important for effecting improvements in sentence structure; it deserves considerable time.

Representative Enabling Objectives

a. Given two related sentences, the student combines them into one compound sentence. (E.g., *The swimming was good. The fishing was very poor* → *The swimming was good, but the fishing was very poor.*)

b. The student explains that when *and, but, for, or, nor, so,* or *yet* is not used as a connective in a compound sentence, a semicolon ordinarily separates the two parts. (E.g., *The swimming was good; the fishing was very poor.*)

c. Given pairs of sentences like *The girls screamed* and *The girls ran,* or *The girls marched around the room* and *The boys marched around the room,* the student combines them and deletes unnecessarily repeated words. ('E.g., *The girls screamed and* the girls *ran. The girls* marched around the room *and* the *boys marched around the room.*) Note: This exercise affords a simple explanation of compound subjects and compound predicates.

d. Given sentences like *I bought a sweater* and *The sweater was blue,* the student combines them in each of two ways. (*I bought a sweater that was blue* or *I bought a blue sweater.*) He analyzes and explains the process used.

e. Given sentences like *My brother is a soldier* and *My brother fought in Vietnam,* the student combines them in each of two ways. (*My brother, who is a soldier, fought in Vietnam* and *My brother, a soldier, fought in Vietnam.*) He analyzes and explains the process used.

f. Given sentences like *This car is here* and *This car is a Ford,* the student combines them. (*This car here is a Ford.*)

g. Given sentences like *The war was over* and *The boys came home,* the student combines them by transforming the one sentence into an adverbial clause. (*After the war was over, the boys came home.*)

h. Given several related sentences, the student combines them, possibly in more than a single way. (E.g., *The man is upstairs. The man is elderly. The man is my uncle. The man likes to tell stories. The stories are about his adventures. His adventures are exciting. His adventures were in Borneo* → *The elderly man upstairs, my uncle, likes to tell stories about his exciting adventures in Borneo.*)

i. In review, the student names and illustrates the kinds of processes that may be used in transforming the basic four types of sentences. (The chief ones are addition of words, deletion of words, substitution of words, rearrangement of sentence parts, and vocal change.)

HISTORY OF THE ENGLISH LANGUAGE

Study of the history of the English language adds breadth and depth to a student's understanding of the workings of the English language. It reveals to him the fact that language changes constantly and that the changes are attributed to the things that happen to people. Language is therefore closely tied to history: If there had been no Norman Conquest or no Renaissance, for instance, today's English would be very different from what it is. In addition, study of language history can help the student to understand the reasons for some of the apparent "oddities" of the language, can familiarize him with relationships between English and other languages, and sometimes can assist him in comprehending literature of a bygone day. Students with such background usually encounter fewer problems with Shakespeare, for example.

Goal 4

The student becomes aware of the relationship between English and other languages.

Performance Objective 4.A

The student explains, orally or in writing, how and why English is a member of the Germanic (Teutonic) branch of the Indo-European family of languages and is therefore a "sister" language of German, Dutch, and the Scandinavian languages.

Representative Enabling Objectives

a. Imagining that they are Angles or Saxons who have come to the British Isles in the fifth or sixth century, students list things in their new environment that may have an effect on their language, and explain how these things may eventually make their language different from what it is. (E.g., unfamiliar plants, animals and topography may lead to changes, and so may contacts with the civilization of the native Celts.)

b. The student points out on a map of Western Europe the areas in which the Germanic languages are the most widely used, and points out on a map of the world (or on a globe) the areas in which the Germanic languages are widely used (Western Europe, most of North America, Australia and New Zealand, India, parts of Africa). (An elaborate chart, including dead languages, is in Thomas Pyles' *Origins and Development of the English Language*, Harcourt, Brace, and World, 1964, p. 80.)

Performance Objective 4.B

The student describes the two main features of the Indo-European language family: inflectional structure and common word-stock.

Representative Enabling Objectives

a. Given a list of English words that contain the form classes, the student discovers that syntactic distinctions such as number, case, and tense are indicated by varying the form of a single word or word-base. Therefore, in English inflection, one adds -*s* to a noun to form the plural or -*ed* to a verb base to indicate past tense.
b. Given a passage of Old English with corresponding modern English text, the student discovers that Old English used many more inflections than does modern English.
c. Given a table that contains examples of the common word-stock of the Indo-European language family, the student does reading and research that enables him to explain how such similarity implies a common origin. (For the above enablers, Robertson and Cassidy, *The Development of Modern English*, Prentice-Hall, second edition, chapter two is a good reference.)

Goal 5

Through his study of language history the student learns the reasons for some of the irregularities or "oddities" of the English language. *See also* IV 17.

Performance Objective 5.A

The student lists a number of English nouns that have plurals other than the customary *s* or *es* and explains why these differences exist.

Representative Enabling Objectives

a. The student lists plurals like *teeth, mice, geese, men,* and *oxen,* and explains that the Old English plural forms of these still survive. (In contrast, others have become regular; e.g., if the OE plural of *book* (*bec*) had endured, we would today say *beek* rather than *books.*)
b. The student lists plurals like *data, criteria, cherubim,* and *libretti,* and with the aid of his dictionary identifies the languages from which these plurals were borrowed.
c. Given a list of words with two plurals recorded in dictionaries (e.g., *memorandum, formula, nucleus, addendum*), the student explains how this situation probably came about.

Performance Objective 5.B

Given words with "odd" spellings (e.g., *debt, doubt, island, sovereign*) the student explains the reasons for the silent letters. *See also* VJ 11.J.

Performance Objective 5.C

Given a list of strong (irregular) verbs, the student traces to Old English the reasons for their irregularities.

Representative Enabling Objectives

a. Given a list containing such verbs as the following, with the OE forms indicated, the student identifies other modern English verbs that can apparently be traced back to the same OE conjugations.

  (ride) ridan rad ridon (ge)riden
    (others: *drive, write, smite, rise,* and less obviously,
        bite, stride, and *strike*)
  (choose) ceosan ceas curon coren
   (also: *freeze*)
  (find) findan fand fundon funden
    (others: *bind, wind*)
  (drink) drincan dranc druncon druncen
    (also: *begin, ring, shrink, sing, stink, swim*)
  (tear) teran taer taeron toren
    (others: *wear, bear, steal, break*)
  (know) cnawan cneow cneowon cnowen
    (others: *blow, throw*)

b. Given such dialectal variations as *holp* (for helped) and *crope* (for crept), the student traces these forms to older versions of the language.

Performance Objective 5.D

Having discovered the fact that some of our modern English verbs retain similarity to Old English, the student, through reading and research, further discovers and explains how the modern English verb makes less use of inflections and how the modern English verb has gone to the *-ed* ending to express past tense.

Performance Objective 5.E

The student develops and justifies a hypothesis concerning the observation that young children frequently create the following past tenses for verbs: *singed, digged, swimmed, drived.*

Performance Objective 5.F

When the student is able to explain the reasons for the creation of new words, e.g., *up-tight, hung-up, right-on;* the alteration of existing words to create new words, e.g., *enthuse, finalize, tax-wise,* he should recognize that the English language is still undergoing changes. In other words, he recognizes the human influence on language.

Representative Enabling Objective

a. Given the context of the civil rights movement, the free speech movement, or a movement the student chooses, the student analyzes the spoken and written lexicons of the influential leaders and defines how these lexicons have developed out of this need. *See also* IV 20.

Goal 6

The student understands that language changes because of what happens to people.

Performance Objective 6.A

The student expresses and justifies, orally or in writing, his hypotheses about how our language might be different if each of the following historical events had not occurred:

The coming of the Angles and Saxons to the British Isles
The Norman victory at the Battle of Hastings
The invention of printing
The Renaissance
English explorations and settlements
English military triumphs in North America
Various inventions and scientific discoveries of the past two centuries.

Goal 7

The student understands the effect of historical and social conditions that affected the English language during the period of 1650–1800.

Performance Objective 7.A

Given the developments that the vernacular language (English instead of Latin or French) was used for scholarly and artistic writing and that the middle class emerged with its anxiety about "correctness" in speech, the student does research and reading which enables him to explain the reasons for the publication of prescriptive dictionaries and Latin based grammar books.

Performance Objective 7.B

Given what the student knows about language change, e.g., Performance Objective 6.A., the student evaluates the "correctness" doctrine as exemplified by prescriptive dictionaries and Latinate grammar books.

Goal 8

The student uses his knowledge of language history to assist in the interpretation of literature of the past.

Performance Objective 8.A

In reading early literature, the student explains transformations which were once in use but which have since been changed. *See also* V 43.J.

Representative Enabling Objectives

a. The student explains the word order frequently used in negative statements in early literature (e.g., "He knows not" instead of modern "He does not know.")
b. The student analyzes the use of multiple negatives in early literature (e.g., Chaucer's use of four negatives in "He nevere yet no vileynye ne saide, in al his lyf unto no maner wight.") and contrasts it with modern practice.
c. The student explains the word order frequently used in questions in early literature (e.g., "Whence came he?" instead of modern "Where did he come from?" or Shakespeare's "Dismay'd not this our captains?" instead of "Didn't this dismay our captains?")
d. The student describes the form for the passive used in much literature before the twentieth century (e.g., "The house was building" instead of the modern "The house was being built.")

Performance Objective 8.B

The student contrasts diction in early literature with modern diction. *See also* III 4.Af and g.

Representative Enabling Objectives

a. Given a passage from Shakespeare, the student substitutes modern words for those that are obsolete or archaic.

b. Given a passage from the King James Bible, the student compares its diction with that of a modern translation. (Or, given the Lord's Prayer or the Twenty-third Psalm in Old English, Middle English, the King James version, and a modern version, the student points out similarities and differences in the diction of the four versions.)

c. Given a passage from a play by such writers as Thornton Wilder or Arthur Miller, the student compares its diction with that of a passage from a play by such writers as LeRoi Jones or Ed Bullins.

Performance Objective 8.C

The student contrasts, orally or in writing, the language of early American literature with that of today.

Representative Enabling Objectives

a. In his reading of seventeenth- or eighteenth-century American prose (e.g., Smith, Mather, Franklin), the student describes how it differs from modern prose in spelling, punctuation, capitalization, sentence structure, and diction.

b. In his reading of fiction by such nineteenth century writers as Poe, Irving, Cooper, and Hawthorne, the student contrasts its language characteristics with those of Hemingway, Salinger, Knowles, Baldwin, Bontemps, or other modern writers, paying especial attention to conversation.

Goal 9

The student becomes aware of similarities and differences between British and American English. *See also* V 14.Ea.

Performance Objective 9.A

While reading British literature, the student compiles a list of British spellings and vocabulary items that differ from American preferences; later he analyzes these and groups them (e.g., the *-our* spellings) as systematically as possible. *See also* VI 11.J.

Performance Objective 9.B

After reading a substantial amount of British literature, the student writes a composition on a topic like "British and American English Aren't Really Different Languages," in which he discusses the question of whether British and American English differences are only superficial or more than superficial.

Representative Enabling Objectives

a. After reading Noah Webster's "declaration of linguistic independence" (reprinted in Mencken and several histories of the language), in which Webster predicted that American would become a language quite different from British English, the members of the class debate the question of the extent to which the prophecy has been fulfilled.

b. Members of the class debate the question of whether H. L. Mencken's use of the title *The American Language* was ill advised. (Reports on some chapters of Raven McDavid's revision of Mencken [Knopf] can be useful.)

Goal 10

The student realizes that contemporary social, political and other historical events have significant effects on the present development of the language.

Performance Objective 10.A

Given the emergence of new industries, e.g., digital computing and aerospace, the student gives examples of how existing words receive new meanings (umbilical cord) and how new terms have been created (xeroxing and lunar module). (The student may receive much input from parents who are engaged in the various industries.)

Performance Objective 10.B

Given the increased acceptability of language used by special groups, the student gives examples of such and explains how and why this is happening. (The pride and push of various minority groups is bringing the general society into contact with many dialectal and colloquial usages both in printed and electronic media, e.g., *right-on, power to the people, rap, up-tight, bag.*)

DIALECT, CHANGE, AND USAGE

Goal 11

The student becomes aware that language changes culturally, i.e., across social groups. *See also* III 4.

Performance Objective 11.A

After examining some regional varieties of American English, the student identifies the elements of a dialect (differences in vocabulary, pronunciation, and grammar). *See also* III 7.Bb; V 14.E.

Representative Enabling Objectives

a. Given sets of sentences such as those below, the student defines the italicized words as he understands them and explains that different words can be used to describe the same object.

  1. The cashier put the groceries in the *sack*.
  2. The cashier put the groceries in the *poke*.
  3. The cashier put the groceries in the *bag*.

  1. Tom ordered a *frappe* at the soda fountain.
  2. Tom ordered a *malted* at the soda fountain.
  3. Tom ordered a *cabinet* at the soda fountain.

  1. Frank ordered a *soda* at the soda fountain.
  2. Frank ordered a *moxie* at the soda fountain.
  3. Frank ordered a *pop* at the soda fountain.
  2. Frank ordered a *Coke* at the soda fountain.
  5. Frank ordered a *soft drink* at the soda fountain.

  1. Mother washed the *spider* after dinner.
  2. Mother washed the *fry pan* after dinner.
  3. Mother washed the *frying pan* after dinner.
  4. Mother washed the *skillet* after dinner.

  1. Mary and Sue rode on the *teeter-totter* at the park.
  2. Mary and Sue rode on the *seesaw* at the park.
  3. Mary and Sue rode on the *teeter board* at the park.

  1. Mother did not allow us to sit on the new *davenport*.
  2. Mother did not allow us to sit on the new *divan*.
  3. Mother did not allow us to sit on the new *couch*.
  4. Mother did not allow us to sit on the new *sofa*.

b. After hearing sentences containing words such as those listed below being pronounced by several native speakers of English from different geographical areas, the student explains that one characteristic of dialect is pronunciation.

  1. route
  2. garage
  3. merry, marry, Mary
  4. Cuba and Africa
  5. park

6. car
7. collar, caller
8. house
9. fish
10. wash
11. pin, pen

c. Given examples of phrases such as those listed below, the student discovers and explains that dialects differ in grammatical aspects.

1.	(a) quarter to (b) quarter of (c) quarter till		2.	(a) wait on (b) wait for	
3.	(a) sick to (b) sick at (c) sick in		4.	(a) behind (b) back of (c) in back of	

Goal 12

The student understands that he, as well as others, is multilingual in the sense of understanding more than one dialect. *See also* VI 10.A.

Performance Objective 12.A

Given examples of words from various professions such as those listed below, the student discovers that there are a variety of names for the same idea.

1. The weatherman makes a *forecast*.
2. The doctor makes a *prognosis*.
3. The scientist makes a *prediction*.

Performance Objective 12.B

Given the opportunity to present pictorial situations necessitating verbal responses from men and women, the student discovers that often men's speech differs from women's speech.

Representative Enabling Objectives

a. Given pictures such as: a baby, a car, a football player, a set of china, the student investigates, by tape recording, the language that men and women use to respond to the pictures; the student then analyzes and interprets the data.
b. The students plan and carry out a research project which investigates the language differences of men and women, boys and girls.

Performance Objective 12.C

Given the challenge of recording the speech used by adolescents with adolescents and of speech used by adolescents with adults, the student analyzes and explains the data that he gathers.

Performance Objective 12.D

Given the challenge of playing various roles, e.g., rock musician, schoolteacher, parent, minister, etc., the student demonstrates his ability to use dialects appropriate to these various roles. *See also* II 1.Ae; V 24.B; V 35.I.

Performance Objective 12.E

The student recognizes variations in his own idiolect by his ability to specify and analyze variations in his word usage and pronunciation in two given situations, e.g., at the school hangout vs. his home. *See also* III 4.Be and f.

Goal 13

The student understands that no one dialect is superior or inferior to any other in its potential for effective communication by its users; however, he further understands and evaluates the value judgments that society attaches to dialects. *See also* V 24.Bb.

Performance Objective 13.A

After examining dialect utterances such as those below, the student demonstrates that he understands the message of each by his ability to explain what each one means. (This may be expanded to research the probable origin of each.)

1. Look in the oven and see if I'm burning.
2. Throw papa down the stairs his hat.
3. It's about five mile down the road.
4. He be my friend.
5. Me cross too much along you.
6. The train she is late.
7. I got me a new deuce and a quarter.

Performance Objective 13.B

Given the tasks of developing a dialect attitude questionnaire and administering the questionnaire to various occupational and social groups, the student then analyzes and explains the data he has gathered.

Goal 14

The student discovers that language is constantly changing in various ways and through various influences.

Performance Objective 14.A

The student discovers that language change is generally related to particular influences and he gives examples that illustrate them.

Representative Enabling Objectives

a. Given a list of words generated or popularized by a specific social, cultural, economic, or technological influence, the student analyzes and discovers how these words can be a model for the creation of new words or new meanings for existing words. Example: *sit-in* becomes the model for such words as (1) *teach-in*, (2) *lounge-in*, (3) *mill-in*, and (4) *be-in*. Example: the generalized application of computer terms such as *input, output, feedback*.

b. The student shows, by giving examples, that the language expands by borrowing words from other languages. Example: *sarong, ikon, steppe, bamboo, vodka, taboo, curry*.

c. The student shows, by giving examples that language changes through the process of analogy, e.g., *"-ize"—radicalize, maximize*.

d. The student shows, by giving examples, that words expand meaning through the processes of pejoration and amelioration.

    1. *discriminating*—from have good taste to judge according to race.

    2. *black*—from general negative connotation to label signifying racial pride.

WORDS AND DICTIONARIES

To be an articulate speaker and intelligent reader, a student needs to understand what words are, what and how they mean, how to send and receive them effectively, and how to look up meanings and other information about words in dictionaries. To be a competent speaker and reader, he will need to develop large speaking and reading vocabularies, and he should be able to add to those vocabularies by knowing how to select among and use different kinds of dictionaries and by developing the habit of looking up new words or attempting to find the meanings of familiar words used in an unfamiliar manner.

Goal 15

The student shows: (a) various ways that people give meanings to words and (b) that dictionaries are a source of information about the meanings, and changes in meanings, of words.

Performance Objective 15.A

After examining words in different contexts, the student explains, orally or in writing, that people give meaning(s) to words and that some of these meanings can be found in dictionaries.

Representative Enabling Objectives

a. Given ten sentences in which the same word occurs in each sentence but obviously has a different meaning in each, the student
   1. shows that people can give many meanings to a word;
   2. shows that he may be able to determine the specific meaning of the word from its context;
   3. looks up the word in a standard desk dictionary to determine what meanings of the word have been recorded;
   4. checks the meaning he assigned to the word in a specific context against the meaning recorded in the dictionary.
b. Given three sentences written during different historical periods which are identified as such, the student shows that a word like *nice* or *silly*, which appears in each of the three sentences, can change meaning in time as well as in context.
c. Given the same word spoken with different emphasis and/or intonation in three different sentences, the student tells what the word means in each sentence and shows that people can change meanings of words by intonation and/or emphasis.
d. Given five example citation slips for the same word (see sample below), the student demonstrates his ability to write lexical definitions for a word. (Suggestion: To give the student the experience of writing a lexical definition for a word that is so new that it will not be recorded in a dictionary, the teacher might prepare five sample citation slips for one of the new words recorded in the most recent *Encyclopaedia Britannica Book of the Year* under the heading, *Words and Meanings.*)

> smaze
>
>   Eric could not see through the smaze— the smoke and haze.
>
>   *—Environment Magazine*
>   May 10, 1970

e. Given five words that have come into the language within the last two years, or given meanings that have recently been added to five words, the student explains, orally or in writing, why he cannot find the new words or the new meanings in a standard desk dictionary.

Goal 16

The student examines several desk dictionaries, analyzes their formats and identifies the basic components of the entry words.

Performance Objective 16.A

The student identifies the basic format of standard desk dictionaries and the basic components of an entry word.

Representative Enabling Objectives

a. After examining entries for the same word (one with only three or four lexical definitions) in at least three different dictionaries, the student identifies these basic components in a dictionary entry:
1. entry word printed in boldface type;
2. syllabification (by syllable dot or space);
3. pronunciation guide (in parentheses or slant lines after the boldface entry word);
4. part of speech label;
5. definitions;
6. restrictive and field labels;
7. etymologies;
8. run-on entries;
9. cross references;
10. usage notes;
11. synonymies.

b. Given the opportunity to compare several dictionaries designed for the same audience (e.g., elementary, intermediate, high school, or collegiate dictionaries), the student demonstrates his knowledge of how dictionaries follow a similar format by explaining, orally or in writing, the following:
1. that entry words are arranged in alphabetical order;
2. that catchwords, headwords, or guide words are printed at the top of each page in the A–Z section to help people find words;
3. that entry words are printed in boldface type;
4. that essentially the same information about words (see 12.Aa) appears in most dictionaries;
5. that all dictionaries contain a guide to the use of the dictionary which may be called an *introduction*, *preface*, or some other name;

6. that dictionaries may also contain information such as an atlas, list of colleges, and so forth. (The standard format calls for such information to follow the A–Z section.)

Goal 17

The student uses the information given in each component of a dictionary. *See also* VI 11.I and J.

Performance Objective 17.A

The student demonstrates his ability to use the following information in dictionary entries: spelling, syllabification, pronunciation, stress marks, parts of speech labels, definitions, restrictive and field labels, run-on entries, cross references, usage notes, and synonymies.

Representative Enabling Objectives

a. Hearing a word he cannot spell, the student finds the most common spelling in a sentence. *See also* VI 11.J.
b. The student shows that some words have more than one acceptable spelling (e.g., *insure, ensure*).
c. When he is not certain how to split a word at the end of a line, the student checks the syllabification of the word in a dictionary and then compares this information with information contained in other dictionaries.
d. Given twenty words transcribed into the phonetic alphabet of the dictionary he is using, the student demonstrates his ability to use the pronunciation key.
e. The student follows the stress marks in the pronunciation guide as he pronounces words that are new to him.
f. The student uses the part of speech label as a guide to help him find a specific meaning of a word.
g. The student identifies various methods of arranging definitions of words (e.g., historical, common meaning according to part of speech classification, synchronic).
h. Given five sentences in which one word is used as several different parts of speech and carries different meanings, the student finds the appropriate lexical definition for the way the word is used in each sentence.
i. The student explains, orally or in writing, the implications of restrictive labels such as *slang* and *informal* as they are used in different standard desk dictionaries.
j. The student recognizes different social attitudes toward certain

words and/or definitions, and he explains, orally or in writing, how different dictionaries reflect or reject such attitudes.

k. The student explains, orally or in writing, why some dictionaries label certain words or definitions as *slang, informal, standard,* and so forth.

l. The student explains, orally or in writing, why some desk dictionaries include usage notes in the entries for certain words and analyzes the attitudes of different lexicographic staffs toward usage.

m. Given a list of ten words that are usually not defined in dictionaries but are recorded at the end of main entries, the student explains, orally or in writing, the value of such run-on entries, and he defines each run-on after studying the main entry.

n. The student explains, orally or in writing, how cross references help him define a word or expand a specific definition of a word.

o. Given a sentence such as "The girl is skinny," the student shows that he can change the meaning of the sentence by substituting a synonym for *skinny*. He checks the shades of meaning of synonyms for *skinny* by looking in a standard desk dictionary. *See also* V 35.

Goal 18

The student shows that dictionaries are a source of information on word history.

Performance Objective 18.A

Given ten words, the student explains, orally or in writing, the origin of each.

Goal 19

The student identifies the purposes of different kinds of dictionaries and compares dictionaries designed for a specific audience or for a specific purpose.

Performance Objective 19.A

Given dictionaries designed for the same audience (e.g., elementary or collegiate) and dictionaries designed for a specific purpose (e.g., a dictionary of slang or a dictionary of acronyms), the student identifies the audience for, and the purpose of, each dictionary and compares, orally or in writing, dictionaries designed for the same audience or purpose.

SEMANTICS

Because language suggests meaning and often suggests more than it says in so many words, it affects human behavior. People frequently react to words as if the words were actually the referents that they symbolize; furthermore, an individual usually assumes that his reaction to or understanding of words reflects the basic meaning of the words. However, research shows that meaning is a highly personal matter relative to an individual's cumulative intellectual, cultural, and social development. The major problems of communication are more semantic than syntactic. Therefore, students can benefit from semantic study because it encourages them to evaluate the implications and assumptions of language in relationship to the context of the communicative environment.

Goal 20

The student discovers that words are symbols whose meanings are arbitrary and varied. *See also* II 1.A; III 7.Ba; III 13; V 36.A; VI 2; VI 6.A; VI 9.

Performance Objective 20.A

The student recognizes that words are symbols when he discovers that a given word can represent many things, some of which are not related.

Representative Enabling Objective

Given words such as *run, set, pool,* and *strike,* the student lists as many meanings as he can for each.

Performance Objective 20.B

The student recognizes that a single object, concept, or idea can be labeled with many different words.

Representative Enabling Objectives

a. Given pictures of various objects such as a factory, policeman, or a cigarette, the student lists as many different words as he can which can name the object.
b. Given concepts such as: "power to the people, devotion to the welfare of one's country, read good books, use good grammar," the

student lists as many words as he can that might label these concepts.

Goal 21

The student recognizes that words affect people in various ways. *See also* V 3.C, 5.A, 6.E, F, G; VI 1.D; VI 6.A; VI 11.A.

Performance Objective 21.A

The student demonstrates that words evoke a response in a given receiver and that this response signals the meaning of that word for that receiver.

Representative Enabling Objectives

a. Given a list of words such as: *liberal, conservative, swinger, stocky, wise, fastidious, sloppy,* the student describes, orally or in writing, what his response would be if each label were applied to him, and why he would respond in this way.
b. The student compares his responses and definitions with those of his classmates and discovers that words elicit different responses in different people because of the meanings they attach to these words.
c. Given a list of words such as *vomit, sweat, rape,* the student investigates the attitudes and responses of various people to these words; he then formulates a credible explanation from his data.

Goal 22

The student recognizes that words influence thoughts, attitudes, and behavior.

Performance Objective 22.A

The student describes, orally or in writing, how words have been used in a specific context to evoke a particular emotive response in the receiver. *See also* III 2.Aa; III 10.Ae; VI 1.D.

Representative Enabling Objectives

a. Given a speech, such as Mark Antony's funeral oration in Shakespeare's *Julius Caesar,* the student identifies the key words and phrases in that speech which Mark uses to influence the citizens to accept his interpretation of the assassination.
b. Given a prose selection, such as The Gettysburg Address, the student describes his response to the selection and analyzes the words and phrases that elicited the response. *See also* V 35.Ea.

c. Given a prose selection such as the example below, the student formulates a hypothesis concerning the attitude of the writer toward his subject and what kinds of responses he is trying to elicit from his readers.

We are sorry too that we created monsters like you, by trying to provide college educations for all. We are sorry we didn't see that everyone couldn't be an educated philosopher, and we should have known that once you got your education you would feel too good to work.

———— letter to the editor
Bloomington, Indiana, newspaper
June 7, 1969

d. Given a current advertisement from radio, TV, newspapers, or magazines, the student identifies the key words and phrases intended to evoke a desired emotive response from the reader.

Performance Objective 22.B

The student discovers that cultural, ideological, or group membership differences can hinder clear communication because individuals with differing viewpoints who use certain words and phrases often do not share a common meaning or interpretation for these words and phrases.

Representative Enabling Objectives

a. Given a tape recording of a role-playing situation such as a discussion concerning a dress and grooming code between the leader of the student strike committee and the high school principal, the class listens for, lists, and analyzes the meanings of the key words used by both speakers.

b. Given an assignment such as viewing Face the Nation, Meet the Press, or Issues and Answers, the student identifies the different meanings that the guest and panelists attach to the same key words. The student then analyzes the effect that this has on his understanding of the issues or ideas being discussed.

Goal 23

The student uses words to influence the thoughts, attitudes, and/or behavior of people.

Performance Objective 23.A

Given a specific purpose and audience, the student chooses appropriate words and phrases to evoke a particular response from the audience. See also II 9; III 10.A1; V 12; VI 13.

Representative Enabling Objectives

a. The student, in a speech or an essay, makes an appeal which attempts to persuade a neutral audience to support a cause, a policy, a position, a candidate, etc.
b. The student modifies a speech or an essay prepared for one kind of audience (neutral) for presentation to a different audience (receptive, hostile).

V

Reading and Responding to Literature

RATIONALE

As we guide high school students in their reading, we may best help them by keeping in mind that our task is:

(1) to serve first as resource persons, putting in their way a wide variety of reading materials and related media with attention to individual needs and interests. These materials, mostly contemporary, should include at least some of the classics and of course much of the printed media, as Ray Bradbury warns in *Fahrenheit 451*.

(2) to capitalize on the "reading readiness" now generated in students by such media as television and cinema; to recognize, through a student's talking, the kinds of reading, in Daniel Fader's phrase, he can be "hooked on."

(3) to serve individuals and small groups as opposed to statistical groups; to recognize that regardless of a school's location (urban, suburban, rural) its students represent, on a spectrum between strength and bankruptcy, a wide range of reading-tastes, abilities, and deficiencies.

The project director in cnarge of this section, Arnold Lazarus, Professor of English and Education, Purdue University, was assisted by several colleagues.

(4) to introduce students to the people in literature, the qualities of human excellence, the real heroes and the phonies; to encourage (never to ignore) readers who question values, who reject whatever is dehumanizing or depersonalizing, as Charles Reich emphasizes in *The Greening of America.*

(5) to help the student discover relationships between literature and life, between experiences in literature and some of his own experiences or observations.

(6) to encourage each student to discover, partly through reading, his own identity; to ask himself such questions as "Who am I?" and "What can I best contribute?"

(7) to involve students in open, informal talking before and after their reading—feedback indispensable to their motivation and growth, and to their productivity in the related arts.

(8) to defend the student's right to read—even materials that may strike us as offensive.

(9) to leave students with skills of judging what they have read —skills developed through performance, which probably ought to be oral and informal before it is written and formal.

(10) to help students read between the lines and beneath the surface levels of meaning in at least a few literary works—help that requires scholarship, on the part of the teacher, along with the art of asking appropriate questions.

(11) to induce in students attitudes toward, and habits of, reading with regularity, discrimination, and enthusiasm long after they have left our classes—habits and attitudes for which the enthusiastic and well-read teacher sets an example.

To read well, a high school student should be able to do more than just get the words off the page—more than just apprehend factual elements like setting, *dramatis personae*, story-line, and allusions. He needs to understand what is implied and assumed beyond what is said. He needs especially to understand how the writer's use of certain techniques affects the meaning and enhances the quality of a literary work. Thus the student should understand such levels of meaning as the symbolic and the allegorical as they work in a particular literary piece; he should understand metaphor, paradox, irony, and satire. He need not, however, define any of these before reading, and then go search for them.

A high school student should also have the opportunity to read a wide variety of literary works (not excerpts and abridgments) carefully and deliberately, responding to them and discussing them in class. But the literary works cited in this catalog and the questions on certain novels, plays, stories, and poems are offered only as examples or possibilities; they should not be construed in any way as a curriculum in which given literary works must be taught.

As for the possibilities of student performance, the following objectives have been arranged within a system adapted by Alan Purves from the Benjamin Bloom and David Krathwohl taxonomies (*Taxonomy of Educational Objectives: Cognitive Domain; Taxonomy of Educational Objectives: Affective Domain*) except that the affective and cognitive domains, by nature inextricable, have been reunited. Similarly, we have resisted discontinuities between "expository" and "imaginative" reading, although we have made a few distinctions between the documentary and the lyrical. Above all, in a departure from the conventional genre (or genre and mode) organization, the system below is student-centered. At least it begins and ends with what the student does or should, ideally, be able to do in his reading. The major student performances in this system consist of the following:

valuing	discriminating
describing	inferring
discovering relationships	evaluating

Each of these kinds of responses is defined and illustrated in its own subsection, but a brief summary is offered here.

SIX KINDS OF RESPONSES TO READING

Valuing

The student shares his feelings; tells what he accepts and admires —and what he rejects—in his reading.

Describing

The student identifies and in his own words describes such literary elements as persons, places, actions, patterns, and rhetorical effects, without necessarily defining them.

Discovering Relationships

The student makes connections (similarities, continuities, reciprocities) between various literary elements and works; between a literary work and his own experiences; between a literary work and another art form (e.g., in the fine arts, theater arts, and electronic media).

Discriminating

The student explains significant differences he recognizes or discovers between various literary forms and works; between a literary work and another art form.

Inferring

The student tells what he has generalized or abstracted (e.g., suggested meaning, vision of life) from what he has read; or he demonstrates his inferences through role-playing and other oral and written re-creations.

Evaluating *

The student, respecting the right of each art form to its own integrity, tells why he does or does not give high marks to a literary work he has read, or to a version of it he has also experienced in the electronic media, or to a review of either he may also have read.

For the convenience of teachers planning a learning-unit or module on poetry, fiction, drama, etc. we conclude this Reading Section with an index of objectives listed by genres.

VALUING

The student shares his feelings; tells what he accepts, admires, cherishes—and what he rejects—in his reading.

Goal 1

The student develops a reading appetite that escalates in its need for satisfaction. (The power of positive reinforcement and the

---

* Evaluating and valuing resist sharp distinctions but do allow different emphases. Valuing emphasizes highly subjective and personal responses; evaluating emphasizes partly subjective, mostly objective, responses based on objective criteria.

need for experiencing a variety of pleasures, including those available in print as well as through electronic media, are here assumed as imperatives of the human condition.)

Performance Objective 1.A

Faced with an attractive variety of literature (e.g., periodicals on the classroom table; paperbacks, hobby books, anthologies, encyclopedias, etc. on the classroom shelves) the student gravitates toward rather than away from them; he browses and reads.

Performance Objective 1.B

The student becomes a card-carrying borrower from the school and public libraries.

Performance Objective 1.C

The student builds a personal book collection.

Performance Objective 1.D

During oral interpretations of plays and the dialog of fiction the student often volunteers, participates with animation, and projects some meaningful interpretations. Occasionally he suggests an imaginative improvement for the reading of one or another of the lines. *See also III 8 * .

Performance Objective 1.E

During choral readings of verse the student participates with gusto, with a kind of compulsive vocalizing. (Note to the skeptical: Even the vocalizing that begins as mischievous mimicry or parody —e.g., of T. S. Eliot's high-falutin "Let us go then, you and I"—can get under the skin, into the muscles, into the bloodstream of a professed anti-intellectual and can convert him in spite of himself, through the power of positive reinforcement, to accept more and more aesthetic experiences and values; such vocalizing has turned on latent taps among the Chicanos, the Blacks, and other minority groups in this writer's high school classes.) *See also III 8.Ae.*

---

* Roman numerals refer to chapters, Arabic numerals to goals, capital letters to performance objectives, and lower-case letters to enabling objectives.

Performance Objective 1.F

The student frequently volunteers to participate in panel discussions of literary works.

Goal 2

In his reading the student seeks answers to such questions as "Who am I?" "How am I the same and how am I different from everyone else?" "What am I here for?" "In literature and life who is to be admired—who are the real heroes and heroines; who are the phonies?"

Performance Objective 2.A

Either before or after the reading and discussions described in 2.B., below, the student participates in writing or in producing a skit dramatizing a conflict between two opposing ethical issues.

Performance Objective 2.B

After reading one or more literary works that stimulate introspection and soul-searching, the student, participating in a symposium or a small buzz group, tells how one or another of the episodes or of the values dramatized therein is or is not compatible with values of his own. (It cannot be emphasized too strongly that the following list is suggestive, not prescriptive. Most of the shorter pieces occur in widely used anthologies.)

SUGGESTED READINGS (MORAL AND ETHICAL VALUES)

Fiction

James Agee, *The Morning Watch*
Sherwood Anderson, "Sophistication"
Harriet Arnow, *The Dollmaker*
William Barrett, *The Lilies of the Field*
Margot Benary-Isbert, *The Long Way Home*
Frank Bonham, *Durango Street*
Ray Bradbury, *Dandelion Wine; Fahrenheit 451*
Pearl Buck, "The Enemy"
Willa Cather, "Neighbor Rosicky"

Walter Clark, *The Ox-Bow Incident*
Arthur Clarke, *Childhood's End*
Samuel Clemens, *The Adventures of Huckleberry Finn*
Richard Connell, "The Most Dangerous Game"
Joseph Conrad, "The Secret Sharer"
Stephen Crane, *The Red Badge of Courage*
Fyodor Dostoevsky, *Crime and Punishment*
Allen Drury, *Advise and Consent*
Ralph Ellison, *The Invisible Man*
Jeannette Eyerly, *Dropout*
William Faulkner, "The Bear"; "The Old Man"; *Intruder in the Dust*
Henry Felsen, *Street Rod; Two and the Town*
Benedict and Nancy Freedman, *Mrs. Mike*
John Galsworthy, "Quality"
Rumer Godden, *The River*
William Golding, *Lord of the Flies*
Nathaniel Hawthorne, "Young Goodman Brown"; "The Minister's
    Black Veil"; *The Scarlet Letter*
Robert Heinlein, *Stranger in a Strange Land*
Ernest Hemingway, *The Old Man and the Sea;* "In Another Country"
John Hersey, *A Single Pebble; A Bell for Adano; The Child Buyer;
    The Wall*
Herman Hesse, *Siddhartha; Demian; Beneath the Wheel*
Aldous Huxley, *Brave New World*
Daniel Keyes, *Flowers for Algernon*
John Knowles, *A Separate Peace*
Harper Lee, *To Kill a Mockingbird*
Sinclair Lewis, "Land"; *Babbitt*
Carson McCullers, *The Heart is a Lonely Hunter; The Member of
    the Wedding*
Florence Means, *It Takes All Kinds*
Herman Melville, "Bartleby the Scrivener"; *Benito Cereno*
George Orwell, *Animal Farm; 1984*
Alan Paton, *Cry the Beloved Country*
Katherine Anne Porter, "Holiday"; "Theft"; "Noon Wine"; *Ship of
    Fools*
Ayn Rand, *The Fountainhead*
Conrad Richter, *The Light in the Forest*
Doris Ritter, *Edge of Violence*
J. D. Salinger, *The Catcher in the Rye*
Irving Shulman, *West Side Story*
Alan Sillitoe, *Loneliness of the Long Distance Runner*

Betty Smith, *A Tree Grows in Brooklyn*
John Steinbeck, *The Pearl; The Red Pony*
Mary Stolz, *A Love or a Season*
J. R. R. Tolkien, *The Hobbit; The Lord of the Rings*
John Updike, *Rabbit, Run*
Leon Uris, *Exodus*
Kurt Vonnegut, *Cat's Cradle; Slaughterhouse Five*
Hugh Walpole, *Fortitude*
Robert Penn Warren, *All The King's Men*
H. G. Wells, "The Country of the Blind"
Eudora Welty, "Petrified Man"; "Why I live at the P. O."
Nathaniel West, *Miss Lonelyhearts*
Esther Wier, *The Loner*
Thornton Wilder, *The Bridge of San Luis Rey*

Drama

Maxwell Anderson, *Valley Forge; Barefoot in Athens*
Aristophanes, *Lysistrata*
James M. Barrie, *The Admirable Crichton*
Robert Bolt, *A Man for All Seasons*
Friedrich Dürrenmatt, *The Physicists*
T. S. Eliot, *Murder in the Cathedral; The Cocktail Party*
William Gibson, *The Miracle Worker*
Susan Glaspell, "Trifles"
Lorraine Hansberry, *A Raisin in the Sun; To Be Young, Gifted and Black* (adapted by Robert Nemiroff)
Lillian Hellman, *The Little Foxes*
Henrik Ibsen, *A Doll's House*
Eugene Ionesco, *Rhinoceros*
Arthur Laurents et al., *West Side Story*
Peter Luke, *Hadrian the Seventh*
Archibald MacLeish, *J.B.*
Arthur Miller, *Death of a Salesman; The Crucible*
Eugene O'Neill, *Ah, Wilderness!*
John Patrick, *Teahouse of the August Moon*
Terence Rattigan, *The Winslow Boy*
Edmund Rostand, *Cyrano de Bergerac*
Jean Paul Sartre, *No Exit*
Dore Schary, *Sunrise at Campobello*
William Shakespeare, *King Lear; Julius Caesar*
George Bernard Shaw, *Saint Joan; Pygmalion; Major Barbara*

Robert Sherwood, *Abe Lincoln in Illinois*
Gore Vidal, *Visit to a Small Planet*
Thornton Wilder, *Our Town*
Tennessee Williams, *The Glass Menagerie*

Biography

James Baldwin, *Notes of a Native Son*
Lerone Bennett, *What Manner of Man?* (Martin Luther King)
Catherine Bowen, *Yankee from Olympus*
Van Wyck Brooks, "Moment of Inspiration"
Claude Brown, *Manchild in the Promised Land*
Marchette Chute, *Shakespeare of London*
Eve Curie, "Four Years in a Shed"
August Derleth, *Still Small Voice*
Leon Edel, *Thoreau*
Louis Fischer, *Gandhi*
Kathryn Forbes, *Mama's Bank Account*
Anne Frank, *Diary of a Young Girl*
Benjamin Franklin, *Autobiography*
Althea Gibson, *I Always Wanted To Be Somebody*
Jerry Gibson, *Big League Bat Boy*
Frank and Ernestine Gilbreth, *Cheaper by the Dozen*
David Hellyer, "Cantinflas"
Rackham Holt, *George Washington Carver*
Langston Hughes, *Famous American Negroes*
Marquis James, *Family Rebel*
J. F. Kennedy, *Profiles in Courage*
George Kent, "Mr. Imagination"
Leonard Kenworthy, *Twelve Citizens of the World*
Charles Lindbergh, *We*
George Putnam, *Soaring Wings* [Amelia Earhart]
Carl Sandburg, *Abraham Lincoln*
Irving Stone, *Darrow for the Defense*
Jesse Stuart, *The Thread that Runs So True*
Henry Thoreau, *Walden*
Louis Untermeyer, "Albert Schweitzer"
Jessamyn West, *To See the Dream*

Other Non-Fiction

The Bible: The Book of Job; The Book of Esther
Robert Benchley, "Good Luck and Try and Get It"

J. Bronowski, "Responsibilities of Scientists"
Carlos Bulosan, "My Father Goes to Court"
Hadley Cantril, *Reflections on the Human Spirit*
Rachel Carson, *Silent Spring*
Arthur C. Clarke, "The Morality of Space"
Jacques Cousteau, *The Silent World*
David Daiches, *A Century of the Essay*
William Du Bois, *The Souls of Black Folk*
Loren Eiseley, *The Unexpected Universe*
Mary Ellman, *Thinking about Women*
Ralph Waldo Emerson, "Self Reliance"
William Faulkner, "Nobel Prize Acceptance Speech"
Kenneth Galbraith, *The Affluent Society; The New Industrial State*
William Golding, "Thinking as a Hobby"
Paul Goodman, *Growing Up Absurd*
John Griffin, *Black Like Me*
John Hersey, *Hiroshima*
J. F. Kennedy, "Inaugural Address"
Arthur Koestler, *The Act of Creation*
R. D. Laing, *The Divided Self*
Norman Mailer, *The Armies of the Night*
Rollo May, *Love and Will*
Marshall McLuhan, *Understanding Media*
James Michener, "What I Learned"
Ralph Nader, *Unsafe at Any Speed*
George Orwell, "Politics and the English Language," *Collected Essays*
Laurence Peter, *The Peter Principle*
Plato, "Phaedrus," *The Republic*
Charles Reich, *The Greening of America*
R. M. Rilke, "Letter to a Young Poet"
Jonathan Swift, "Grand Academy of Lagado"
T. S. Szaz, "Moral Conflict and Psychiatry"
James Thurber, *The Thurber Carnival*
Tom Wolfe, *The Pump House Gang*

Verse

Matthew Arnold, "Dover Beach"
W. H. Auden, "The Unknown Citizen"
Stephen Benet, *John Brown's Body*
The Bible, "Twenty-Third Psalm"
Robert Browning, "My Last Duchess"; "Rabbi Ben Ezra"

E. E. Cummings, "anyone lived in a pretty how town"
Emily Dickinson, "Bring Me the Sunset in a Cup"
T. S. Eliot, "Prufrock"; "The Hollow Men"
Mari Evans, *I Am a Black Woman*
Robert Frost, *Death of the Hired Man*
Kahlil Gibran, *The Prophet*
Robert Graves, "Devil's Advice to Story Tellers"
Thomas Hardy, "The Man He Killed"
A. E. Housman, "Eight O'Clock"
Langston Hughes, "Evenin' Air Blues"
G. M. Hopkins, "Spring and Fall"
Rudyard Kipling, "If"
Robert Lowell, "At the Altar"
John Masefield, "Being Her Friend"
Edgar Lee Masters, *Spoon River Anthology*
David McCord, "The Sportsman"
Edna St. Vincent Millay, "Recuerdo"
Marianne Moore, "In Distrust of Merits"
Ogden Nash, "Kindly Unhitch that Star, Buddy"
Wilfred Owen, "Arms and the Boy"
Henry Reed, "Naming of Parts"
Edwin Robinson, "Richard Cory"; also Paul Simon's version
Theodore Roethke, "My Papa's Waltz"; "The Waking"
Carl Sandburg, "Money"
Karl Shapiro, "Auto Wreck"
Sara Teasdale, "Tears"
Dylan Thomas, "A Refusal to Mourn the Death, by Fire, of a Child
    in London"
Elinor Wylie, "Address to My Soul"
W. B. Yeats, "Sailing to Byzantium"; "The Second Coming"

Goal 3

The student values reading as a humanizing experience, as an act that adds zest and meaning to his life, a habit that affords him not only wider access to what people are saying (wider access than is ordinarily available through television and cinema) but also more private opportunity for thought about what to accept and reject. (The reader can, in short, make choices; he can read whatever books and periodicals he pleases, not just those prescribed by pressure groups like those in his school, community, or elsewhere.)

Representative Entering Performance Objectives

Entering Objective A. Within his own sense of values the student has made at least a start in adapting to his purposes his rates and techniques of reading various kinds of materials (e.g., report cards, love notes, directions or instructions, bulletin notices, newspapers, magazines, textbook assignments, paperbacks, etc.) He may linger over a love note but skim through the headlines of a newspaper.

Entering Objective B. Given a selection which he can not finish reading, the student states, from among a number of possibilities, the reason(s) for this. (The work seemed too difficult, nonrelevant, or inappropriate for his age group; he felt lazy, etc.).

Performance Objective 3.A

In an informal panel or in a written "interest inventory" the student tells which kinds of books and periodicals he likes best (e.g., sports, comics, classic comics, science fiction, hobby books). He may also explain why he chooses to read given kinds of books and periodicals—*any* kind of book, periodical, pamphlet, etc. from anywhere on the spectrum (e.g., *Mad* Magazine, *Ebony*, religious pamphlets, organizational newsletters, etc.).

Performance Objective 3.B

After reading any literary work containing characters (play, narrative, narrative verse), the student talks about why he liked or disliked one character or another. For his journal he may also draw a cartoon or write a brief caricature. *See also* VI 1.Ba.

Performance Objective 3.C

After reading some such account of events as John Hersey's *Hiroshima* or Norman Mailer's *The Armies of the Night,* the student tells how he feels about the events and about the tone(s) in which they were depicted.

Performance Objective 3.D

After reading a poem, narrative, or play with which he strongly identifies, the student orally shares it (or an excerpt) with the class.

He may also tell why the work has such personal value for him (e.g., what events in his life the work reminded him of, etc.).

Goal 4

The student values human experiences enough to read about them not only as they are depicted fictionally in narrative and drama but also as they are reported or interpreted in biography and auto-biography, no matter how controversial.

Performance Objective 4.A

The student reads such works as James Baldwin's *Notes of a Native Son*, Eldridge Cleaver's *Soul on Ice*, the *Autobiography of Malcolm X*, etc., with a view to seeing which of these writers' values he wishes to accept, which reject. The student then airs his feelings in a panel discussion with other students. (Aside from social, economic, and political values, all three of these writers are concerned with intellectual and aesthetic values and especially the educative values of reading. All three, despite originating in socially disadvantaged environments, are remarkably articulate and well read. Although being well read does not in itself guarantee *any* reader's articulateness in communicating, the reverse is generally true—i.e., the articulate person is generally well read. Any person who reads widely and well enhances his possibilities of communicating orally and in writing. In fact—aside from indispensable practice in speaking and writing—reading contributes to literate and articulate communication much more than do textbook exhortations to avoid mistakes, as hundreds of educators have observed. In their autobiographies authors and other achievers testify to that assumption. Here, for example, is James Baldwin:

I was born in Harlem thirty-one years ago. I began plotting novels at about the time I learned to read . . . In those days my mother was given to the exasperating and mysterious habit of having babies. As they were born, I took them over with one hand and held a book with the other . . . In fact, I read just about everything I could get my hands on . . .

When one begins looking for influences one finds them by the score . . . I hazard that the King James Bible, the rhetoric of the storefront church . . . and something of Dickens' love for bravura have something to do with me . . .

But in the work of Faulkner . . . Robert Penn Warren, and most significantly in the advent of Ralph Ellison one sees the beginnings of a more genuinely penetrating search . . . to utilize language, and brilliantly, some of the *ambiguity* and *irony* of Negro life . . .

I love America more than any other country in the world, and exactly for this reason I insist on *the right to criticize her* . . . One must find one's own *moral center* . . . I consider that I have many responsibilities, but none greater than this: *to last,* as Hemingway says, and get my work done . . . I want to be an honest man and a good writer. (Emphasis added.)[1]

Representative Enabling Objective

Given some such testimony as the above, the student engages in a dialog with other students, addressing himself to such questions as the following: Why is reading important, if it is? To whom is it important? What is it important for? What kinds of reading seem to be the most productive? How do we know? Assuming that James Baldwin is an educated person, what elements of his testimony contribute clues to some of the answers? Did the passage suggest answers to (or move me to raise) questions like "Who am I? (Machine? Product? Person?) What does 'human being' mean? What is meant by 'loving one's neighbor'? Is the opposite of love, indifference? What did reading this passage (book) do for my sense of conscience (other moral senses)?"

Goal 5

The student respects his own and everybody else's right to read. (Note: The following "Reader's Bill of Rights" is offered as a supplement to the NCTE's leaflet, *The Student's Right to Read.*)

The Reader's Bill of Rights

The student recognizes his right to read whatever invites his attention for whatever reason.

The student has the right to read for the sheer fun of reading, without necessarily having to explicate.

The student, while accepting the common reading task of a class, demonstrates his own independence by selecting reading materials for his own pleasure.

The student chooses books according to his interest and ability, not according to some preconception of the quantity or quality of classroom related reading.

The student recognizes that a variety of literary expressions is appropriate to a culturally diverse society. The student resists any attempt to abridge or curtail the publication or distribution of any

[1] From James Baldwin, *Notes of a Native Son* (New York: Bantam Books, 1969). Copyright, 1955, by Beacon Press, and used by special permission.

literary expression and has in fact developed negative attitudes toward censorship.

The student recognizes that literary ability is not the exclusive possession of a cultural elite. He recognizes his own potential as a literary critic, even if not as an artist.

Performance Objective 5.A

Having read a work like *Hair, Catch 22,* or *Soul on Ice,* the student defends, in a panel or debate, the right of other people to read it regardless of its potential offensiveness.

Performance Objective 5.B

Given a story that seems to the student to be in bad taste, the student reads through to the end to determine whether his first suspicion is justified and then writes, in his notebook or journal, a brief note about his decision.

Goal 6

The student respects not only his own experiences and responses but also (a) other readers' experiences and responses and (b) the experiences and responses depicted in a wide variety of literary works. *See also* VI 11.F.

Representative Entering Performance Objective

Entering Objective A. Participating in an informal group discussion, the student demonstrates such courteous behavior as (a) listening to the other speakers and (b) responding—i.e., agreeing or disagreeing— to points made by others before offering his own opinions and feelings. *See also* III 7.C.

Performance Objective 6.A

The student accepts the possibility that two or more interpretations of a given literary work (e.g., Robert Frost's "Stopping By Woods") are quite verifiable by details in the work and offers his own oral interpretation as a viable alternative.

Performance Objective 6.B

Having read a given work that depicts an experience he may not have had (e.g., *Lord of the Flies*), the student accepts it as possible (i.e., he does not dismiss all vicarious experience as unimportant and unreal).

Performance Objective 6.C

Given a play (e.g., a Japanese Noh play or a verse play) in a form different from what he is used to, the student does not dismiss the play out of hand; he accepts it and starts reading it.

Performance Objective 6.D

After reading an experimental story (e.g., one by Jorge Luis Borges, Robert Walser, or Donald Barthelme), the advanced student expresses his respect for such experimentation, no matter whether he gives it high or low marks.

Performance Objective 6.E

Given a student's refusal to talk about a story, a second student, without becoming objectionably personal, explains what may be blocking the first student from talking about the work.

Performance Objective 6.F

Given a controversial play (e.g., William Hochhuth's *The Deputy*) which evokes an angry response, the student orally hypothesizes on the causes of that response.

Performance Objective 6.G

Given a play about a topical phenomenon (e.g., *Hair*), the student orally distinguishes between the play and his reaction to what the play is about (e.g., He does not say, "I think that's a bad play because it's about Hippies.")

Performance Objective 6.H

After reading a play, the student sorts out his value-responses to the play as aesthetic event and to the events themselves (e.g., between his sorrow at a character's death and his enjoyment of the acting).

Performance Objective 6.I

After reading an essay (e.g., one by Ralph Nader, or Loren Eiseley, or Rachel Carson), in which the author makes evident his convictions about an issue (e.g., pollution), the student tells how he feels about the issue and the author.

Performance Objective 6.J

After hearing two or more responses to a teacher's question(s) about a story or a play the class has read, the student tells why he feels that one or another of the responses is or is not justified.

Representative Enabling Objective

After reading Gore Vidal's *Visit to a Small Planet* and after hearing two or more responses to some such questions as: "Why do you agree or disagree with Spelding that a young man's chief goal in life should be to 'get up and go'? Why do you agree or disagree with Kreton that there is murder in the hearts of all earthlings, that we are all savages?" the student tells why he feels that one or another of the responses is or is not justified.[2]

Goal 7

The student develops a sense of humor, at least in part through what he reads and responds to.

Performance Objective 7.A

In reading tall tales (e.g., those about Paul Bunyan, Mike Fink, Casey Jones, etc.) the student tells what he likes, if anything, about this kind of humor (e.g., perhaps the pleasant assumption by both the narrator and his audience that most of the exploits described consist of exaggeration for its own sake).

Performance Objective 7.B

In reading a literary work in which a pompous character is satirized (e.g., Malvolio in *Twelfth Night*, the Duke and the Dauphin in *The Adventures of Huckleberry Finn*, etc.), the student tells what he likes, if anything, about this kind of humor (e.g., the pleasant

---

[2] From the *Purdue Project English Unit on Visit to a Small Planet* (Skokie, Illinois: National Textbook Company, 1972). Copyright, 1972, by Purdue Research Foundation and used by permission.

ways in which other characters manage to deflate the inflated. "Affectation is the only true ridiculous," as Henry Fielding says.)

Performance Objective 7.C

In reading selections whose humor is based on incongruity (e.g., the pseudo-advertisements in *Mad* Magazine; many of Mark Twain's stories and essays; the essays of Stephen Leacock, James Thurber, Robert Benchley, S. J. Perelman, and Harry Golden; the light verses of Ogden Nash, Phyllis McGinley, and Richard Armour), the student tells what he likes, if anything, about this kind of humor (e.g., the "pleasant disappointment of expectation" that Max Eastman emphasizes in *The Importance of Laughter*).

Performance Objective 7.D

In reading works in which the writer takes comparatively more space and time to build humorous situations (e.g., *A Midsummer Night's Dream*), the student tells what he likes, if anything, about this kind of humor.

Representative Enabling Objective

After reading and orally interpreting *A Midsummer Night's Dream*, for instance, the student writes his personal responses, in a brief paper (200 words), to the humor of incongruity arising out of the clash of competing worlds in the play (e.g., the world of the tradesman vs. the world of the pixies; the world of the lovers vs. the world of parental and political authority, etc.).[3]

Performance Objective 7.E

In reading works that combine fantasy with humor and satire (e.g., J. R. R. Tolkien's *The Hobbit*, Ray Bradbury's *The Martian Chronicles*, Kurt Vonnegut's *Cat's Cradle*), the student tells why he is willing, if he is, to suspend his disbelief, to accept imaginative distortions of the literal.

Performance Objective 7.F

After reading a poem like Dorothy Parker's "Resumé," which combines a sense of humor with a list of devices and methods for com-

---

[3] From the *Purdue Project English Unit on A Midsummer Night's Dream* (Skokie, Illinois: National Textbook Co., 1972). Copyright, 1972, by Purdue Research Foundation and used by permission.

mitting suicide, the student tells why he likes or dislikes the poet's attitudes toward suicide and life.

Performance Objective 7.G

The advanced student writes a brief paper (about 300 to 400 words) on what he likes or dislikes about gruesome humor—the "black humor" of one or another of such writers as Jules Feiffer, Thomas Pynchon, Terry Southern, and James Purdy.

DESCRIBING

The student identifies and, in his own words, describes such literary elements as characters, places, actions, patterns, and rhetorical effects without necessarily defining them.

Goal 8

The student describes a piece of writing in his own terms. *See also* III 8.

Representative Entering Performance Objectives

Entering Objective A. The student identifies the meanings of words in context (not from a "vocabulary list").

Entering Objective B. The student identifies some of the characteristics of certain literary pieces, at least on surface levels; he identifies a play, for example, as a piece of writing consisting of acts and scenes, intended to be performed through the speeches and actions of the characters.

Performance Objective 8.A

When referring to a specific form of literature (e.g., poem, play, short story) the student uses appropriate terms, though not necessarily a set of prescribed terms.

Goal 9

In his reading the student apprehends at least the literal and factual levels of meaning.

Performance Objective 9.A

While reading a play or a piece of fiction, the student identifies and describes the setting—i.e., the time, place, cultural features, and the like.

Performance Objective 9.B

In grasping the literal sense of a poem, the student describes the scene or the setting; he talks about "where" the poem happens.

Representative Enabling Objectives

a. Given a poem with a real-world setting such as William Stafford's "Travelling Through the Dark," the student describes the time, the geography, and other literal details that can be located in the text. (In a class discussion he may also infer some of the less explicit elements of setting.)
b. Given a poem with a "surreal" setting, such as S. T. Coleridge's "Kubla Khan," the student describes the scene. He may also re-create parts of the out-of-this-world scene by composing a poster-collage, using magazine pictures that illustrate elements of the setting.

Performance Objective 9.C

In reading fiction, drama, and narrative verse, the student sorts out and identifies, at least at face value, the cast of characters—i.e., who is who.

Representative Entering Objective

Entering Objective A. The student demonstrates his understanding that characters in fiction and drama, unlike personalities in history and biography, are intended to be realistic in the sense that they are "like" real-life persons. He may talk about persons in his experience that a character is "like."

Performance Objective 9.D

After reading or hearing a piece of narrative literature, the student retells the story in his own words, resisting as much amplification of detail as possible. The student may sometimes describe the plot by means of graphic diagrams (triangles, ramps,* etc.) in a chalk talk at the board.

---

* See plot graph in Freier, *Adventures in Modern Literature,* 5th Edition (New York: Harcourt, Brace, and World, 1963), p. 534.

Representative Enabling Objectives

a. After reading or hearing a play (e.g., Lorraine Hansberry's *A Raisin in the Sun*), the student demonstrates his understanding of the plot by retelling it briefly—perhaps using a one-sentence summary for each of the acts.
b. After reading a narrative poem (e.g., *The Odyssey*) the student, using a set of duplicated maps, which he has prepared, retells the main events; or he may write a brief "book for children," retelling the main events to a child in grade 6.

Performance Objective 9.E

While reading a piece of fiction, the student comments on such other significant literal details as what a character does and does not do or say.

Representative Enabling Objectives

a. While reading a novel like *Huckleberry Finn*, the student answers questions like these:

In Chapter 6, Pap rails against a government that would let a free Negro vote. On what grounds does he make this objection? What is Huck's first reaction to Jim's announcement that he has run off? At this point, why does Huck declare he won't tell on Jim? [4]

b. After reading a novel like *The Light in the Forest*, the student demonstrates his ability to apprehend specific information by answering questions like these:

Where is the land of the Tuscarawas? Left alone with the white soldiers, True Son sees a clear and beautiful mental picture of the land of the Tuscarawas. Which sentences in the description show that he is observant, that he loves nature? How does True Son react to Del Hardy? According to the Indian trio—Little Crane, Half Arrow, True Son—as they talk in Chapter 4, what are some of the peculiar traits of white men? Why do the three Indians think white men are nearsighted, hard of hearing, and heedless like children? [5]

Performance Objective 9.F

Having read any literary work containing an allusion, the student identifies it and describes how it contributes to the meaning. (In a

[4] From *Teaching Literature in Grades Ten Through Twelve,* edited by Edward B. Jenkinson and Phillip B. Daghlian. (Bloomington: Indiana University Press, 1968.) Reprinted by permission of the Indiana University Press.
[5] From *Teaching Literature in Grades Seven Through Nine* edited by Edward B. Jenkinson and Jane Stouder Hawley. (Bloomington: Indiana University Press, 1967.) Reprinted by permission of the Indiana University Press.

discussion he may judge in his own words whether the allusion has also contributed imaginatively to the work's economy.)

Representative Enabling Objectives

Given the Biblical allusion, in John Knowles' *A Separate Peace*, to the tree of the knowledge of good and evil in Eden, the student identifies this allusion and may also show how it appropriately relates to the chief characters' fall from innocence.

Performance Objective 9.G

Given a piece of non-fiction, the student reads for specific information. He uses such reference tools as the library card catalog, encyclopedias, biographical references like *Who's Who, Current Biography*, etc., special indexes, and the like, to help him investigate topics related to issues raised in class.

Representative Enabling Objectives

a. The student identifies (in a series of suggested interesting topics) the key ideas to be looked up in an index, card catalog, or encyclopedia.
b. Given several challenging questions or topics for investigation, the student uses the *Reader's Guide to Periodical Literature;* he identifies and reads some magazine articles related to each topic.

Goal 10

The student follows the logic of any literary work, especially the logic of nonfiction.

Performance Objective 10.A

Having read a non-fictional work like Rachel Carson's *Silent Spring,* or Ralph Nader's *Unsafe at Any Speed,* or Lawrence Peter's *The Peter Principle,* the student states in his own words the work's controlling idea and some of its supporting arguments.

Performance Objective 10.B

The student identifies the logical sequence in a piece of nonfiction prose—i.e., whether the sequence is inductive, deductive, or dialectical, and he supports his description by citing or paraphrasing thesis statements and illustrative excerpts.

Representative Enabling Objectives

a. After reading an essay like E. B. White's "The Decline of Sport," the student identifies its logical sequence as inductive and supports his description by citing two or three of the essay's opening examples (several sports events being played and recorded simultaneously on multiple electronic media) that lead to the essay's culminating thesis (Our sports-mad society needs to rediscover simpler, more agrarian pleasures).

b. After reading an essay like Robert Louis Stevenson's "Walking Tours," the student identifies its logical sequence as deductive and supports his description by citing the essay's opening thesis (Walking should be its own reward rather than a means to a utilitarian end) and two or three of the illustrative advantages (exercise, reflection, sight-seeing).

c. After reading an essay like Stephen Leacock's "I'll Stay in Canada," the student identifies its logical sequence as dialectical and supports his description by citing the essay's opening thesis (Canada has more to recommend it than does England), the ensuing antithesis (Canada lacks some few of the attractions available in England and the United States), and the closing synthesis (All things considered, I'll take Canada).

Goal 11

The student understands that the "I" in fiction and poetry is more often than not a fictive narrator rather than the author himself. (See, under *Discriminating*, the related and more challenging Performance Objective 27.F.)

Performance Objective 11.A

In reading a poem or a piece of fiction containing a narrator (e.g., Edgar Allan Poe's "The Tell-Tale Heart") the student identifies and describes him.

Goal 12

The student understands the role of "point of view" or "narrative focus"—what it contributes to the meaning and tone of a literary work; how it limits artistically what the narrator can know and say. (*See also* II 9; III 7.C; VI 13 and 14; VII 14.)

Performance Objective 12.A

Given a piece of fiction (e.g., F. Scott Fitzgerald's *The Great Gatsby,* or Harper Lee's *To Kill a Mockingbird,* or Conrad Richter's

Sea of Grass), the student identifies its "point of view" or "narrative focus," specifying not only whether it is "first person" or "third person" but also identifying the narrator's *degree of participation* in the story (i.e., as one of the main or minor characters, as the "central intelligence," or as a mere observer).

Representative Enabling Objective

After reading a novel like John Knowles' *A Separate Peace*, the student demonstrates his understanding of point of view by answering questions like these:

> What are the differences between Gene as a boy and as a mature narrator? Can you always tell whether Gene is relating how he felt at the time an event happened or how he feels about it fifteen years later? In the following passage, for instance,
>
>> The summer session closed, officially came to an end. But to me it seemed irresolutely suspended, halted strangely before its time. I went South for a month's vacation in my home town and spent it in an atmosphere of unreality, as though I had lived that month once already and had not been interested by it the first time either.
>
> is Gene using the words to describe how he felt at the time or how he now knows that he felt? Is there a reason for his feeling as he does? Does he know the reason at the time? Does he know it now? [6]

Goal 13

The student recognizes or discovers certain conventional structures of poetry.

Performance Objective 13.A

Given a poem with a regular pattern (such as that of a limerick, a haiku, a ballad, a sonnet), the student identifies and describes the pattern.

Representative Enabling Objectives

a. Given a limerick like "There was a young man from Japan," the student describes it as a five-line verse with the first, second, and fifth lines rhyming and sharing the same meter; the third and fourth lines rhyming and sharing the same meter.

b. Given a haiku, the student describes it as a three-line poem, with no rhymes but with the first and third lines each containing five

[6] From "An Approach to *A Separate Peace* and *Demian*" by Donald A. Seybold and Edward B. Jenkinson in *New Ways to Teach Literature*, edited by William Evans. (New York: Bantam Books, 1972.) Reprinted by permission of Bantam Books.

syllables; the second line, seven syllables. (In a later discussion, the student may compare haiku and cinquains and say which form he judges to be the more interesting.)

c. Given a ballad stanza, the student describes it as a four-line verse, which alternates four-stress lines (lines one and three) with three-stress lines (lines two and four); and with only the second and fourth lines rhyming. A musically inclined student may demonstrate the ballad rhythm by means of a guitar.

Performance Objective 13.B

To demonstrate his understanding that set patterns of poetry are accepted by poets who wish to do something successful within these limits, a student volunteer may invent his own pattern (of stanza, rhyme scheme, meter, word count, and the like) and compose a poem within these self-imposed restrictions. (In a discussion he may later judge some of the advantages and disadvantages of variations on, or breaking with, patterns.)

Goal 14

In any piece of writing the student understands the language; not only its vocabulary but also, and especially, its syntax, rhetoric, and sound-effects.

Performance Objective 14.A

Given a selection (e.g., O. Henry's "Gift of the Magi") containing both figurative and non-figurative language, the student identifies and in his own words interprets the figurative language. (See, further, the related and more challenging Performance Objective 32.C.)

Performance Objective 14.B

After reading a book like Daniel Keyes' *Flowers for Algernon,* the student identifies and talks about the sentence fragments at the end of the story, commenting on their intended and their actual effect.

Performance Objective 14.C

After reading a novel, the student demonstrates his understanding of the author's way with words by responding to appropriate questions.

Representative Enabling Objective

After reading a novel like Conrad Richter's *The Light in the Forest*, the student answers questions like these:

> Instead of writing that M. Butler is a wealthy man, the author gives a description of the Butler farm as Del sees it. Why do you think this is more effective than if the author had simply written that Mr. Butler is rich? Why do you think that this is a more specific description than one which would have simply used the words *rich, very rich,* or *wealthy?* [7]

Performance Objective 14.D

After reading, or hearing a recording of, a poem, the student talks about its language—its rhetoric, syntax and sound-effects.

Representative Enabling Objectives

a. After reading or hearing a poem like Edgar Allan Poe's "The Raven" or Sidney Lanier's "Song of the Chattahoochee," the student in his own words describes various sound-effects that impress him, without necessarily naming such effects as alliteration, assonance, consonance, onomatopoeia and the like. He may also demonstrate in an oral reading how the line-ends may create tension or excitement.

b. The student tells how a condensed utterance might appear in its "natural" (i.e., less condensed) form (e.g., "Breathes there a man with soul so dead" as opposed to "Is there anyone alive with such a small spirit that . . .").

Performance Objective 14.E

While reading a play or a piece of fiction, the student identifies some of the dialog and the dialect, and talks about the uses of both. (Compare Performance Objective 32.D.) *See also* IV 11.A; VI 10.

Representative Enabling Objectives

a. In reading G. B. Shaw's *Pygmalion*, the student identifies Cockney expressions repeated by Eliza and her father, and translates them into standard English. Another student or a small committee may compile a "Cockney Phrase Book."

b. After reading a novel like *To Kill a Mockingbird*, the student explains how important the use of dialect is in a novel by answering questions like these:

> The first word spoken is "hey," a Southern expression for "hello," equivalent to the Northern "hi." What other regional expressions occur in this

[7] From *Teaching Literature in Grades Seven Through Nine*, edited by Edward B. Jenkinson and Jane Stouder Hawley. (Bloomington: Indiana University Press, 1967.) Reprinted by permission of the Indiana University Press.

first exchange of dialog? . . . Why does the narrator give the ages of the children as "almost six," and "nearly ten," and "goin' on seven" (pp. 10–11)? [8] *See also* III 4.

DISCOVERING RELATIONSHIPS

The student makes connections (similarities, continuities, reciprocities) between various literary elements and works; between a literary work and his own experiences; between a literary work and another art form (e.g., in the fine arts, theater arts, and electronic media).

Goal 15

In whatever he reads the student recognizes or discovers relationships—at first those that are obvious, then those that yield to his deepening insights.

Representative Entering Performance Objectives

Entering Objective A. The student identifies contextual clues. Reading a sentence like "The solitary meal was a dreary pastime," the student recognizes that in this context the words *solitary* and *dreary* inform each other. He seeks further clues in the preceding and in the following sentences and paragraphs, and he checks his guesses against possible confirmation in a dictionary.

Entering Objective B. Encountering some such sentence as "The zither sounded tinny, as did the player-piano, whose ragtime and jazz assailed the air," the student classifies under *musical instruments* the zither as well as the piano; under *music*, the ragtime as well as the jazz. He also guesses right in matching *assailed* with *made an unpleasant* (rather than *pleasant*) *sound*.

Performance Objective 15.A

The student recognizes that regardless of context, certain art forms (e.g., stories, narrative poems, dramas, television and cinema plays) are related in form and contain such related elements as setting, plot, and characters. He may demonstrate this recognition by

---

[8] From *Teaching Literature in Grades Seven Through Nine.* Reprinted by permission of the Indiana University Press.

listing, on the chalkboard, some of these elements in the interpretation of a given literary work by two different media.

Goal 16

In any literary work the student not only apprehends the elements of setting (Goal 9) but also sorts and compares those elements within his own frame of experience; he recognizes relationships between the happenings, customs, beliefs, and mores of a past, future, or remote setting and those of his own contemporary world. (*See also* V 9.)

Performance Objective 16.A

Given a literary work treating some of the re-created mores and issues of the past (e.g., Arthur Miller's *The Crucible* or Edgar Lee Masters' *Spoon River Anthology*) the student orally or in writing compares and contrasts one of these past mores or issues with those of today. (In a related discussion, the student may also try to identify the authors' biases toward mores, issues, and cultures, as Darwin Turner suggests in "Literature and Society's Values," *English Journal*, May, 1971.)

Representative Enabling Objective

While reading Miller's *The Crucible*, the student discusses some of the ways in which the Colonial Salem witch-hunting depicted in that play persists in the notion of "guilt by association" and other reflected guises today. (As a challenge, the student may also write an editorial on who he believes are the good guys and who the bad guys in society today; these editorials may need to be preceded by some library research.)

Performance Objective 16.B

Given a literary work treating some of the imagined mores and socioeconomic issues of the future (e.g., George Orwell's *1984* or Aldous Huxley's *Brave New World*), the student states in his own words which predicted mores and issues seem to have already arrived in more or less adapted form.

Performance Objective 16.C

Having read a work centering in a different social, ethnic, or religious culture from his own (e.g., Rudyard Kipling's *Kim*, Herman Hesse's *Siddhartha*, John Hersey's *Hiroshima*, Alan Paton's *Cry, the*

Beloved Country, Willa Cather's *My Antonia*) the student explains which features of the other culture or life cycle are similar to those of his own. A group of students may also produce a related costumes and artifacts exhibit.

Goal 17

The student recognizes or discovers relationships between two or more characters in a literary work; how they interact and change; how *they* create the drama (rather than vice versa); in fact, "our emphasis in teaching literature," says J. N. Hook, "should be on the people in it."

Performance Objective 17.A

In reading fiction or drama whose characters include family members, the beginning student identifies the characters related through family and those related through friendships, love, rivalry, and the like.

Representative Entering Performance Objective

For Joseph Krumgold's *And Now Miguel,* the beginning student, after identifying who is who among the characters, talks about Miguel's attempt to establish a meaningful relationship between himself and his father—also between himself, his older brothers, and his uncle.

Performance Objective 17.B

Given any work with dramatic structure (play, novel, story), the student identifies the conflict between one character and another (or between a character and himself or between a character and society) and states in his own words how this conflict relates to the work's total meaning and effect.

Representative Enabling Objective

In reading Shakespeare's *King Lear,* the student identifies the following related conflicts: (1) between Cordelia and her short-sighted, self-centered father; (2) between Cordelia and her insincere sisters Goneril and Regan; (3) between those unscrupulous sisters themselves, at first as competitors for the handouts of Lear, later as rivals for the affections of Edmund; (4) between King Lear and the two heartless daughters once he is disillusioned about them; (5) between Lear and Cordelia, at first, but later between Lear and himself, agonizing over his symbolic blindness toward Cordelia—a blindness that is physically consummated by Regan's husband. The student may also explain how all these related conflicts contribute to the audience's sense of horror over the consequences of several characters' ruthless selfishness.

Performance Objective 17.C

In reading a literary work containing character foils (e.g., Edgar Lee Masters' *Spoon River Anthology*, John Knowles' *A Separate Peace*, Herman Hesse's *Demian*), the student identifies emphasized likenesses and differences among the traits of certain characters.

Representative Enabling Objectives

a. After reading *Spoon River Anthology*, the student first lists some of the contrastive traits of Lucinda Matlock and Elizabeth Childers; or Fiddler Jones and Doc Hill; or Bill Piersol and Hod Putt; or Jonas Keane and Albert Schirdling; then participates in a related role-playing episode "scripted" by one or two other students.[9] *See also* III 1.A d.

b. After reading, or listening to recordings of, Shakespeare's *Julius Caesar* and Andrew Webber and Tim Rice's *Jesus Christ, Superstar*, the student writes a brief essay comparing and contrasting the archetypal betrayer represented by Brutus and Judas. The student may also comment on the characterization of Judas as a kind of Uncle Tom.

c. While reading *Demian*, the advanced student identifies the contrast between Emil's this-worldly anxiety and Demian's out-of-this-world detachment, then the gradual reciprocal exchange and blend of their traits.

Performance Objective 17.D

After reading two or more literary works (e.g., John Steinbeck's *The Pearl* and Ernest Hemingway's *The Old Man and the Sea;* or H. G. Wells' "Country of the Blind" and Herman Melville's *Billy Budd*) containing archetypal characters (e.g., the outsider and the scapegoat), the student writes a paragraph comparing and contrasting one or more ways in which these archetypal characters are related. (Other scapegoat archetypes include Piggy in William Golding's *Lord of the Flies*, Tom Robinson in Harper Lee's *To Kill a Mockingbird*, and Mrs. Hutchinson in Shirley Jackson's "The Lottery.") See, further, the Grosset *Modern English Glossary*, 1971.

Goal 18

The student recognizes or discovers relationships between story lines and archetypal experiences.

[9] From the *Purdue English Unit on Spoon River Anthology*.

Performance Objective 18.A

After reading two or more literary works (e.g., The Book of Ruth and Albert Camus' *The Stranger*) treating a similar archetypal experience (e.g., alienation), the student writes a brief paper comparing and contrasting some of the ways in which this experience was handled. (Note: Camus' alienated Mersault may also be compared with Ray Bradbury's Bazarov in *The Martian Chronicles* or even with T. S. Eliot's Prufrock.)

Performance Objective 18.B

Having read two or more literary works centering in such archetypal experiences as alienation (e.g., Ernest Hemingway's "In Another Country" or Franz Kafka's "Metamorphosis"), initiation (e.g., J. D. Salinger's *The Catcher in the Rye* or Alberto Moravia's *Two Adolescents*) and ritual sacrifice (e.g., Richard Connell's "The Most Dangerous Game" or Shirley Jackson's "The Lottery") the student discusses some of the ways in which one of the fictional episodes is related to a real-life episode he has experienced or observed.

Representative Enabling Objectives

a. After reading *The Catcher in the Rye*, the student writes a journal entry or personal essay comparing one of his own initiations (into dancing, or smoking, or driving, and the like) with Holden's abortive sexual initiation. Or the student may discuss one of his more formal initiations into a social or religious group (communion, bar mitzvah, and the like).

b. After reading "The Lottery," the student writes a journal entry or a personal essay comparing the feelings of the stoning-victim with the feelings (terror and helplessness) that must be felt by a knifing-victim in a large city when onlookers and by-passers refrain from "becoming involved." To document his paper the student may mount on it a newspaper clipping illustrating how a literary episode can be close to an experience in real life.

Goal 19

The student recognizes and discovers relationships between themes in various literary works.

Performance Objective 19.A

Having read two literary works (e.g., *Macbeth* and *Antigone*) with the same theme (e.g., "the individual against fate"), the student writes a brief essay comparing and contrasting some of the ways in which the two works are related.

Representative Enabling Objective

After reading Shakespeare's *Julius Caesar* and Andrew Webber and Tim Rice's *Jesus Christ, Superstar,* the student writes a paragraph on the ways each play handles the theme of the fickleness of crowds. (A humorous version of this theme is depicted by James Thurber in his short sketch, "The Day the Dam Broke.")

Performance Objective 19.B

Given a play treating a crucial issue (e.g., Susan Glaspell's "Trifles" or Thornton Wilder's *Our Town* or Henrik Ibsen's *A Doll's House*), the student states how one or another of the opinions expressed by a character is related to the theme of the play as a whole. The student may also give his own opinion about the issue discussed.

Goal 20

The student discovers relationship(s) between a work's meaning and its use of certain literary conventions.

Representative Entering Performance Objectives

Entering Objective A. The student remembers from the folk stories he has heard or read in his childhood that an expression like "Once upon a time . . ." signals the opening; that a conventional expression like ". . . and they lived happily ever afterward" signals the end. Or he identifies the comparable signals of "panning in" and "fading out" on the screens of television and cinema.

Entering Objective B. From the stories he has read or heard the student is familiar with such conventions as the hero's having a best friend, the heroine's having a friend or relative in whom she confides, and the like.

Performance Objective 20.A

Given a literary work that uses an *in medias res* sequence, the student, without necessarily naming or defining that convention, identifies the time-relationships between various scenes or episodes of the action. (In answering his own question "What happened next?" the student resists spelling out all the details.)

Representative Enabling Objectives

a. In reading *The Odyssey*, or *A Tale of Two Cities*, or *All the King's Men*, all of which use flashbacks, the student reconstructs the chronological sequence of events. He may also state one reason why the author apparently preferred to start the narative in a non-chronological sequence.
b. After reading Nathaniel Hawthorne's *The Scarlet Letter*, the student explains how and why Hawthorne uses the device of having childhood scenes pass through Hester's eyes as she endures shameful exposure on the scaffold.
c. Having read John Knowles' *A Separate Peace*, the student answers questions like these: Does Gene tell the story in chronological order? Why or why not? Does the story seem to have a kind of rhythm? Does it progress at a steady pace? How is the pace controlled? [10]
d. After reading Peter Luke's play *Hadrian VII*, in which the first and last scenes are more related chronologically than are all the intervening scenes, the student reconstructs and explains the true chronological sequence.

Performance Objective 20.B

Given a play containing a chorus, the student explains the latter's relationship to the meaning of the play as a whole.

Representative Enabling Objective

In reading T. S. Eliot's *Murder in the Cathedral*, the advanced student explains the way(s) in which the chorus comments on the action (i.e., expresses its aproval and disaproval) and probably also serves as the author's own "mouthpiece."

Performance Objective 20.C

Given a work that uses the literary convention of recurrence (e.g., Friedrich Dürrenmatt's *The Physicists*), the student explains at least one of the effects of this convention on (a) the characters and (b) the audience.

Performance Objective 20.D

Given a poem containing a refrain (e.g., Edgar Allan Poe's "The Raven" or William Morris's "Two Red Roses Across the Moon"), the student explains how this convention not only marks off sections of the poem but also relates to the reader's sense of expectancy. When-

---

[10] From "An approach to *A Separate Peace* and *Demian*" by Seybold and Jenkinson. Reprinted by permission of Bantam Books.

ever germane, the student also explains a poet's deliberately varying a refrain and how such a variation relates to the reader's sense of expectancy (e.g., pleasant disappointment of expectation).

Performance Objective 20.E

Having read a "well-made" play or novel, the student identifies as a literary convention the early introduction of background information ("exposition" in a play; expository second chapter in a novel); also the conventional early "planting" of details necessary for the ultimate credibility of the whole work. (In a discussion the student may later assess the art, or lack of art, demonstrated by the writer who chose to use one or another of these conventions.)

Goal 21

The student discovers relationships between a work's content and its form.

Performance Objective 21.A

Given a frame narrative (e.g., Thornton Wilder's *The Bridge of San Luis Rey*) or a story within a story (e.g., Joseph Conrad's "Heart of Darkness"), the student explains the ways in which the parts relate to the whole.

Performance Objective 21.B

Given a "well-made" three-act play like Eugene O'Neill's *Beyond the Horizon* or R. C. Sherriff's *Journey's End*, the student shows the relationship(s) of the three-act structure to the play as a whole—e.g., how the first act is devoted to setting up the action, the second to unfolding it, and the third to resolving it.

Performance Objective 21.C

For a work of fiction or drama, the student explains a relationship of the plot to the meaning and tone of the work as a whole.

Representative Enabling Objectives

a. After reading Richard Connell's short story "The Most Dangerous Game," the student explains how the "cat and mouse scenes," in which the aggressive hunter gets closer and closer to his human victim, teasing him with approaches and retreats, contribute not only to the atmosphere of tension and suspense but also to the major moral question about the hunters and the hunted.

b. While reading Lorraine Hansberry's play *A Raisin in the Sun*, the student explains how the white reader's feeling of guilt (or the black reader's resentment) is aroused through the suspensive scenes in which the black protagonists' hopes for decent housing are now encouraged, now frustrated.

Performance Objective 21.D

Given an essay (e.g., George Orwell's "Marrakech") in which one of the main structural devices is juxtaposition, the advanced student creates a picture essay that illustrates both the device and the subject matter of the essay.

Performance Objective 21.E

Having read two or more literary works containing dialog (plays, stories, novels), a group of students demonstrate, by means of oral interpretative presentations, one or two of the ways in which the form and content of such dialog is related to its meaning and tone.

Representative Enabling Objectives

a. Having read a farce comedy like Sean O'Casey's *The End of the Beginning*, two students orally reproduce the conversational ping-pong (repartée), thus demonstrating its relations both to the farcical situation and to the humorous nature of the two chief characters.
b. Having read a problem play like Shakespeare's *Hamlet*, a student orally interprets one or two of the soliloquies, demonstrating how they relate not only to the unfolding action but also to the tragic flaw in the main character(s). Next, two students orally interpret some of the comic repartée between Hamlet and Polonius; next, two students orally interpret some of the mock-comic but poignant and tragically ironic repartée between Hamlet and Ophelia. Finally two students orally interpret the comic repartée of Tom Stoppard's *Rosencrantz and Guildenstern Are Dead*. Other members of the class may then comment on how the dialog's form and content, in each reading, were related to the tone and meaning.

Performance Objective 21.F

Given two or more essays (e.g., Randall Jarrell's "The Taste of the Age" or Loren Eiseley's "Science and the Unexpected Universe," or Norman Mailer's "Superman Comes to the Supermarket") the student explains in his own words how the essayist's choice of examples and anecdotes is related to his mood and meaning.

Performance Objective 21.G

Given a personal essay (e.g., "My Father Goes to Court" by Carlos Bulosan) in which two antithetical portraits are sketched (e.g., one of the rich and one of the poor), the student explains in his own words how the antithesis (sometimes simply a juxtaposition) produces a single effect.

Performance Objective 21.H

For poems the student explains a relationship of the structure to the meaning and tone of the poem as a whole.

Representative Enabling Objectives

a. Given a concrete poem like William Burford's "A Wish," the student identifies the physical shape of the poem (a triangular conifer) and tells how the lines printed in the shape of a Christmas tree prompt the reader to associate that visual image with the concomitant sensuous details inside and outside the poem. (Another, more subtle, concrete poem is E. E. Cummings' "Loneliness, a Leaf Falls.") As a challenge, the student may compose a concrete poem of his own, a creative activity that has proved popular and successful in many high schools.

b. Given a poem like Edgar Allan Poe's "The Raven," the student identifies the "Nevermore" refrain with its echoing variations at the end of each stanza and explains how the hammering repetition of this gruesome echo adds insult to the injury already suffered by the speaker in the loss of his beloved Lenore. The student may also read the postscript poem "Lenore" and explain the relationship between "Guy De Vere" (third line of this poem) and the speaker in "The Raven."

Performance Objective 21.I

The student discovers and explains the relationship of word-position, in poems, to meaning and tone.

Representative Enabling Objectives

a. After reading, or listening to a recording of, Dylan Thomas' "Do Not Go Gentle," the student explains how the line-ends and the beginnings of subsequent lines are related; (e.g., they play with each other in such rhetorical games as echoing and punning.)

b. Given some such free verse as William Carlos Williams' "This is Just to Say" or "Tract" or "The Red Wheelbarrow," the student states in his own words why the lines end where they do. He may also try rearranging the lines to see what is gained and what is lost.

c. After reading, or listening to a recording of, a poem containing a *line* (not a sentence) ending with a verb (e.g., "flew" that ends the tenth line of John Keats's sonnet "Written on the Day that Mr. Leigh Hunt Left Prison"), the student explains the meaning of the verb in relation to its own line, then in relation to the sentence of which it is a part and to the poem as a whole. In Keats's sonnet the *line* ending with *flew* relates to the physical act of Leigh Hunt's release from prison, but the run-on meaning of *flew* in its sentence and in the poem's whole context relates also to Hunt's more ethereal flight with kindred spirits, especially "With daring Milton through the fields of air." (According to such poets as Theodore Roethke, Donald Hall, and Philip Booth, the line-ends—more than the sentence-ends—are among the most strategic and "sensitive spots" for creating planned ambiguities.)

Performance Objective 21.J

Given a poem containing more lyrical than dramatic structure— at least manifestly—the student nevertheless identifies the tension between two diametric forces or feelings in the poem and states in his own words how this tension relates to the tone and meaning of the poem. *See also* VI 14.B.

Performance Objective 21.K

Given a poem with an established pattern (e.g., sonnet, ode, ballad, ballade, haiku, limerick, etc.) the student explains how the pattern makes some of the content inevitable.

Representative Enabling Objectives

a. Having read a limerick that requires a word to rhyme with "Tech" and "wreck," the student explains why some such word as "neck" or "heck" might be inevitable. (In a discussion the student may also cite two or three limitations of rhyme.)
b. Having read a sonnet like John Milton's "When I Consider . . ." the student states in his own words the relationship between the first eight lines (containing the *problem* of the poet's blindness) and the last six lines (containing the *resolution* of the problem: "They also serve who only stand and wait.")

Goal 22

The student recognizes or discovers the role of imagery in creating relationships between the author or speaker and the reader.

Performance Objective 22.A

For a poem or song, the student identifies one of the images (i.e., objects appealing to any of the senses) and explains at least one relationship (perhaps a shared feeling) that this image creates between the poet or speaker and himself.

Representative Enabling Objectives

a. After reading, or listening to a recording of, Robert Browning's "How They Brought the Good News . . ." the student identifies the rhythms of galloping ("Past Looz and past Tongres, no cloud in the sky") and explains how these rhythms re-create for him the very motion of the galloping horse on which the speaker is riding.

b. After reading May Swenson's poem "Southbound on the Freeway," the student identifies the imagery of the "red eyes turning," explains how it re-creates for him the speaker's (perhaps also his own) vision of, and feeling about, police cars, then lists some related images of his own.

c. After reading Walt Whitman's "When lilacs last in the dooryard bloomed," the student identifies the three most emphasized images (the lilacs, the bird, the western star) and their sensuous appeals (fragrance, music, spectacle) and comments on what the speaker is trying to re-create through these images.

d. After reading Alastair Reid's poem "Pigeons," the student explains how the images (the pigeons and the statues) relate to each other (among several relationships, one is that the pigeons and the statues resist change), and how the imagery re-creates in the reader the poet's admiration for these pigeons whether the reader has hitherto liked or disliked pigeons. (Although it is not necessary for the student to define *Objective correlative,* much less to read T. S. Eliot's and W. B. Yeats' theories about it, any reader's enjoyment of poetry can be enhanced when he discovers (1) relationships between imagery and the *feelings* imagery generates and (2) the phenomenon that the poet's emotion indirectly transmitted and re-created through such correlatives usually turns out to have a more powerful effect on the reader than that of the poetaster who transmits his feelings in direct statements, exclamations, and exhortations.) See, further, the Grosset *Modern English Glossary,* 1971.

Goal 23

For any literary work the student discovers connections between the speaker's voice or role and the work's meaning and tone. *See also* VI 8.B.

Performance Objective 23.A

The student explains orally or in writing at least one way in which the narrator, faithful to a certain role or speaking voice, affects the tone of the whole work.

Representative Enabling Objectives

a. In reading *The Adventures of Huckleberry Finn,* the student identifies the narrator, Huck, and explains how Huck's *speaking voice* (faithful to the role of a semi-literate but shrewd and compassionate adolescent) affects the tone of the whole novel; in his explanation, the student addresses himself to answering such questions as the following:

What does Huck's phrase "a tolerable slim old maid" add to the description of her in chapter 1? Why is it important that these are Huck's words? How would the meaning be changed if we thought that it was Mark Twain calling her a "tolerable slim old maid"? Would the humor be lost? [11]

b. In reading Thornton Wilder's *Our Town,* or Robert Bolt's *A Man For All Seasons,* the student explains the ways in which the narrator in his role as stage manager not only sets the tone of the play but also tends to monitor how the audience should feel about it—at least those members of the audience who identify with the narrator.

c. In reading Robert Browning's "My Last Duchess," the student identifies the "I" not as the poet Browning but as the Duke and explains at least one of the ways in which the Duke as narrator (with his condescending, sometimes sarcastic, tone) enables the poem to reveal the Duke's relationship with his last Duchess. (Contrast this *dramatis personae* "I" with the *persona* "I" in 27.F and G.)

Performance Objective 23.B

The student explains a relationship between the speaker in a poem and one of the poem's probable meanings or implications. (Compare Performance Objective 27.G.)

Representative Enabling Objectives

a. Having read Frost's "Stopping by Woods on a Snowy Evening," the student explains at least one of the relationships between the speaker (e.g., a senior citizen, perhaps a member of a profession, expressing nostalgia and tension) and one of the poem's statements

---

[11] From *Teaching Literature in Grades Ten Through Twelve,* edited by Edward B. Jenkinson and Philip D. Daghlian. (Bloomington: Indiana University Press, 1968.) Reprinted by permission of the Indiana University Press.

(e.g., the responsible speaker reluctantly gives priority to his obligations rather than to his private desires).

b. Having read Robert Frost's "Canis Major," the student explains at least one of the relationships between the speaker (e.g., a former underdog suddenly turned rebel) and one of the poem's probable implications (e.g., The role of underdog may prompt one to romp, finally, as an Overdog). (The student who has also read Arthur C. Clarke's *Childhood's End* may comment on the expressed and implied hierarchy of Overlords and their Masters in the star universe beyond our solar system.)

Goal 24

The student relates the language of a literary work (i.e., its vocabulary, syntax, and rhetoric) to the work's tone and meaning.

Performance Objective 24.A

For a given literary work (e.g., *The Pump House Gang*) the student lists a few frequently repeated expressions and ideas (e.g., "Me-dah," "jaysus," and "How old will you be in 1984?") and explains how they relate to the tone and meaning of the work.

Performance Objective 24.B

Given a literary work containing characters (story, novel, play, narrative poem), the student relates the character's language to the characterization, specifying whether such language contributes to an individualist or to a "stock" character, or to a more complicated mixture. *See also* IV 12.D and 13.

Representative Enabling Objectives

a. Having read *Treasure Island*, the student lists some of the characteristic expressions used by Jim Hawkins (the young son of an innkeeper) and some used by Long John Silver (the mutineer). The student explains that although Jim uses a few clichés, the jargon used by Long John ("Aye, aye, mates," "Shiver me timbers," "Take your bearings," etc.) relates him characteristically to seamen, if not to pirates. A perceptive student may qualify the latter relationship with the observation that Long John is not quite so much the "stock" pirate as are his accomplices; that Silver is individualistic enough to needle Jim with such ironic and equivocal remarks as "None of us won't hang you, mate" and "Lad, no one's a-pressing of you." [12]

[12] From the *Purdue Project English Unit on Treasure Island* (Skokie, Illinois: National Textbook Company, 1972). Copyright, 1972, Purdue Research Foundation and used by permission.

b. In reading *The Adventures of Huckleberry Finn,* the student who finds Pap (as most readers do) a thoroughly despicable person with no redeeming human characteristics, explains how much of this impression is created by what Pap says and how much by the way he says it.

Performance Objective 24.C

Given some narrative prose consisting of one or two extra-long sentences as in William Faulkner, the student states at least one of the relationships (e.g., suspensiveness) between such rhetoric and the unfolding of the story (as in *Light in August*).

Performance Objective 24.D

Given narrative prose containing many conjunctions and a chain of compound sentences (as in Ernest Hemingway's "In Another Country") the student states how such rhetoric, echoing the rhetoric of the King James Bible, relates to the story's tone and meaning.

Performance Objective 24.E

Given an essay or article with an idiosyncratic syntax (e.g., the elliptical prose of R. W. Emerson) the student quotes some excerpts and explains how these help to create the tone (crispness, epigrammatic quotability, etc.) and meaning.

Performance Objective 24.F

Given a narrative prose or verse selection containing verbal phrases at ends rather than at beginnings of sentences, the student identifies the phrases that spell out concretely what is introduced only generally in the initial main clauses.

Representative Enabling Objective

Given the following excerpt from *The Odyssey,* "Once more Odysseus crossed the wine-dark seas, his men working the oars, the water dripping from the wood," the student underscores the last two phrases and explains that such words as *men working, oars, water dripping* concretely "render" the generalization "Odysseus crossed the . . . seas." [13]

Performance Objective 24.G

In any literary work the student shows the relationship(s) between the metaphor(s) and the main idea(s) of the work as a whole.

---

[13] From the *Purdue Project English Unit on The Odyssey.* (Skokie, Illinois: National Textbook Company, 1972.) Copyright, 1972, Purdue Research Foundation, and used by permission.

Representative Enabling Objectives

a. After reading Mark Twain's *Life on the Mississippi*, the student, given the passage beginning "The face of the water, in time, became a wonderful book—a book that was dead language to the uneducated passenger . . ." identifies the related images of the metaphor ("water's face" and "book") and states in his own words the relationship of the metaphor to the whole work. (E.g., "An experienced pilot can read the Mississippi like a book.") [14]

b. After reading Mark Twain's *The Adventures of Huckleberry Finn*, the student writes a brief expository paper developing his interpretation, for instance, of The River as Metaphor or The Raft as Metaphor and its relation to the meaning of the novel as a whole. (Academically talented twelfth graders may also compare their interpretations with Leslie Fiedler's critical essay on *Huckleberry Finn* in *Love and Death in the American Novel* or with Lionel Trilling's essay in *The Liberal Imagination*.)

Goal 25

The student explores relationships between a literary work and other art forms.

Performance Objective 25.A

After reading literary works rich in sensuous details, the student brings to class such artifacts (paintings, posters, collages, and the like) as are related to the works read. He displays these artifacts and talks about them, pointing out some of the relationships.

Representative Enabling Objectives

a. After reading a narrative like *The Red Badge of Courage*, the student re-creates some relationships between the red (or blood) images by making a collage (hearts, cardinals, roses, flags, raw meat, etc.), displaying it and explaining it to the class.

b. Having read a poem like Marianne Moore's "The Steeple-Jack," which begins "Dürer [the Medieval German painter fond of sharp details and primary colors] would have seen a reason for living in a town like this," the student relates the poem's drollery and pristine colors with similar qualities in paintings like those by Marc Chagall,

---

[14] From the *Purdue Project English Unit on Life on the Mississippi.* (Skokie, Illinois: National Textbook Company, 1971.) Copyright, 1971, Purdue Research Foundation, and used by permission.

brings to class a print of Chagall's (e.g., "I and My Village" or "The Poet") and points out relationships between such Chagallité and Marianne Moore's expressionism in "The Steeple-Jack."

Performance Objective 25.B

After reading, or listening to, poems and folk songs closely related to music, the student or a group of students tape-record a choral reading (or singing) and play the latter for the class. The group's spokesman explains to the class some of the relationships between the works and the musical effects. *See also* III 8.B.

Representative Enabling Objectives

a. Having read a folk ballad like "Barbara Allen" or "John Henry," the student composes original music for it, sings it (perhaps with guitar accompaniment), and explains to the class a relationship or two (e.g., repetitions, nostalgic notes) between the words and the music.
b. Having taped their choral reading of a poem or song like Paul Simon's "Feeling Groovy" or John Lennon and Paul McCartney's "In My Life" and having played the tape for the class, a group of students or their spokesman explains some of the relationship(s) between the works and their choral readings.

Performance Objective 25.C

After reading a novel or a story containing much dialog, a group of students re-create a scene in a script of their own and produce it for the class. Some students and classes may also make a related film.

Representative Enabling Objectives

a. After reading Marjorie Rawlings' *The Yearling*, a student rewrites in play form one of the scenes containing dialog (e.g., Jody, his father, and his mother confronting the possibility that the yearling deer will have to go), which a student-director then casts and produces for the class.
b. Having read a short short story (e.g., Saki's "The Open Window"), a student-director, with the help of a student cast and crew, writes a play or a movie script, produces it, and presents it for the class, perhaps explaining some of the limitations and possibilities of re-creating a literary work in dramatic and cinematic art forms. *See also* VI 2.

DISCRIMINATING

The student explains significant differences he recognizes or discovers within and between various literary forms and works; between a literary work and another art form.

Goal 26

The student distinguishes among the common forms of literature without necessarily defining them.

Representative Entering Performance Objectives

Entering Objective A. Given a short story (e.g., Edgar Allan Poe's "The Tell-Tale Heart") and a poem (e.g., Poe's "The Raven") the beginning student tells which one looks like verse, which like prose.

Entering Objective B. Given a piece of fiction (e.g., Lewis Carroll's *Alice's Adventures in Wonderland*) and a play (e.g., James Barrie's *Peter Pan*), the beginning student tells which is which.

Entering Objective C. Given a narrative-descriptive paragraph (e.g., from Barrie's "Peter and Wendy") and an explanatory paragraph (e.g., from a how-to or hobby book), the beginning student identifies the passage that tells a story.

Performance Objective 26.A

Given a pair of unabridged pieces of writing (e.g., an essay and a news report; a classical myth and a fable) the student lists some of the differences between the pair.

Performance Objective 26.B

Given a short story (e.g., John Steinbeck's "The Leader of the People") and an essay containing much narration (e.g., E.B. White's "The Decline of Sport"), the student identifies the story and the essay; in his own words he also explains one of the differences. (E.g., although each piece contains narration and a theme, only the story depicts the development of a main character.)

Performance Objective 26.C

Given a personal essay like Joseph Wood Krutch's "The Flowering Desert" and an article like Raymond Ditmars' "Desert Sidewinders," which are concerned with much of the same subject-matter, the student explains at least one of the differences in the treatments. (E.g., the article contains more documentation or more objectively presented information; the essay contains more subjective description or personal reflection more lyrically presented.)

Performance Objective 26.D

Given an expository essay (e.g., Arthur C. Clarke's "The Morality of Space") and a satirical essay (e.g., Jonathan Swift's "A Modest Proposal"), the student lists some of the differences in content and treatment.

Performance Objective 26.E

Given such different modes and forms as fantasy (e.g., J. R. R. Tolkien's *The Hobbit*), science fiction (e.g., Robert Heinlein's *Tomorrow the Stars*), and a *Saturday Review* or *New York Times* editorial (e.g., "The Population Explosion"), the student explains why fantasy and science fiction almost always push past what is known or accepted by scientists.

Performance Objective 26.F

After reading a tragedy (e.g., Robert Bolt's *A Man for All Seasons*) and a comedy (e.g., G. B. Shaw's *Pygmalion*), the student explains some of the similarities and differences between comedy and tragedy.

Performance Objective 26.G

After reading a tragedy (e.g., Shakespeare's *Macbeth*) and its parody (e.g., Barbara Garson's *Mac Bird*) the student identifies at least one of the differences between those two literary modes. He may choose a parody of any other mode (comedy, romance) or of any other literary form (fiction or non-fiction, prose or verse).

Performance Objective 26.H

After reading two such different forms of poetry as a ballad (e.g., the folk ballad "Barbara Allen") and a long narrative poem (e.g., Robert Frost's *Death of the Hired Man*), the student lists at least one attribute that both forms have in common (e.g., both tell a story) and at least one of the differences (e.g., the shorter poem is more lyrical—lends itself to singing and instrumentation; the longer poem has more character delineation).

Goal 27

Given a common form of literature, the student distinguishes among its most representative features.

Representative Entering Performance Objectives

Entering Objective A.   Remembering from his childhood two such verses as "Lullaby and Goodnight" and "Simple Simon Met a Pieman," the student has long ago identified the verse that would be more appropriate to accompany rope-skipping.

Entering Objective B.   Remembering from his childhood a stanza like the one beginning "Mary had a little lamb," the student has identified the lines that rhyme and those that do not.

Entering Objective C.   Given a play (e.g., Thornton Wilder's "The Happy Journey"), the student distinguishes between dialog and stage directions.

Entering Objective D.   Given any piece of writing containing quoted matter and unquoted matter, the student identifies at least the mechanically signalled difference (e.g., quotation marks or a passage set off by deep indentation).

Performance Objective 27.A

Given any piece of literature containing a story line (e.g., short story, novel, play, narrative poem) the student distinguishes between the story line and the theme.

Performance Objective 27.B

Given a piece of literature containing an expressed or implied philosophic statement about any experience in life, the student distinguishes between the general theme (usually expressible in a phrase) and the more amplified thematic idea (usually expressible in a statement). In a discussion the student may also tell why he accepts or rejects the moral assumptions or values and the author's bias reflected in such a thematic statement.

Representative Enabling Objective

In reading Katherine Anne Porter's short story "Theft," the student distinguishes between the general theme ("private vs. public welfare" or "self-interest vs. altruism") and the implied philosophical statement or conclusion ("A person needs to look after his own interests lest he be stepped on.") Although some such conclusion is the "moral" of this story, the student committed to Judaeo-Christian values may well reject such "morality."

Performance Objective 27.C

After reading a work of literature, the student explains, in his own terms, some of the distinctions between the work's literal and its sub-surface meanings. (See, further, Goal 36.)

Representative Enabling Objective

In reading Tennessee Williams' play *The Glass Menagerie*, the student distinguishes between (a) the "givens" of a crippled Laura and a normal mother and (b) the undercurrents of a not-so-abnormal Laura and of an even more crippled mother—a mother emotionally hobbled through her ambitions for, and fantasies about, her daughter.

Performance Objective 27.D

In reading or hearing some poems with various meters (e.g., "Take, O take those lips away," "That time of year thou mayst in me behold," "This is the forest primeval, the murmuring pines and the hemlocks,") the student distinguishes each meter by tapping his pencil, perhaps, on his desk—light taps for light stresses, heavier taps for heavier stresses. In academic classes the students may also distinguish these meters in traditional terms (e.g., trochaic, iambic, dactylic, and so on).

Performance Objective 27.E

After reading a play written in prose (e.g., Robert Sherwood's *Abe Lincoln in Illinois*) and a play written in verse (e.g., Maxwell Anderson's *Valley Forge*) the student identifies some of the differences in the forms. If he uses traditional terms, he should also distinguish between blank verse and free verse. In a discussion he may also cite an advantage and a limitation of prose and of verse plays.

Performance Objective 27.F

Given a poem containing (1) a narrator (e.g., The Duke in Robert Browning's "My Last Duchess") or (2) a narrator representing only one side of a poet's personality through a speaking voice (e.g., the "I" in Theodore Roethke's "The Waking"), the student explains in his own words the distinctions between these speaking voices.

Performance Objective 27.G

After reading several poems by one poet (e.g., Robert Frost's "Birches," "Departmental," and "Canis Major"), the student orally distinguishes the different speaking voice in each poem. (Note: Such essays as T. S. Eliot's "The Three Voices" and John Hall Wheelock's "The Four Voices" are available in anthologies of literary criticism and are summarized in the Grosset & Dunlap *Modern English Glossary,* pp. 320–321.)

Performance Objective 27.H

In reading a romantic play like Shakespeare's *Romeo and Juliet* or a farce comedy like Sean O'Casey's "The End of the Beginning," the student identifies the passages of ping-pong dialog (without necessarily calling them "repartée" or "stichomythy") and explains how such snappy word-exchanges differ in tone and spirit (e.g., in playfulness) from longer-winded dialogs and monologs.

Goal 28

While reading such literature as fiction, drama, and narrative verse, the student not only sorts out the *dramatis personae* at face value (Goal 9) but also distinguishes among the subtler traits that distinguish one character from another.

Representative Entering Performance Objective

The student distinguishes the "good guys" from the "bad guys"; qualities of human excellence, from less humane attributes. In reading a Western story like *Shane,* the student identifies significant differences in the ways in which the hero and the villain treat their horses. (This skill of discriminating good from evil in two or more characters is a prerequisite to the much more sophisticated skill of sorting out humane and inhumane qualities in one complicated character, who almost always embodies both good and evil.)

Performance Objective 28.A

The student identifies qualities of good and evil within a single major character in fiction and drama ranging in difficulty from Nathaniel Hawthorne's "Young Goodman Brown" and Katherine Anne Porter's "Noon Wine" to G. B. Shaw's *Saint Joan* and Henrik Ibsen's *An Enemy of the People.* In a discussion the student may also cite distinctions between an individualized characterization and a stereotype.

Performance Objective 28.B

When reading a literary work containing a narrator, the student distinguishes him from other characters and from the author.

Representative Enabling Objectives

a. In reading Ring Lardner's "Haircut," the student distinguishes the author from the narrator, who is here the barber. Another student may draw, on the chalkboard, a cartoon or a diagram representing the comparative positions of the author, the barber-narrator, and the reader—also the "distances" between them.
b. In reading Thornton Wilder's *The Bridge of San Luis Rey* (or Joseph Conrad's *Lord Jim*), which uses more than one narrator, the student identifies the narrators and explains how each narrator differs from the others.
c. Given two stories told in the first person (e.g., Conrad's "Heart of Darkness" and Ernest Hemingway's "In Another Country") the student distinguishes between the narrator as bystander-commentator (Marlow in "Heart of Darkness") and the narrator as active participant (the young American in "In Another Country"). (To begin with, the student need not define such phenomena as "omniscient narrator," "limited participant," and "central intelligence," although he may later use these labels inductively.)

Performance Objective 28.C

In any literary work containing characters, the student distinguishes among them not only by their jobs or social stations but also by their attitudes and life styles.

Representative Enabling Objective

In reading a play like Wilder's *Our Town*, the student distinguishes between Editor Webb's attitude and Dr. Gibbs' attitude toward making a living; between Dr. Gibbs' and the town drunkard's; between those living and the articulate dead. (See George Miller's suggestions for selecting or rejecting *Our Town* as instructional material according to where one is teaching. "The Blackboard Jungle . . ." *College Composition and Communication,* May, 1970).

Performance Objective 28.D

In apprehending characterizations, the student distinguishes orally or in writing between a character's self-image and the impression he or she has made on other characters. (Compare, for instance, Becky Sharp in Thackeray's *Vanity Fair;* Mr. Darcy, in Austen's *Pride and Prejudice,* whose original working title, incidentally, was *First Impressions.*)

Representative Enabling Objective

The student composes a skit consisting of a soliloquy for a character he re-creates (e.g., Abraham Lincoln, as in Stephen Vincent Benet's *John Brown's Body*) and a dialog in which two other speakers (e.g., Tad and Mary) talk about the soliloquist. The student–playwright then casts and produces the skit for the class.

Performance Objective 28.E

In discriminating among characters, the student states his distinctions not only on what a character says or on what another character says about him, but also on what a character does.

Representative Enabling Objective

After reading Friedrich Dürrenmatt's play *The Physicists,* which is not only a murder thriller, but also a critique of contemporary society, the student makes for each of the three main characters a brief list of (a) his actions, (b) his comments on these actions, and (c) his comments on each other character's actions.

Performance Objective 28.F

While reading a literary work written in a past century, the student distinguishes between the past significance of certain archetypal characters and the present significance of similar archetypes.

Representative Enabling Objective

While reading Shakespeare's *The Merchant of Venice,* the student identifies Shylock as the archetype of the Jewish usurer and distinguishes him from the Jewish usurer or any other usurer of today—i.e., identifies certain changes of public attitude, also persistent non-changes, toward Jews in general and usurers in particular. Similarly, the student identifies the intellectual woman Portia as much more exceptional in her time than is the intellectual woman today.

Goal 29

The student distinguishes among the ideas (issues, opinions) he meets in any piece of writing.

Performance Objective 29.A

The student identifies and sorts out a contrariety of representative ideas expressed in the literary work he is reading.

Representative Enabling Objective

After reading an essay like Charles Lamb's "Dissertation on Roast Pig," in which a father's and a son's attitudes are contrasted (or an essay like Robert Benchley's "Good Luck and Try and Get It," in which fun is poked at various superstitions), the student reads aloud to the class excerpts of his own choosing in such a way as to show how the contrastive notions differ. *See also* III 8.

Performance Objective 29.B

The student identifies and sorts out a contrariety of representative ideas implied (or partly expressed, partly implied) in the literary work he is reading.

Representative Enabling Objective

Confronted with two or more contrastive ideas on one topic (e.g., issues of bureaucracy undergirding Robert Frost's humorous poems "Departmental" and "A Considerable Speck"), the student orally identifies the implied differences of opinion and attitude. He may also dramatize the difference(s) in a skit or short story of his own composition.

Goal 30

The student discriminates between logical and illogical notions in whatever he reads. *See also* III 12.

Performance Objective 30.A

The student discriminates between circular reasoning and viable reasoning without necessarily defining those terms.

Representative Enabling Objective

Given a character (e.g., in a novel of Charles Dickens) who says, "We are without funds because we haven't a farthing left," the student explains that being without funds means practically the same thing as "not having a farthing left" and that therefore one such phrase cannot be a *reason* for the other. The student then composes a more viable because-clause (e.g., "because we were robbed").

Performance Objective 30.B

The student discriminates between *sequiturs* and *non-sequiturs* without necessarily defining those terms.

Representative Enabling Objectives

Given a brief scene from a narrative or play in which John says to Mary, "My wallet was lying right here just before you came in. Just after you came in, my wallet was gone. Come on, hand it over!" the student explains why John may have been jumping to an erroneous conclusion. (It is not necessary for the student to label this kind of non-sequitur a *post hoc*, though he may wish to call it a "hasty conclusion" or some such appropriate synonym.)

Goal 31

The student distinguishes among the various world views ("visions of life") he encounters in the literature he reads.

Performance Objective 31.A

After reading two representative authors reflecting contrasting visions, the student identifies and orally explains the differences.

Representative Enabling Objectives

a. Having read Walt Whitman's *Leaves of Grass*, or several of Whitman's poems that extol "The American Dream," and having read some of the fiction of Theodore Dreiser (e.g., *An American Tragedy, Sister Carrie, The Financier,* etc.) reflecting that novelist's disillusionment with the American dream, the student (without necessarily mentioning or defining *naturalism*) explains one of the main differences between Whitman's vision of life and Dreiser's vision.

b. Having read some of Ernest Hemingway's works (e.g., *The Old Man and the Sea, The Sun Also Rises, Death in the Afternoon, The Green Hills of Africa,* etc.) and some of William Faulkner's (e.g., "The Bear," *Intruder in the Dust, The Reivers, The Hamlet, The Unvanquished,* etc.), the student explains (preferably in an expository paper) one of the main differences between Hemingway's vision of life (e.g., man as superman; or . . .) and Faulkner's (e.g., man as prevailing and enduring through his humaneness; or . . .).

Performance Objective 31.B

After reading two or more works about one topic, issue, or setting, the student explains the various points of contrast in those works' moral visions.

Representative Enabling Objective

After reading two or more works on World War I (e.g., Eric Remarque's *All Quiet on the Western Front,* Hemingway's *A Farewell to Arms,* R. C. Sheriff's *Journey's End*), the student lists various points of contrast in the moral visions presented.

Performance Objective 31.C

In his reading, the student orally distinguishes between a comic vision and a tragic vision of life.

Representative Enabling Objective

After reading Sophocles' *Oedipus the King* (or Katherine Anne Porter's "Pale Horse, Pale Rider") and Aristophanes' *Lysistrata* (or Eudora Welty's "Why I Live at the P. O."), the advanced student tells some of the distinctions he has discovered between a tragic vision and a comic vision of life (e.g., the tendency of the tragic vision to be more *feelingful,* the comic vision to be more *rational;* the tendency of a character in comedy to take himself more seriously than he is taken by the narrators and the readers. As Frye suggests, both visions sometimes meld.)

Performance Objective 31.D

In works by or about one given author, the student orally distinguishes between that author's public vision and private vision.

Representative Enabling Objective

After reading a biographical essay like Thoreau's *Walden* and identifying its romantic, return-to-nature vision of life; then reading Leon Edel's biography of Thoreau, which interprets *Walden* as a grossly unreliable account of Thoreau's actual experiences at Walden, the student explains in his own words at least one main difference between Thoreau's public vision and his private vision of life. (This distinction can also be related to the *persona* adopted by Thoreau in *Walden*—the *persona* and the writer hardly ever being truly identical.)

Performance Objective 31.E

In reading literary criticism (e.g., reviews in *Saturday Review* or *The New York Review of Books*) the academically talented student identifies and discriminates among the reviewers' reference-frames.

Representative Enabling Objective

Given Theodore Morrison's essay-review "Dover Beach Revisited," an academically talented student (who has previously read Matthew Arnold's poem "Dover Beach") reads aloud, to the class, first the poem and then his own selected excerpts from the essay in such a way as to teach his peers the effects that different attitudes and reference-frames (e.g., Freudian, Marxist, New-Critical) can have in interpreting a poem like "Dover Beach." (Later a panel of students can review Frederick Crews' *The Pooh Perplex,* a humorous look at various "schools" of criticism.)

Goal 32

The student discriminates between alternative possibilities of meaning and tone that depend upon rhetorical, syntactic, and lexical distinctions.

Representative Entering Performance Objectives

Entering Objective A. The student reads at a level of competence that includes his habitual use of context clues.

Entering Objective B. The student has developed an ear for discriminating between questions, declarative statements, requests, exclamations, exhortations, and so on, not only in listening and in speaking but also in reading, whether orally or silently.

Performance Objective 32.A

In any literary work the student distinguishes orally between a question intending an answer and a question not intending an answer ("rhetorical question"); between a request and an exhortation; between any statement at face value and its actual meaning if different from its surface meaning.

Representative Enabling Objective

Reading, in *The Odyssey,* Nestor's report to Odysseus's son, Telemachos, in which the wise elder says, "Could any mortal man tell the whole story?" the student identifies the intent and tone of Nestor's question as purely "rhetorical." [15]

Performance Objective 32.B

The student distinguishes figurative from non-figurative language.

Representative Enabling Objective

Given a passage like the following from Walter V. T. Clark's *The Ox-Bow Incident,* which contains some figurative and some non-figurative language, the student identifies the figurative expressions.

[15] From the *Purdue Project English Unit on The Odyssey* (Skokie, Illinois: National Textbook Company, 1972). Copyright, 1972, by Purdue Research Foundation, and used by permission.

Having heard myself speak, I realized that . . . there had been something in the kid's raving which had made the canyon seem to swell out and become immaterial until you could think the whole world, the universe, into the half-darkness around you: millions of souls swarming like fierce tiny pale stars, shining hard . . . To me his idea appeared just the opposite of Davies'. To the kid, what everybody thought was low and wicked . . . was a mere disguise of their evil.[16]

Performance Objective 32.C

Without being rehearsed in trivial distinctions between simile and metaphor, the student discriminates between a less imaginative and a more imaginative comparison.

Representative Enabling Objective

Given the following comparisons (1) "The boy looked like a man" and (2) "The boy looked like a bulldozer," the student nominates the latter comparison as more imaginative than the first. (In comparisons—whether simile, metaphor, personification—the *actual likeness* of two compared objects is relatively prosaic, whereas the more imaginative comparison depends upon the *actual unlikeness* of the two compared objects—except for one surprisingly believable aspect, that of "right surprise.") See, further, the Grosset *Modern English Glossary*, 1971.

Performance Objective 32.D

When he reads dialog in fiction, drama, and narrative verse, the student discriminates by means of pitch, stress, and pause, between alternative meanings dependent upon intonation.

Representative Enabling Objective

Orally reading the passage in *The Yearling*, in which Mr. Baxter asks Jody "How come you to take off such a fur *piece* [down the road]?" the student does not put more stress on *fur* than on piece.[17] (Oral interpretation is to be distinguished, of course, as is eye-dialect, from the dialectologist's random field recordings.)

Performance Objective 32.E

While reading any literary work, the student distinguishes between logical intentions and actual rhetorical effects. In his own words the student explains the difference(s) between a character's

---

[16] From the *Purdue Project English Unit on The Ox-Bow Incident* (Skokie, Illinois: National Textbook Company, 1972). Copyright, 1972, by Purdue Research Foundation and used by permission.

[17] From the Purdue Project English Unit on *The Yearling*.

intentions, for instance, and the actual impressions he creates, in spite of everything, upon his audience.

Representative Enabling Objective

After reading, in Shakespeare's *A Midsummer Night's Dream,* Bottom's production of "The Tragedy of Pyramus and Thisbe," the student distinguishes orally between Bottom's concept of himself as an actor in a tragi-serious piece and the actual funny effects that his performance produces. (The student may or may not label this phenomenon "irony" or "dramatic irony," but there is no harm in his doing so as long as he realizes that this is only one of several aspects of irony.) [18]

Performance Objective 32.F

The student identifies and distinguishes between the documentary and the lyrical, especially when those two modes are used in one literary work.

Representative Enabling Objective

In reading some such non-fiction as Paul Goodman's *Growing Up Absurd,* Norman Mailer's *The Armies of the Night,* or Gordon Parks' *A Choice of Weapons,* the student identifies at least one of the documentary and one of the lyrical passages.

Performance Objective 32.G

In reading poetry and other lyrical works and passages, the student distinguishes between normal word order and deliberately transposed order without necessarily using such labels as "attributive," "epithet," "transferred epithet," and the like.

Representative Enabling Objective

After reading a poem such as Dylan Thomas's "Fern Hill," which contains several transferred epithets, the student identifies at least one of them (e.g., "whinnying stable") and restates the concept in its non-transferred form (e.g., "whinnying horses").

Performance Objective 32.H

In reading works of a given century or era, the student distinguishes between expressions contemporary with that era and expressions, especially poeticisms, that are now archaic.

---

[18] From the *Purdue Project English Unit on A Midsummer Night's Dream* (Skokie, Illinois: National Textbook Company, 1972). Copyright, 1972, by Purdue Research Foundation and used by permission.

Representative Enabling Objectives

a. After reading, in Shakespeare's *Romeo and Juliet,* Juliet's speech beginning "O Romeo, Romeo! Wherefore are thou Romeo!/ Deny thy father and refuse thy name;/ Or, if thou wilt not . . ." (Act II, Sc.i.), the student rewrites the speech in contemporary standard English or in contemporary slang.

b. Reading, in a recent newspaper, a poem or a feature piece containing such poeticisms as *o'er* (for *over*), *e'er* (for *ever*), *e'en* (for *even*), *'neath* (for *beneath*), and the like, the student identifies them as archaic. He may also, in a discussion, tell whether he believes the writer was using such archaisms consciously or unconsciously—i.e., deliberately, in parody; or lazily, in mistrust of his own contemporary voice.

Goal 33

The student distinguishes the works of various writers on the basis of style.

Performance Objective 33.A

Given two passages (unmarked as to authors) from two different authors he has read in depth, the student identifies the authors.

Representative Enabling Objective

Given an unidentified but representative passage from Faulkner (e.g., a long involuted sentence from *Absalom, Absalom*) and an unidentified but representative passage from Hemingway (e.g., the opening paragraph from *A Farewell to Arms*) the student correctly identifies the authors.

Performance Objective 33.B

In a genre that the advanced student has read in depth (e.g., the short story) he identifies and explains some stylistic features that distinguish one author from another.

Representative Enabling Objective

Given two or three short stories (e.g., Poe's "The Murders in the Rue Morgue," Doyle's "Sherlock Holmes gives a Demonstration," and Donald Barthelme's 'The Phantom of the Opera's Friend") the student identifies some of the stylistic clues that distinguish these stories from one another (e.g., Poe's meticulous vocabulary; Doyle's habit of having Watson "rubber-stamp" Holmes' casually uttered, clever statements; Barthelme's understatement or "soft-sell" and his uncommitted, purposely openended comments on his characters' behavior).

INFERRING

The student tells what he has generalized or abstracted (e.g., suggested meaning, vision of life) from what he has read; or he demonstrates his inferences through role-playing and other oral and written re-creations.

Goal 34

The student draws inferences from the explicit statements, actions, and events in whatever he reads.

Representative Entering Performance Objective

Entering Objective A. The student understands the explicit statements, actions, and events in his reading. To demonstrate that he understands what is said explicitly, for instance, in a paragraph developing a point, he identifies and underscores the sentence that makes the point.

Performance Objective 34.A

Given a passage from an article containing information organized inductively but with the author's concluding statement deleted, the student writes the conclusion in his own words and afterwards compares his version with the author's to see whether the two match, even if not word for word.

Performance Objective 34.B

Given a paragraph that illustrates some such explicitly stated topic sentence as "Diesel-fueled buses pollute the air," the student infers and states in his own words one of the paragraph's implications (e.g., "Let's get rid of diesel-fueled buses" or "Let's get rid of diesel fuel" or "Let's develop a non-polluting power for running buses and other vehicles," etc.). (Such an inference as "Let's get rid of buses" can be used to teach and learn the fallacy of "throwing the baby out with the bath water," a fallacy that misleads certain critics of performance objectives.)

Performance Objective 34.C

Given an editorial or position paper (perhaps from one's school newspaper) with an expressed main theme, the student infers not only (1) the main implications but also (2) the underlying or "hidden" assumption and states 1 + 2 in his own words.

Representative Enabling Objective

Given a school newspaper editorial written by the chairman of the Students' Curriculum Committee, the reader encounters the following concluding statement: "Practically all authoritative research points to zero transfer between knowledge of grammatical terms and competence in communicating." The reader infers and states in his own words (1) the main *implication* "Grammar courses must go." and (2) the main *assumption* "The chief purpose of studying grammar is to improve one's skills of communicating." (In a panel discussion or a debate the student may argue for or against accepting such an assumption. Most linguists reject it, preferring to defend grammar study for its own sake.)

Performance Objective 34.D

After reading an essay or an editorial (e.g., one or another of the Sierra Club's editorials like "Who Owns the Forests?" or "Who Owns the Mountains?") the student infers and states in his own words the main theme.

Performance Objective 34.E

After reading any literary work (narrative, drama, verse), the student infers and states in his own words the main theme or thesis or moral center.

Performance Objective 34.F

Having read a modern play (e.g., William Gibson's *The Miracle Worker* or Tennessee Williams' *The Glass Menagerie*) with explicit, if minimal, description of the stage designs, the student draws a "set" appropriate for visualizing the action.

Performance Objective 34.G

To demonstrate that he has correctly inferred the dramatic structure of a play (or of a narrative with a plot), the student draws a simple diagram (e.g., a two-sided mountain with its peak as the climax) of the work's action, along with appropriate labels. (Compare the cartoon-model in Freier, et al., eds., *Adventures in Modern Literature*, 5th Edition. Harcourt Brace Jovanovich, p. 534.)

Performance Objective 34.H

After reading one act of a play or one chapter of a novel, the student writes a one-sentence prediction, based on what has occurred so far, of one event that may occur later. (Note: The student and the teacher should respect the *author's givens*—should not, that is, speculate about what might have happened if the protagonist had been a different kind of person.)

Performance Objective 34.I

Given a novel with a setting in the future, the student, after reading the first chapter or two, infers and predicts an outcome. (Orwell's *1984*, since too close to many aspects of the present, is perhaps not appropriate for this particular objective.)

Representative Enabling Objective

After reading the first two chapters of Herman Hesse's *The Glass Bead Game*, the advanced student infers and predicts the ultimate "move" made by Joseph Knecht, protagonist and Master of the Game.

Goal 35

The student draws inferences from the partly explicit, partly implicit, statements, actions, and events in whatever he reads, especially from such meanings as are implied by context and tone.

Representative Entering Performance Objectives

(Same as A and B under Goal 15, above.)

Performance Objective 35.A

Given a list of possible implications from a clear and brief editorial he has read, the student correctly rejects (draws a line through) each implication not revelant to, or supported by, the specimen editorial.

Performance Objective 35.B

Given a paragraph illustrating a point that is only suggested rather than explicitly stated, the student in his own words writes the explicit statement ("topic sentence"). (Many a paragraph suggests rather than states a topic statement. In fact, most paragraphs suggest only a topic question, which the paragraph's statements attempt to answer. See "Paragraph," the Grosset *Modern English Glossary,* 1971.)

Performance Objective 35.C

The student points to places in poems where ellipsis or condensation occurs (e.g., in poems by Browning or Dickinson) and spells out, in the light of the context, what the compression has implied.

Representative Enabling Objective

Given Dickinson's poem "Bring Me the Sunset in a Cup," the student supplies the "I dare you to . . ." or "I challenge you to [bring me the sunset in a cup]" that the context implies.

Performance Objective 35.D

Given such comic strips as "Peanuts" and "Pogo," the student, recognizing that these comics carry deeper meanings than what is on their surfaces, infers and, in his own words, states some of the implied meanings.

Representative Enabling Objective

Given the Pogo cartoon with the caption, "We have met the enemy, and they are us!" the student states what is implied.

Performance Objective 35.E

In reading a narrative or a play in which the speaker means something different from what he says, the student infers (from the speaker's attitude) the appropriate meaning and demonstrates it in an oral interpretation.

Representative Enabling Objectives

a. By reading aloud Antony's funeral oration (Shakespeare's *Julius Caesar*), the student demonstrates Antony's intention of conveying the opposite impression to what his actual words say ("And Brutus is an honorable man.")

b. In reading some such passage as the following in *The Ox-Bow Incident* . . .

He [young Tetley] looked lonely and unhappy . . . "Cold wind," I [Art Croft, the narrator] began. "It's a lot more than wind," he said . . . "You can't go hunting men like coyotes after rabbits and not feel anything about it. Not without being like any other animal. The worst animal."

"We don't have to hunt men often," I told him. "Most people get along pretty well together."

"Oh, we love each other," he said. "We labor for each other, suffer for each other, admire each other . . ."

the student demonstrates that he understands the last speaker (Tetley) is saying the opposite of what he means. The student may read the passage aloud in an ironic-sarcastic tone.[19]

Performance Objective 35.F

While reading a given narrative or play, the student states what he infers about the characters from their ambivalent, ambiguous, or cryptic actions and dialog.

Representative Enabling Objectives

a. After reading Vidal's *Visit to a Small Planet*, the student writes his inferences in response to some such questions as the following: What is the evidence, in this play, that Kreton has done some research on the "Small Planet" (Earth) before landing here? Which part of his research was apparently not very thorough? When Kreton in his conversation with Spelding refers to "this period of your [Earth's] development" a Kretonic theory is implied. What might this theory be? [20]

b. After reading Melville's *Benito Cereno* or Robert Lowell's dramatization of it, the student demonstrates his skills of drawing inferences by correctly answering some such questions as these: Why couldn't Captain Delano have recognized at first the real roles of Benito and Babo? What inferences had Delano made about Benito's apparel and "small yellow hands"? When "suddenly Delano thought that one or two of them [the Spanish sailors] returned his glance with a sort of meaning" what were these sailors trying to reveal that they dared not communicate orally? During the shaving scene how does Babo manipulate both Benito and Delano? What, ultimately, is Melville condemning in this narrative? [tyranny of one human over another].[21]

[19] From the *Purdue Project Unit on The Ox-Bow Incident* (Skokie, Illinois: National Textbook Company, 1972). Copyright, 1972, by Purdue Research Foundation, and used by permission.

[20] From the *Purdue Project English Unit on Visit to a Small Planet* (Skokie, Illinois: National Textbook Company, 1972). Copyright, 1972, by Purdue Research Foundation, and used by permission.

[21] From Arnold Lazarus, ed., *A School Edition of Melville's Benito Cereno Together with Captain Delano's Journal* (unpublished).

Performance Objective 35.G

While reading a literary work involving a character's inner conflict (as distinguished from conflict between one character and another), the student infers, and in his own words states, the two poles of this inner conflict (e.g., desire vs. duty).

Representative Enabling Objective

While reading *A Separate Peace,* the student infers and states Gene's inner conflict between love and hate for Phineas. To further demonstrate his inferences about inner conflict, the student writes a character sketch of Gene.

Performance Objective 35.H

After reading a given novel (e.g., Steinbeck's *The Pearl*) or short story (e.g., Saki's "The Open Window"), the student composes a scene or episode that is only hinted at in the text itself. (Some of the students ordinarily thought of as "least capable" sometimes demonstrate not only skills of inferring and intuiting but also powers of creating.)

Performance Objective 35.1 (Dramatic Improvisations)

Through oral interpretation, at first, the student demonstrates what he has inferred about a given character's convictions, prejudices, and life style. Later, in a script-free role-playing episode, the student—given a contemporary issue (e.g., pollution, overpopulation, campus unrest, women's liberation, reform in education)—orally reacts as he believes the character whose *persona* he now momentarily inhabits would react.

Goal 36

Given a narrative, a play, or a poem that relies heavily on imagery, metaphor, allegory, and symbolism to communicate its meaning(s), the student infers and states some of these subsurface meanings. (Although all language is symbolic in the sense that it represents a level of abstraction at least once removed from an object referred to, the language of poetry, drama, and fiction is symbolic in the sense that it represents, through suggestion rather than explicit statement, multiple meanings several times removed from the given objects and images.)

Representative Entering Performance Objectives

Entering Objective A. Before exploring for allegorical and symbolic possibilities of meaning, the student demonstrates his understanding of the literal meaning. Given the image *rope,* for instance, in *Moby Dick,* the student states that the first and obvious meaning of the rope connecting whaling ship to rowboat is "lifeline." (All too often the search for symbolic meaning is premature, as Terence Martin has observed in his CEEB film *Teaching Moby Dick.*)

Entering Objective B. In reading Steinbeck's "The Gift" (in *The Red Pony*) the student identifies Carl Tiflin's literal reference to the vultures in contrast to Jody's symbolic interpretations.

Performance Objective 36.A

In interpreting a given image in a literary work, the student—after stating the more or less obvious literal meaning—infers and states what he believes to be one or two possible symbolic meanings.

Representative Enabling Objectives

a. When reading *The Yearling,* the student infers and states in his own words several possible meanings for the *flutter-mill* as suggested in this narrative.
b. When reading a play like O'Neill's *Emperor Jones* or a poem like Lindsay's "The Congo," the student infers and states in his own words some symbolic meaning(s) of the drum beats beyond what they signal explicitly.
c. When reading Williams' *The Glass Managerie,* the student infers and states in his own words several possible meanings for *glass* and for *menagerie* as suggested in this play.
d. After reading a story like James Joyce's "Clay," the student explains in his own words one of the allegorical meanings of the story (e.g., Maria as a spinster figure, representing a one-to-one relationship with spinsters in general) as distinguished from multiple symbolic meanings of *clay* (e.g., malleability, or entrapment, or death, and so on).

Performance Objective 36.B

Given poetry with extended figures or patterns of recurring imagery (e.g., money and barter images in Shakespeare's sonnets, falling leaves in W. D. Snodgrass's "Spring") the student infers the metaphoric and symbolic meanings and states several of them in his own words. (As W. B. Yeats, T. S. Eliot, and other poet-critics have observed, most poets consciously or unconsciously build from image to metaphor to symbol; and Northrop Frye would add, "from symbol to archetype to myth." This progression, known as the image-metaphor-symbol complex, need not of course be defined or even named by the student, although the teacher may wish to remind himself of it.)

Representative Enabling Objective

Given the poem "Stopping by Woods on a Snowy Evening," the student infers and states in his own words the meaning(s) of the recurring image *woods* not only as a metaphor for the speaker's lingering-place but also as a symbol of the speaker's and all human beings' wishful thinking or return-to-the-womb daydreaming ("The woods are lovely, dark, and deep"). Another meaning, which the details in this poem can support, is that the woods symbolize inextricable indebtedness, assuming that the phrase "miles to go before I sleep" means through the woods of indebtedness.

Performance Objective 36.C

After reading a literary work containing several layers of meaning —literal, allegorical, symbolic, mythic and the like—the student writes a brief explication.

Representative Enabling Objectives

a. After reading a work like Katherine Anne Porter's *Ship of Fools* (or Steinbeck's *The Pearl* or Ernest Hemingway's *The Old Man and the Sea*), the student explains in his own words how reading that work as an allegory can modify a reader's interpretation of its meaning.
b. After reading George Orwell's *Animal Farm*, the student explains that it is an animal story only on the surface; that as an allegory it parallels several episodes in the Russian Revolution as well as man's tendency in general to seize and abuse power.
c. After reading a work like Edward Albee's *Who's Afraid of Virginia Woolf*, the advanced student identifies (1) the surface level of meaning, (2) an allegorical level of meaning, and (3) one of the symbolic levels of meaning. Then he explains in his own words how all these levels contribute, like levels in a mansion, to an overall unifying meaning. (See, further, the article "Levels of Meaning," pp. 174–177, *Modern English Glossary*, Grosset & Dunlap, 1971.)

Goal 37

The student draws inferences from an imaginative work whose genre or mode signals meanings beyond those signalled by exposition or reportage alone. The student reads beyond the literal, beneath the surface; he infers meanings that depend upon his understanding of paradox, irony, satire, allegory, parody, and the like, which remain at bottom a kind of game playing.

Representative Entering Performance Objectives

Entering Objective A. The student, recalling how he participated during his childhood (if he did) in hop scotch and rope jumping and in playing such games as "Simon Says," "Buck, Buck," and "Red Rover, Come Over," talks about some of the sensations (kinesthetics) he enjoyed—for example, the rhythmical stepping, hopping, jumping; saying or singing the magical words, passwords, rhymes, spells, incantations; relating ritually with the members of his group. (In a later discussion he may also talk about some of the ways in which game-playing and role-playing help re-create or interpret poems, plays, stories—in fact, life itself.)

Entering Objective B. The student has as a child responded imaginatively—or has at least enjoyed listening to—stories containing riddles and paradoxes (e.g., "Rapunzel," "The Magic Top," "The Seven Ravens"), to Biblical and other parables, to Mother Goose rhymes; to folk tales and songs from his own ethnic subculture; and to verses like those in May Swenson's collection *Poems to Solve*. (As a child the student may not only have listened to but also followed the text as he was being read to, as John Holt suggests in *How Children Learn*, pp. 110–114. Holt and others add that the more fascinated the child is with the material, the less likely he is to degenerate into a "deficient" reader or one requiring "remediation.")

Entering Objective C. In childhood or early adolescence the student has read one or more of such works as *The Wizard of Oz, The Wind in the Willows*, the *Pooh* books, the *Mary Poppins* stories, the *Dr. Doolittle* books, *Charlotte's Web, Alice in Wonderland*, and the like.

Performance Objective 37.A

Given a selection containing paradox and innuendo (e.g., a Volkswagen advertisement, a Bill Mauldin cartoon, a selection from *Mad* Magazine, a column by Art Buchwald, etc.) the student infers what was meant beyond what was said and in his own words states what was suggested. (He need not use or define such terms as *double intente, double entendre, planned ambiguity, pleasant disappointment of expectation*, or even the terms *paradox* and *innuendo*.)

Performance Objective 37.B

Given a poem containing several serious or poignant paradoxes and ironies (e.g., P. B. Shelley's "Ozymandias," W. B. Yeats' "Sailing to Byzantium," Dylan Thomas' "Do Not Go Gentle," Theodore Roethke's "The Waking"), the student reconstructs in his own words at least one of the statements that the poem suggests.

Performance Objective 37.C

Having read any work containing paradoxes (e.g., the Biblical parable of the Prodigal Son or G. K. Chesterton's essay "Tremendous Trifles"), the student identifies the apparent inconsistencies and comments on why he believes, if he does, that they nevertheless make sense.

Performance Objective 37.D

After reading any satirical work (e.g., Jonathan Swift's "A Modest Proposal," Kurt Vonnegut's *Slaughter House Five* or "The Report on the Barnhouse Effect") the student infers what has been satirized and explains it in his own words. (He need not define *satire* or its chief tool, *irony*.)

Representaitve Enabling Objective

After reading Kurt Vonnegut's satirical story "The Report on the Barn-house Effect," the student answers some of the following questions: In what way is this selection a report, and in what way isn't it a report? What sort of fun is the author poking at scientists through his special use of the word *effect* and through his characterization of Professor Barnhouse? What is this story ridiculing mainly—i.e., what is its most serious, implied charge against bureaucratic groups in relation to the welfare of the public? What current practice is satirized, for instance, in that aspect of the Barnhouse effect that "enables the professor to single out (certain) individuals and objects instead of slaughtering whole populations"? What immunity does the author somewhat glee-fully expect to enjoy through having the story told by a narrator other than himself—by a psychology student serving as one of Professor Barn-house's assistants?

Performance Objective 37.E

After reading an allegory, the student infers and explains what each character represents.

Representative Enabling Objective

After reading or listening to a reading of some such allegorical verse as E. E. Cummings' "anyone lived in a pretty how town," the student infers and explains (1) why *did* in "he danced his did" must have been used as a noun (2) what this noun may be naming and (3) who is represented by such characters as Anyone, No-one, and the Some-bodies.

Performance Objective 37.F

After reading a parody the student identifies the author and the work being imitated and in his own words explains the fun (gentle or barbed) which the imitator pokes at his model.

Representative Enabling Objectives

a. After reading Shakespeare's *Macbeth* and Barbara Garson's *Mac-Bird*, the student identifies not only the Macbeth characters being parodied but also the celebrated persons in real life. The student may also judge which *MacBird* barbs are gentle parody; which, cutting satire.

b. After reading Shakespeare's *Hamlet* and rereading the scenes involving Rosencrantz and Guildenstern (Act II, sc. ii; Act II, scenes i and ii; Act IV, scenes i, ii, iii, and iv), then reading Tom Stoppard's play *Rosencrantz and Guildenstern Are Dead*, the student comments on, and in oral interpretation demonstrates, the cloddishness of the characters being parodied.

Goal 38

The student develops a sense of humor.

Performance Objective 38.A

Given a joke that makes him laugh or that he at least enjoys, the student infers the reason and states it in his own words (e.g., "The punch line was a surprisingly pleasant switch from what one would ordinarily expect.")

Performance Objective 38.B

In reading any literary work, the student infers and identifies ironic humor.

Performance Objective 38.C

In reading any literary work, the student infers and identifies the tall tale, and he comments on some of the implied as well as the explicit elements of the humor of exaggeration.

Representative Enabling Objectives

a. In nearly all folk tales about such personalities as Paul Bunyan, Johnny Appleseed, Mike Fink, Pecos Bill, John Henry, Casey Jones, and the like, the student identifies and talks about the humorous exaggeration, especially in its relation to the bigness of the settings. (Such humor may not always be incongruous exaggeration, of course.)

b. In reading Mark Twain's *The Adventures of Huckleberry Finn*, the student identifies and talks about the transparent bragging and tall tales of the Duke and the Dauphin. (Here the humor emanates from *affectation* and *incongruous* exaggeration, which the reader can easily infer.) Using the Duke and the Dauphin dialog, a student may write a skit, which a student director may then cast and produce for the class.

Performance Objective 38.D

In reading a serious drama or work of fiction, the student identifies and re-creates through oral interpretation, a scene containing comic relief. He may then comment on what tension the comedy is relieving.

Representative Enabling Objectives

a. In *Macbeth* (Act II, sc. iii) after Macbeth has murdered Duncan, the drunken porter comically curses whoever is knocking at the gate. The student then explains this contrast in mood.

b. In *The Adventures of Huckleberry Finn* the Duke and the Dauphin scene can be explained as a comic change of pace from the tensions of Jim and Huck's escape.

Goal 39

The student makes accurate and appropriate inferences from the language, especially the rhetoric and vocabulary, in whatever he reads or hears.

Performance Objective 39.A

In any literary work (and in the mass media) the student identifies euphemisms without necessarily defining them.

Representative Enabling Objective

Reading fiction or non-fiction that calls a "concentration camp" a "relocation center," (e.g., in George Orwell's "Politics and the English Language") or that speaks of "training the natives how to operate the equipment" ("how to shoot guns"), the student identifies the euphemisms, translates them into more explicit language, and comments on whether or not they are socially and morally responsible. The class may also be divided into small groups, with the members of each group contributing a section (e.g., A–G) to a "Dictionary of Current Euphemisms."

EVALUATING

The student, respecting the right of each art form to its own integrity, tells why he does or does not give high marks to a literary work he has read, or to a version of it he has also experienced in the electronic media, or to a review of either that he may also have read.

Goal 40

In developing his critical tastes in reading, the student experiences, whenever possible, television and cinema versions of literary works he has read (or intends to read) and makes thoughtful comparisons. The student and the teacher may need to be reminded, however, that each medium, each art form, has a right to its own integrity. The student and the teacher may also wish to reread Marshall McLuhan's *Understanding Media,* with a view to reconsidering how much they wish to accept or reject of McLuhan's observations about the newer ("cooler") media in comparison with the printed ("hotter") media, perhaps commenting on his use of those temperature epithets.

Performance Objective 40.A

After experiencing a cinema or television version of a literary work he has read (e.g., John Galsworthy's *The Forsyte Saga* or Gore Vidal's *Visit to a Small Planet*) the student writes a brief critical comparison, praising whatever he believes was well done and making suggestions for elements he believes could have been done better.

Performance Objective 40.B

After reading a work like G. B. Shaw's *Pygmalion* or T. H. White's *The Once and Future King* and then experiencing a stage or screen version (e.g., *My Fair Lady* or *Camelot*), the student—respecting each medium's right to its own integrity—writes a brief critical review (about 300 words) in which he judges where each medium gained a little or lost a little.

Goal 41

In developing his powers of evaluating what he reads in the printed media and what he experiences in such media as cinema or television, the student cultivates the habit of reading reviews and of testing the various reviewers' judgments against his own experiences and judgments.

Performance Objective 41.A

Before seeing a cinema or television play, the student reads a review or two of it (e.g., in *Scholastic* or *Saturday Review,* or *Life,* or *TV Guide,* or *Christian Science Monitor*). On the basis of these reviews, he may decide to pass up the cinema or TV play. If he does attend, he compares—in a brief oral or written critique—his own judgment with that of the reviewer.

Performance Objective 41.B

Given two illustrated reviews (e.g., one from *Saturday Review* and one from *Life*) or two illustrated essays (e.g., one in *Life* and one in the *New York Review*), the student orally compares them with respect to integration of picture and text, reverence and irreverence. He may also prepare a graphic presentation of his own.

Performance Objective 41.C

In an informal panel (or in a brief written critique) the student judges how much the medium or manner of a given work contributes to the work's message or impact.

Goal 42

The student judges to what extent an essayist or an editorial writer has been informed or misinformed, thorough or incomplete (and perhaps equivocal), logical or illogical, convincing or unconvincing, relevant or irrelevant. The student supports his claims with examples and evidence. (Teachers' reference: Mortimer Adler, *How to Read a Book.*)

Performance Objective 42.A

Given an essay (e.g., George Orwell's "Shooting an Elephant") in which the author has selected events to suit his thesis, the student lists one or more important events that have been omitted, as one way of pinning down the author's biases.

Performance Objective 42.B

Given a biographical or autobiographical essay (e.g., Rackham Holt's *George Washington Carver* or Jesse Stuart's *The Thread That Runs So True*) the student lists some expressions the biographer has used in describing his subject, then some alternative expressions for the subject as he might be otherwise described.

Performance Objective 42.C

Given an essay on a political or controversial topic, the student separates the issue from the writer's feelings about the issue and writes a brief explanatory statement about this distinction. A group of students may then wish to debate the issue.

Goal 43

The student judges as objectively as possible certain works that he has read.

Representative Entering Performance Objectives

Entering Objective A. Before anyone can meaningfully evaluate various authors' achievements, he must have read closely and widely.

Entering Objective B. The student distinguishes between an objective judgment like "It was good" and such a subjective judgment as "I like it." (The student and the teacher have orally discussed the difference between judgments based on objective criteria and judgments based on intuition.)

Performance Objective 43.A

After reading a work of his choice, the student states his opinion of the work's effectiveness or lack of effectiveness in evoking a response from him. (He may also wish to consider whether or not his personal values have stood in the way of the transaction, as Louise Rosenblatt puts it, between the author and himself.)

Performance Objective 43.B

Given the question "What is this selection about?" the student responds with a critical observation rather than with a mere summation of plot or of the factual level(s) of meaning, assuming that the teacher has made this stipulation beforehand, especially before essay-type examinations. (A student's grasp of factual elements can be measured in short-answer or multiple-choice quizzes.)

Representative Enabling Objective

In evaluating Aldous Huxley's *Brave New World*, the student, in response to the question "What is this book about?" may begin with some such statement as follows: "This book is Huxley's vision of what human, or semi-human, life may be like if certain radical changes are forced upon it by people who control the earth's ecological, political, and economic resources."

Performance Objective 43.C

Having read, or on the screen witnessed, a number of stories and plays in which the boy meets a girl, falls in love with her, and despite complications marries her (e.g., as in Shakespeare's *Romeo and Juliet* and Erich Segal's *Love Story*), the student discusses features of the treatment of this formula that failed or succeeded in rising above banality.

Performance Objective 43.D

In his own words the student states why he judges as successful or unsuccessful, serious or trivial, any literary work (or any elements of it) that he has read.

Representative Enabling Objective

After reading *Visit to a Small Planet*, the student responds to some such questions as the following: In your experience of the play as a whole, why would you rate as "successful" or "unsuccessful" Kreton's witticisms about "cats vs. dogs" (opening of Act II)? At the end of the play the "Small Planet" (Earth) is rescued from Kreton by the surprise intervention of the Second Visitor from outer space. Do you regard this surprise rescue (a kind of rescue that ancient critics called "deus ex machina") as believable or unbelievable? Why? Did the playwright "plant" any elements earlier in the play to make such an ending convincing? If so, which elements? [22]

22 From the *Purdue Project English Unit on Visit to a Small Planet* (Skokie, Illinois: National Textbook Company, 1972). Copyright, 1972, by Purdue Research Foundation, and used by permission.

Performance Objective 43.E

After reading any play, short story, or novel, the student states why he judges one or another of its characters or experiences as "true to life" or not. (Note: Academically talented students may wish to explore the contrariety of views about *illusion of reality, verisimilitude,* etc., which are discussed in such references as Walter Jackson Bate, ed., *Criticism: The Major Texts;* L. S. Hall, *A Grammar of Literary Criticism;* David Daiches, *Critical Approaches to Literature;* and the Grosset and Dunlap *Modern English Glossary.*)

Performance Objective 43.F

After reading a literary work containing characters (play, narrative, narrative verse), the student states why he judges a given character (e.g., Willie Loman in *Death of a Salesman* or Willie Stark in *All the King's Men*) (a) as believable or not and (b) as either distinguishable or else *sounding like too many other characters in the same work.*

Performance Objective 43.G

Given the words to a piece of contemporary rock verse (e.g., Paul Simon's "The Sounds of Silence" or "The Dangling Conversation") and after listening to a recording of it with or without music, the student writes a short critical paper (about 200 words) in which he compares and contrasts the contemporary piece with a short poem of an earlier vintage (e.g., Edna St. Vincent Millay's "Recuerdo"). One of the features the student may well concentrate on is that of the life styles—customs, manners, moral attitudes, sports and pastimes—expressed or reflected in each poem. The student states why he accepts or rejects one or more of the values in either milieu.

Performance Objective 43.H

Given a short poem, in which the poet's choice of words is almost always crucial, the student evaluates the poet's choice of at least three crucial words by consulting a thesaurus, listing alternative words, and writing a sentence in favor of each original or of the student's choice of alternative(s).

Performance Objective 43.I

Given a contemporary poem (from a recent *Poetry* magazine or *Saturday Review* or *New Republic*), the student states orally or in

writing why he judges the poem (a) obtrusive, noisy, or jingly; or
(b) unobtrusive—perhaps because of the run-on lines (*enjambe-
ment*) instead of end-stopped lines; perhaps because of conversational tone.

Performance Objective 43.J

Having read a number of poems (some contemporary, some Vic-
torian), the student inductively determines the criteria for defining
diction (or not defining it) as poetic; he also arrives incidentally at
a definition of the derogatory term *poeticism*. (Robert Lowell and
other contemporary poets regard as maudlin such poeticisms as
"o'er," "e'er," "ne'er," and " 'Twas," and the non-colloquial inversion
of subject-verb to verb-subject. Nevertheless, the critical point here
is that the language—i.e., the vocabulary, syntax, etc.—of poetry does
not differ essentially from the language of prose. The differences
between poetry and prose are much more subtle and complex, and
they resist pinning down.)

Performance Objective 43.K

After reading a contemporary essay or article (e.g., Norman
Mailer's *Armies of the Night* or John F. Kennedy's "Inaugural Address") the student assesses the author's *moral awareness* and states
what he accepts or rejects in the author's moral position.

Performance Objective 43.L

For any essay the student, in making a judgment about the appropriateness of the examples, lists them and briefly comments on
them. If possible he offers alternative examples for the ones he
downgrades.

Performance Objective 43.M

The student demonstrates maturity in his critical judgments
about an author's qualities of originality or uniqueness by assessing
and stating how much the writer adheres to, or departs from, or
freshly combines, elements of a well-established genre, mode, style,
rhetoric, literary convention, vogue, school, etc. (e.g., romantic,
neoclassical, metaphysical, Gothic, baroque, Faulknerian, etc.).
(Since there is nothing totally new under the sun, nothing totally
original, and since a writer's originality consists mainly in the suc-

cessful new way(s) he has modified something old—perhaps cast it in a fresh light or environment, perhaps created a new combination, a new amalgam—the critic's and the student-critic's task remains in part the identifying of old as well as new features in a writer's work.)

Performance Objective 43.N

To demonstrate that he has identified an author's (e.g., William Faulkner's or Ernest Hemingway's or Thomas Wolfe's) uniqueness of style, the student writes a paragraph in imitation of it, then tries out his anonymous piece on two or more students to see if they can identify the author in question. (Whatever else imitation—even parody—may be, it is usually a judgment of praise in the sense that it assumes that the imitated author has achieved individuality.)

Representative Enabling Objective

Having read several works by Faulkner, the student demonstrates his grasp of the author's characteristic rhetoric and idiolect (e.g., Faulkner's involuted sentences containing many parenthetical embedments) by writing a paragraph imitating Faulkner's style but using content close to the student's own experiences (e.g., shopping for a used car). The result will be a parody. The student then tests his imitation on the class to see if they can guess who the model author is.

Performance Objective 43.O

After reading a contemporary poem (e.g., by Gary Snyder, Denise Levertov, or X. J. Kennedy) or story (e.g., by John Cheever, David Barthelme, or Joyce Carol Oates), the student states why he judges it original or not.

Performance Objective 43.P

Given a play which accommodates a variety of interpretations (e.g., the plays of Friedrick Dürrenmatt and Berthold Brecht), a mature student argues the validity of any two or three interpretations.

Performance Objective 43.Q

After reading a contemporary novel (e.g., by John Barth, or Saul Bellow, or John Cheever, or Bernard Malamud, or Philip Roth, or John Updike), the student discusses, in a panel of other students, why he judges the novel as serious or trivial.

Performance Objective 43.R

(For the student who reads a language besides English.) Given a translation and an original (e.g., of one or another of such works as Albert Camus' "The Guest," Jacques Cousteau's "Shark Closeups," Gunter Grass' *The Tin Drum*, Thomas Mann's "Railway Accident," Alberto Moravia's "Agostino," Jorge Luis Borges' "The Circular Ruins," Isak Dinesen's "The Ring," Bjönstjerne Björnson's "The Brothers," Ingmar Bergman's "The Seventh Seal," Anton Chekhov's "The Proposal," etc.) the student judges and explains any qualities that distinguish, or that fail to distinguish, the translation. He supports his judgments with examples from the original and the translation.

Performance Objective 43.S

Given a translation of a literary piece (e.g., the King James Bible, which some pupils have yet to realize is a translation from Hebrew and Greek), the student explains that it is quite possible for any original work to lose a little or gain a little in translation. (E.g., in several books of the New Testament, especially in the epistles of Paul, where the expression "God is no respecter of persons" appears frequently, the *persons*, a transliteration of the Graeco-Latin word *persona*, meaning *mask*, has lost a little in translation.)

Goal 44

From time to time the student re-examines his former judgments and either confirms or revises them.

Performance Objective 44.A

After rereading a literary work which he has read several years ago (e.g., *David Copperfield, Alice in Wonderland*, etc.) the student writes a brief review (about 200 words) explaining what, if anything, has changed in his latest judgment of the work. (The student's change in judgment may be owing less to objective criteria than to changes in his personal values.)

Performance Objective 44.B

Given two interpretations of a work he has already read, the student rereads (or rethinks) the literary work in question to see what his latest judgment may be and reports his decision in a brief (200 word) paper.

Performance Objective 44.C

Hearing in a conversation or a panel discussion two or three character analyses that conflict with his own interpretation, the student rereads the literary work in question and orally reports his reconsidered analysis.

Performance Objective 44.D

Hearing in a conversation or a panel discussion two or three interpretations of a controversial piece (e.g., *Animal Farm* or *Lord of the Flies*), the student rereads the literary work in question (or a particular portion of it) and orally reports his reconsidered judgment.

A GENRE INDEX TO OBJECTIVES IN READING AND RESPONDING TO LITERATURE

(Numbers refer to objectives, not to pages.)

Novels

5A, 6B, 7B, 7D, 7E, 9E, 9F, 12A, 14B, 14C, 14Eb, 16B, 16C, 17A, 17Cc, 17D, 18A, 18B, 18Ba, 20Ab, 20Ac, 21A, 23Aa, 24Ba, 24Bb, 24Gb, 25Aa, 25Ca, 26E, 28, 28Bb, 28D, 30A, 31Aa, 31Ab, 31B, 32B, 32D, 33A, 34I, 35Eb, 35Fb, 35G, 35H, 36Ca, 36Cb, 37 entering C, 37D, 38Cb, 38Db, 43B, 43C, 43F, 43Q, 44A, 44D.

Short Stories

6D, 7A, 11A, 14A, 18Bb, 20, 21Ca, 25Cb, 26, 26B, 27B, 28Ba, 28Bc, 31C, 33B, 35H, 36 entering B, 36Ad, 37 entering B, 37D, 38Ca, 43O, 43R.

Plays

5A, 6C, 6F, 6G, 6J, 7B, 7D, 9Da, 14Ea, 16A, 17B, 17Cb, 19A, 19B, 20Ad, 20B, 20C, 21B, 21Cb, 21Ea, 21Eb, 23Ab, 26F, 26G, 27C, 27E, 27H, 28E, 28F, 31C, 32E, 32H, 34F, 35Ea, 35Fa, 35Fb, 36Ab, 36Ac, 36Cc, 37Fa, 37Fb, 38Da, 40A, 40B, 43C, 43D, 43F, 43P.

Poems

1E, 6A, 7F, 9Ba, 9Bb, 9Db, 13Aa, 13Ab, 13Ac, 14Da, 16A, 17Ca, 20Aa, 20D, 21Ha, 21Hb, 21Ia, 21Ib, 21Ic, 21Ka, 21Kb, 22Aa, 22Ab, 22Ac, 22Ad, 23Ac, 23Ba, 23Bb, 24F, 25Ab, 25Ba, 25Bb, 26H, 27D, 27F, 27G, 28A, 28C, 28D, 29B, 31Aa, 32A, 32G, 35C, 36B, 37B, 37E enabling, 43G, 43.

Biography

4A, 9G, 24Ga, 31D, 42B.

Essays and
Other Non-Fiction

3A, 3C, 6I, 7C, 9G, 10A, 10B, 21F, 21G, 24A, 26B, 26C, 26D, 27G, 29A, 31E, 32F, 34D, 35D, 37A, 37C, 39A, 40, 41A, 42A, 43K, 43R.

VI

Writing

RATIONALE

The objectives in this section of the catalog emphasize writing as a process—a very complex process that involves a number of skills, attitudes, and abilities. Many of these are difficult to observe and understand, and we teachers of writing are only beginning to get new insights into the whole process of writing that can be translated into effective teaching techniques.

With this in mind we have attempted to write objectives that treat writing as an organic process, a complex activity that requires the writer to become a self-aware self-evaluator. The objectives encourage the student to look closely at his subject, his purpose, his role, his language, and his audience. The whole process of writing is related to the environment in which it is produced, and the student writer must come to terms with writing in the context(s) in which it will be written and read. The writer must be aware of not only linguistic and rhetorical principles, but cultural, sociological, and personal factors that affect him as a writer, the audience for whom he is writing, and the subject matter about which he is writing. Every objective in this section should be seen as an attempt to help students become aware of as many of the elements in the process of writing as possible, and also to help them understand how these elements are related to, and influenced by, each other.

Words as a subject of study will appear in many sections of this

The project director in charge of this section, Donald A. Seybold, formerly Assistant Director of the Indiana University English Curriculum Study Center, was assisted by several consultants and directors.

book. In this section we are concerned with words from the point of view of the student as writer who is confronted several times in every sentence with the problem of choosing the "right" words. *Right* is not the right word here; like its opposite "wrong," it is too broad, too vague. And besides, words are not just right or wrong; they may be more or less appropriate or effective or expressive. Both student and teacher need specific criteria for judging and discussing words.

The writer does not choose his words in a vacuum. He is doing a specific kind of writing, guided by a specific point of view and tone. As he writes, he must make individual choices about words in the light of his overriding point of view, tone, and role.

The writer must make similar choices, and develop the same kind of critical awareness and criteria for finding material to write about, deciding what is relevant and what is not, organizing what he chooses to include, and approaching his purpose and audience. The philosophy underlying the writing objectives is that these are not simple choices to make; that contrary to what some writing texts suggest, such decisions cannot be made arbitrarily and then prescribed as the answer for every writing situation.

Instead, we hope that the student will be encouraged and helped to make discoveries about such questions and problems that will be useful to him and flexible enough to aid him in every writing situation that he might encounter. Of course, central to this inductive process is the need for the student to write instead of merely analyzing writing. He must write often and with a great deal of feedback from other students, the teacher, and, whenever possible, the audience for whom he is writing. When he does analyze writing, it should most often be his own; at least as often as he analyzes professional writing, he should be looking also at the writing of his peers.

The order of the objectives suggests a teaching sequence, but it is not intended to imply that this is the only or the best way to approach the teaching of writing with every group of students. Because it is finally impossible to separate the complex interrelated aspects of writing into discrete sequential units of instruction, the order here is only suggestive; and because there must be an order, it must always be somewhat arbitrary. The first six goals tend to be introductory and comprehensive to a degree. They tend to encompass most of the major concepts that will be dealt with more specifically in later goals and objectives. In this way they can be seen as a kind of foundation or undergirding, but it is not essential, nor even recommended that the teacher start at the beginning and work sequentially through the objectives. Writing cannot be taught in such a neat way, and the sequence of the objectives does not intend to suggest that it can. Instead, the teacher must engage in early and continuing diagnosis of student writing to determine what objectives most need emphasis at a given time. The teacher is encouraged to use only those objectives that his students have not yet reached and to go about working toward the objectives in the order which seems most effective and efficient to him and his students.

Goal 1

The student recognizes and uses the act of composing as a way of ordering, understanding, and communicating his experience.

Performance Objective 1.A

The student experiments with various arrangements of miscellaneous concrete objects, shapes and colors, and non-verbal items to make statements, convey moods or tone, convey information, or in some other way to affect an audience. *See also* II 7.A and 12.A; V 25.*

Representative Enabling Objectives

a. Given five or six objects, such as an empty bottle, a piece of wood, a child's crayon, a phonograph record, a banana, and a spark plug, the student arranges them in some manner, or in some way uses them to make a statement, etc.
b. Given several objects of various shapes and colors, the student arranges them in some manner that makes a statement, conveys a mood, etc.
c. Given a selection of pictures, photographs, magazines, clippings, etc., the student creates a collage.

Performance Objective 1.B

The student writes for self-expression.

Representative Enabling Objective

Given class time and encouragement from the teacher, the student makes frequent entries in a journal. The student keeps the journal in whatever format he chooses and shares its contents with others only when he wishes to do so. (For some representative student journal-entries see Tate & Corbett, *Teaching H. S. Composition,* p. 221).

* Roman numerals refer to chapters, Arabic numerals to goals, capital letters to performance objectives, and lower-case letters to enabling objectives.

Performance Objective 1.C

The student uses writing to record information.

Representative Enabling Objective

The student takes notes both in school and outside when necessary for him to remember, to be accurate, or to provide a record of some event or idea. He takes notes in a format useful to him.

Performance Objective 1.D

The student uses writing to communicate information and/or to persuade others. *See also* III 16.Ac; IV 21.A and 22.Ad.

Representative Enabling Objectives

a. The student frequently writes about things of interest to him and submits his writing to his classmates or some other audience.
b. The student takes public stands on issues that concern him by writing letters to the editor of the local or school newspaper, or through some other medium available to him.

Goal 2

The student recognizes that each medium and technique of composing and communicating has both strengths and weaknesses. *See also* II 1.A, 2.A and 11; V 25.Cb.

Performance Objective 2.A

The student experiments with various media.

Representative Enabling Objectives

a. The student composes a photographic or pictorial essay to present to the class.
b. The student composes, from original work or existing recordings, a musical essay that conveys a mood, tone, or message to the audience. *See also* V 25.B.
c. The student makes a film and presents it to the class.
d. The student creates a pantomime performance for two or three people and presents it to the class. *See also* III 3.Ac.
e. The student writes a story, a play, or a script for a television or radio show.

Performance Objective 2.B

The student identifies some of the potentials, capabilities, and limitations of various forms of composition and communication. *See also* III 2.C.

Representative Enabling Objectives

a. After experiencing several presentations through various media, the students discuss the strengths and limitations of each. They should discuss such things as:

(1) Which medium handles action most effectively?
(2) Which medium conveys mood and tone most powerfully?
(3) Which handles abstraction most clearly?
(4) How could two or more media be effectively combined?

b. (The following is merely an example of the kind of comparisons that could be made between and among various media. The pantomime is chosen merely as an example; film, music, photographs, etc. could be used in any combination. Further, it is not necessary to answer each question or carry the discussion to the detail the questions might suggest.)

Given a pantomime performance, then a script for the pantomime, then an enactment of the script, the student either orally or in writing indicates:

(1) the options, potentials, and limitations involved in communicating a situation to an audience without using language;
(2) the demands made upon a receiver in such a situation that are not present or not as difficult when speech accompanies non-verbal communication;
(3) the potential problems of interpretation for both sender and receiver using a non-verbal medium;
(4) the problems that are solved by adding written dialog to the action;
(5) the options, potentials, and limitations which are added with a written script;
(6) the new problems that are created for sender and receiver;
(7) the demands upon each that change when a written script is used;
(8) the limitation of reading what is intended to be seen and heard;
(9) the options, potentials, and limitations involved in communicating dramatically using both verbal and non-verbal media;
(10) the demands made upon the sender and receiver in such a situation;
(11) how these demands are different from those when pantomime or print only is the medium;
(12) the ways in which non-verbal and verbal media are related and dependent;
(13) the ways in which the addition of language affects the original action of the pantomime;

(14) the ways in which the original pantomime determines or affects the dialog;

(15) the demands of interpretation made upon the sender and receiver that change from pantomime to drama to written script;

(16) the degree to which the dialog fits the pantomime;

(17) the degree to which the dialog adds accurate interpretative information to the actions;

(18) the degree to which the dialog adds additional information to the actions;

(19) the degree to which the dialog changes the actions or the meaning of the actions;

(20) the advantages and disadvantages of each mode of communication.

Goal 3

The student is aware of the factors that must be considered when one is composing material to be communicated to others. *See also* II 3.A; VII 1.A.

Performance Objective 3.A

The student identifies the various components that are part of the process of communication, and explains the relationships that exist between each.

Representative Enabling Objectives

a. The student identifies significant elements in the process of communication and labels them with such terms as sender, receiver, medium, message, purpose, and role or speaking voice.

b. The student discusses and explains how the various elements interact and affect each other.[1]

Goal 4

The student recognizes that writing as a form of composition and communication is a process with many complex elements. He seeks to make himself more conscious of the ways in which he goes about performing the operations of communication, especially as a writer. He explores the potentials and restraints inherent in language as he

---

[1] For a sophisticated treatment of 3.A and B that could be very useful to the teacher, see Kenneth Burke, especially Part I of *Language as Symbolic Action* and the Introduction to *A Grammar of Motives*. Also see *Rhetoric: Discovery and Change*, Young, Becker, and Pike. These books are definitely not for students, but they can be very helpful to teachers. Students may benefit from Walker Gibson's *Persona* (Random).

manipulates it as a writer and communicator. *See also* II 2.A; IV 4; V 15 and 25.

Performance Objective 4.A

The student identifies similarities and differences between manipulating objects to make a statement and manipulating language to communicate.

Representative Enabling Objectives

a. Given a random selection of about six or eight objects and a random selection of twenty-five words, the student arranges each set to communicate an idea, statement, or mood to an audience. *See also* VI 1.Aa.
b. After completing an exercise such as that in 4.Aa, the student explains which task was easier, how the two were similar, how the second was different from the first, and why.

Performance Objective 4.B

The student explains that various words fulfill various functions and perform in specific roles in a given discourse. He analyzes and discusses these functions and roles according to a grammatical system agreed upon by the class.

Representative Enabling Objectives

a. Given a random selection of ten words that name objects, the student explains what arrangements and statements are possible and impossible.
b. Given a random selection of ten verbs, the student explains what arrangements and statements are possible and impossible.
c. Given a random selection of nouns and verbs, the student makes as many arrangements as possible with the words he has. He explains which combinations are grammatical, which are logical, which are true. He explains why they need not be all three.
d. The student adds words to the combinations in the previous exercises and explains what function they perform and where they might be added to communicate various messages.

Performance Objective 4.C

The student defines what is meant by grammatical categories and syntactic patterns and explains how a writer uses this knowledge to make his writing more effective. (This performance may of course follow rather than precede much of the student's own writing.)

Performance Objective 4.D

The student recognizes and identifies various ways in which words combine in sentence patterns, and he demonstrates this knowledge by using a variety of syntactic patterns and sentence structures in his own work.

Representative Enabling Objectives

a. Given passages of student and professional prose, the student identifies sentence fragments and distinguishes between those he finds acceptable and those non-acceptable. During discussion, the student formulates and describes his criteria for discriminating between the two.
b. Given examples of his own and other students' work, the student identifies sentences that could be combined to produce greater clarity, smoother rhythm, less monotony, or a different effect. The student combines such sentences in various ways to produce a desired or needed change. The student does this in his own writing as he revises.
c. Given examples of his own and other students' work, the student identifies passages that he considers vague, confusing, or ambiguous. The student suggests changes in sentence structure, word choice, punctuation, etc., that make the passage more clear or concrete. The student makes similar changes in his own work as he revises.

Performance Objective 4.E

The student discovers and identifies ways in which sentences are combined and organized into paragraphs.[2]

Representative Enabling Objectives

a. Given a set of related but unorganized sentences, the student arranges them and explains why he has ordered them the way he has.
b. The student examines various ways of organizing the same sentences and explains what factors must be considered in choosing the most effective organization for a particular effect or purpose.
c. After examining his own paragraphs as well as those of other students and also professional writers, the student identifies and defines various ways paragraphs are structured and developed.

---

[2] Some of the ideas for this and previous objectives under Goal 4 are derived from the work of Francis Christensen. Teachers will find valuable suggestions for augmenting these objectives in *Notes Toward a New Rhetoric,* Francis Christensen (New York: Harper and Row, 1967), especially the devices for rendering.

Performance Objective 4.F

The student writes paragraphs that are not just collections of sentences, but are structured to present an orderly development of the topic to the reader. (Later, in revising, he deletes the irrelevant.)

Representative Enabling Objectives

a. Given material for writing a description of a particular object or place, the student organizes the material in various ways (i.e., specific to general; most important to least important; by smell, touch, etc.; from top to bottom of object, etc.). The student identifies the organizational principle which he thinks would be most effective for a particular purpose and/or audience, or for a particular esthetic effect.
b. Given various topics upon which to write, the student develops paragraphs and distinguishes among paragraphs by identifying his main points and the sentences that add information, clarify, emphasize, or enumerate.

Performance Objective 4.G

The student develops a sense of what the reader must be told about his subject and asks questions that help him to develop and organize his paragraphs according to the reader's needs. Such needs are primarily logical and structural, but may also be sensuous.

Representative Enabling Objectives

a. Given the same topic for readers of different knowledgeability about the topic, the student reorganizes his paragraphs to better suit the needs of a particular audience. He explains why he chooses a particular organization for a specific group.
b. The student explains how he might change his paragraphing if his paper were being printed in narrow newspaper columns rather than on 8½" by 11" pages.

Performance Objective 4.H

The student discovers, identifies, and explains how the various relationships among words, sentences, paragraphs, and whole discourses are controlled by "rules" and manipulated by the writer at the same time.

Representative Enabling Objectives

a. In his writing, the student experiments with various ways of organizing words in a sentence. He willfully breaks "rules" to achieve new effects.
b. In his writing, the student organizes sentences into paragraphs in various ways to achieve various purposes and effects. He recognizes the need to be consciously aware of the tension between his own logical and intuitive organization and the needs of the reader. The more he desires communication, the more the needs of the reader must be considered.
c. In his writing, the student recognizes and consciously makes connections among various parts of a piece of discourse (i.e., the beginning and end, transitions, examples, signposts, etc.).

Goal 5

The student recognizes and consciously makes use of the dynamic and organic relationships among his purpose for writing, the mode of his discourse, his role or speaking voice, the subject of his writing, and the audience for whom it is being written.[3]

Performance Objective 5.A

The student takes a single topic and writes about it to achieve different aims or purposes.

Representative Enabling Objectives

a. Given a topic such as a popular music group, a political candidate or issue, an athletic team, a new car, an ecological or economic issue, the student writes about it in order:

   (1) to express his own opinions, feelings, and ideas;
   (2) to explain objectively the issues or attributes of the object or topic;
   (3) to persuade an audience to accept a particular point of view about the topic.

b. The student creates a drama or short story in which the topic, issue, or object is treated in a fictional way.

---

[3] Many of the ideas and some of the terminology of the objectives under this goal are based upon or drawn from *A Theory of Discourse*, James L. Kinneavy (New York: Prentice-Hall, 1971). This monumental work is essential background for all teachers of writing. See also *Writing As a Process of Discovery*, Jenkinson and Seybold (Bloomington: Indiana University Press, 1970) and Janet Emig, *The Composing Processes of Twelfth Graders* (NCTE: 1971).

Performance Objective 5.B

The student writes about a single topic using various dominant modes of discourse.

Representative Enabling Objective

Given a film, or book, or some other medium, the student writes:

(1) a brief historical account (narration) of the making or writing of the film or book, or how it takes its place in the history of the genre;

(2) a brief analysis (description) of the structural, symbolic, etc. elements of the film or book;

(3) a brief criticism (evaluation) of the film or book;

(4) a paper in which the film or book, etc. is placed into some kind of theoretical system (classification) by which it can be compared to other similar and dissimilar books and films.

Performance Objective 5.C

The student identifies the various kinds of distance that can exist between himself and his subject.[4]

Representative Enabling Objectives

a. The student writes about an event as he observes it, recording as accurately as possible what happens.

b. The student writes about an event after it has occurred and gives an accurate account of what happened.

c. The student, drawing from his past experience, writes an essay in which he makes generalizations about what happens when certain conditions obtain. (He can talk about sports, politics, music, etc.)

d. The student writes an essay in which he theorizes upon what might or will happen if . . . (This can be on a scientific, philosophical, economic, political problem, etc.)

Performance Objective 5.D

The student identifies the various kinds of distance that can exist between him and his audience.

Representative Enabling Objective

The student identifies various audiences for whom he might write and lists and explains the various distance problems he might face in trying to communicate with each. Such problems might include:

[4] This objective and the one that follows are based on *Teaching the Universe of Discourse*, James Moffett (Boston: Houghton Mifflin Co., 1968). Against "pre-teaching," Moffett advocates students' inductive discovery.

spatial distance
ideological distance
language distance
chronological distance
ethnic distance
occupational distance
racial distance
educational distance

He then writes for several different audiences.

Performance Objective 5.E

The student writes with an obvious conscious awareness of his purpose, role, mode, audience, and subject.

> Most of the goals and objectives in this Writing Section are directly or indirectly related to those in other sections. The objectives under Goal 6, for instance, are only suggestive of those language objectives relevant to writing. The teacher should see Chapter IV for appropriate objectives, other than those indicated here.

Goal 6

The student becomes aware of the particular attributes of words that give language its power, flexibility, and usefulness as a means of discovering, composing, creating, and communicating.

Performance Objective 6.A

The student recognizes that the "meaning" of a given word may have as many as three aspects: it *refers* to a class of objects; it *denotes* the defining characteristics of the objects in that they belong to that class (as defined by a dictionary); it *connotes* or suggests what the individual or people in general associate with objects of that class. *See also* III 7.Ba; IV 20.A and 21.

Representative Enabling Objectives

a. Given words in context, such as those in the following list, the student identifies the referent or lack of one and lists as many meanings as he can for each word. The student further discusses the various denotative and connotative meanings of each word.

unicorn	elephant
electron	nurse
socialism	school

b. Given several sets of synonyms (words that have essentially the same denotation and referent) such as those that follow, the student identifies the connotative meaning(s) of each word in each set and explains which word of each set he would use to evoke a particular response from an audience.

(1) boy, lad, stripling, minor
(2) friend, pal, buddy
(3) thin, skinny, slim, emaciated

Performance Objective 6.B

The student recognizes the differences between concrete and abstract words and uses them effectively and appropriately in his writing. (Ultimately he renders abstractions by means of concrete objects. See V 22.Ad.)

Representative Enabling Objectives

a. Given a selection of prose (preferably his own), the student distinguishes between concrete (e.g., *cow, book*) and abstract (e.g., *decision, loyalty*) nouns.
b. Given a selection of prose (preferably his own), the student distinguishes between concrete and abstract verbs, adjectives, and adverbs.
c. The student distinguishes among several words and phrases used at various levels of abstraction, such as:

Kathy wore hot pants to class.
Seniors are very casual in their choice of clothes.
College students wear wild outfits.
Young people have no respect for rules or proper dress.
The behavior of the younger generation is shameful.

d. The student uses concrete and specific language whenever possible and appropriate in his writing. When necessary and appropriate he uses abstract language, but only when it is made clear and specific through example and/or definition. (See V 22.Ad.)

Performance Objective 6.C

The student distinguishes between words and phrases that are used to make factual statements in a given context and those that convey opinion. *See also* III 13.

Representative Enabling Objectives

a. Given a series of sentences such as those below, the student fills the blanks with those words or phrases that convey specific factual information rather than opinions.

(1) Mr. Smith is a _____ teacher.
(2) That building is _____.
(3) Jim is a _____ player.
(4) _____ friends are few and far between.

b. In statements from various examples of expository prose that contain a mixture of fact and opinion, the student identifies and distinguishes between each.

c. After pursuing such investigations as those suggested in a. and b., the student establishes and examines the criteria for determining whether a statement is fact (observation/report) or opinion (judgment) or a mixture of both. Such criteria might include:

(1) Reports emphasize denotative meanings; judgments emphasize connotative meanings.
(2) Reports are true or false and can be verified; judgments are believed or not believed and cannot be verified.
(3) Judgments tend to be more persuasive in purpose; judgments are more subjective than reports.

d. Using the criteria developed for distinguishing between reports and judgments, the student examines several advertisements from magazines and catalogs and determines whether they are reports or judgments or combinations of each.

e. The student writes several advertisements or other short persuasive pieces using both reports and judgments and in class discussion decides which is more effective in achieving its purpose and why.

f. The student checks the use of his words in all of his writing to determine whether they are conveying observations or judgments and makes certain they are not performing one function when they are supposed to be performing the other.

Goal 7

The student uses language with accuracy when he writes. *See also* III 10; V 42; VII 14.Aa and 15.

Performance Objective 7.A

Given a situation and a purpose that require it, the student writes a detailed, accurate, factual account of what he has observed.

Representative Enabling Objectives

a. Given the assignment to select any object in the classroom or the immediate area,[5] the student writes a detailed objective description

---

[5] For instance, the class could be taken to another part of the school or out into the neighborhood. (Cf. Walker Gibson, *Seeing and Writing*, Longmans, 1961.)

of it. The accuracy and objectivity of the description will be determined by the ability of the class to identify the object and by their determination of whether the description is an observation or a judgment, and why.

b. Given the assignment to select any classmate or other available person as a subject, the student writes a detailed objective description of that person. The accuracy and objectivity of the description will be determined by the ability of the class to identify the person and by their determination of whether the description is an observation or a judgment, and why.

c. Given an observable incident such as an accident, a fight between two fellow students, a portion of a sports event, or a simulated incident, the student writes a detailed objective account of what happened. Whenever possible, his account will be checked against other accounts of the same incident. The language of the account will be critiqued by the class in small group discussion and/or the teacher.

d. After viewing a short incident in a film (made by the class, if possible), the student writes an accurate, objective account of what he has seen. He then watches the film again and compares his account to determine its accuracy.

e. The student compares the capabilities and limitations of the visual accuracy of a motion picture with the capabilities and limitations of the verbal accuracy of language.

Goal 8

The student uses language honestly when he writes.[6] *See also* III 11. (The objectives under this goal are one attempt to get at the nebulous problem of style in a more positive and concrete way than most writing instruction does. The objectives also attempt to deal with the contiguous problem of false and inflated diction contained in much student writing.)

Performance Objective 8.A

After reading and analyzing several pieces of writing which he has produced, which his classmates have written, and/or which he

---

[6] For excellent ideas and techniques for implementing the objectives under Goal 8, see: Janet Emig, *Composing Processes of Twelfth Graders* (NCTE, 1971); Ken Macrorie, *Writing to Be Read, Telling Writing*, and *Uptaught* (New York: Hayden Book Co., Inc., 1968, 1970, 1970). Walker Gibson, *Persona* (Random, 1969), *Tough, Sweet and Stuffy* (Bloomington: Indiana University Press, 1966); Monroe Beardsley, "Style and Good Style," in Tate and Corbett, eds., *Teaching H. S. Composition* (Oxford, 1970).

has found in print, the student develops criteria for defining honest writing.

Representative Enabling Objectives

a. After he has written a short descriptive account of a person or object, or an expository account of some topic or issue, the student tape records an oral account of the same person, object, topic, or issue without using his written account. He compares the language of the written and oral accounts and decides which is more honest and why he thinks so. (This may be more effective if the oral account comes first.)

b. Given examples of various accounts of the same subject, from his classmates, several newspapers, or some other source, the student explains, orally or in writing, which is most honest and why he thinks so.

Performance Objective 8.B

The student writes in language and in a voice that honestly expresses his subject in language that is clearly related to himself and the experiences he is writing about. *See also* V 23.

Representative Enabling Objectives

a. After he has written, the student asks another student to read his paper and paraphrase what he has read. The writer compares the paraphrase with the written original to see if it is an accurate rendering of what he has written.

   If it is not, the student discovers why by looking at the language he has used and comparing it with that of the paraphrase and that which he might have used if he had been speaking instead of writing. He makes changes where he thinks it is necessary and attempts to get an accurate paraphrase from another student.

b. The student rereads his writing to find dishonest, pretentious, and false writing. He revises to make the language and the voice more honest. One test he applies is to ask, How would I have said this orally? Is the oral account different from the written? If so, in what ways? Is the oral rendition more honest? Why? Would the oral account be appropriate in written form? If not, can it be changed to be appropriate? If not, how else might I say it that would be more honest than the first attempt?

c. The student rereads his writing, asking himself what kind of person the voice of the writing belongs to. Is it me or is it, at least, the person that I want to project in this particular piece of writing? If not, why not? How can I project the voice I want to project? [7]

---

[7] It might be useful here for the teacher to have the students submit samples of their writing to Walker Gibson's style machine in *Tough, Sweet, and Stuffy*.

Performance Objective 8.C

The student distinguishes between factual honesty and stylistic honesty, or the manner in which the facts are expressed.

Representative Enabling Objective

Given examples of writing that present factual truths, the student distinguishes those in which the language is pretentious, false, or dishonest. The student identifies the linguistic features which he believes separate the two.

Goal 9

The student explores and discovers ways in which oral language and non-verbal gestures are related to and conveyed by the written language. *See also* II 1.A; III 2; IV 20.A; V 36.A.

Performance Objective 9.A

Having witnessed an event in which the actions and gestures of the participants convey significant meaning, the student re-creates those actions and gestures through a written interpretation. *See also* II 13; IV 20; V 9.

Representative Enabling Objectives

a. Having prepared a written account of the physical actions of some event, such as a classroom pantomime or a portion of an athletic contest, the student gives an oral summary of what he has seen and recorded. He compares a transcript of his oral summary with his written recording of the event to discover the similarities and differences between the two. (He may compose his oral draft on a tape, as Tovatt and Miller describe in "The Sound of Writing," *Research in the Teaching of English*, Fall, 1967.)

b. Given an event with significant gestures, such as a pantomime, a film without sound, a sporting event, etc., the student writes an interpretation of the meaning of the gestures and actions that he has observed. Such an interpretation cites specific correspondences between the gestures and the meaning they conveyed to the student, along with the reasons for interpreting each as he did.

c. Given several written interpretations of the same event, the student compares and contrasts the various interpretations, including:

   (1) a discussion of the actions and gestures which tended to be interpreted in the same way by all students;

   (2) a discussion and definition of symbolic and conventional gestures;

(3) a discussion of those actions and gestures that tended to be given several—sometimes conflicting—interpretations;

(4) a discussion of the various ways that non-verbal communication can be translated into writing.

Goal 10

The student experiments with and uses different styles and voices in his writing. *See also* III 1.Ae, 4, and 16; IV 11.A and 12.D; V 14.E.

Performance Objective 10.A

The student writes dialog that successfully conveys to his reader the individual distinctions among speakers in a narrative. The student uses the written language to convey recognizable speech habits, such as word choice, idiom, sentence structure, and idiosyncratic phrases and patterns. *See also* IV 12.

Representative Enabling Objectives

a. Given hypothetical situations and paired roles to play, the student assumes one role in a pair (i.e., speeder/policeman, waiter/diner, teacher/principal, hippie/football player), and then each pair improvises a short dialog. Their dialog demonstrates clear linguistic clues to the role they are playing.

b. After listening to a dialog between two distinct role-figures, the student identifies those linguistic elements that help him distinguish each role and the relationships between each pair. The student then discusses in writing how each role characterization might be improved through changes in the language of the dialog. He defends each change that he suggests.

c. The student listens to the speech of five different people and transcribes on paper a brief portion of what he hears. The student then revises each passage to emphasize the speech differences of each person. He then identifies the changes he has made, the categories that such changes might fall into, and his reasons for making particular changes in the speech of each person. (The identity of the speaker may be an important factor here. Does he attempt to distinguish teachers from students, executives from laborers, etc.? If so, how is this done and what validity does it have?)

d. Given a hypothetical situation in which one person is describing an event to another person, the student writes a dialog describing the event as told by such role-players as the following or by alternative roles the student may prefer:

(1) an ardent boy to his girlfriend

(2) a boy as mentor to another boy (or to a younger brother or sister)

(3) a devoted boy to his mother
(4) a rebellious boy to his father
(5) a busybody girl as informer to each of the above

Goal 11

The student directs his writing to various audiences. *See also* III 7.Bc and 16.Ac.

Performance Objective 11.A

Except when he has written something like a personal diary or journal entry, the student shares his writing with others in the class to get their reactions and comments aside from a teacher's feedback.

Performance Objective 11.B

The student frequently writes for various audiences.

Representative Enabling Objectives

a. The student extracts a passage from his journal and rewrites it for his classmates.
b. Given an account of an important event in his life that he has written for his own use or amusement, the student revises it to serve a particular purpose for a specific audience.
c. Given a topic of concern to the student, he writes a paper or a letter to the editor, when appropriate, for an audience who he feels needs to read his views on the topic.
d. When he has written a short story, a poem, or an article that he likes, the student submits it to an appropriate publication (school paper or magazine, newspaper or magazine, etc.).

Performance Objective 11.C

The student identifies and analyzes the audience for whom he is writing.

Representative Enabling Objective

The student asks questions that define the essential and relevant characteristics of his audience, such as:

(1) Is this a homogeneous or heterogeneous group?
(2) What is the age of the group? Does this have any bearing on what I will say and how I will say it? If so, what?
(3) Are there socio-economic, educational, or cultural factors that are important to consider when writing about this topic to this particular audience?

(4) Is the audience likely to be receptive, hostile, or neutral to what I have to say? Is this significant considering the purpose I hope to achieve?

(5) What don't I know about the group that I ought to know? How can I find this information?

Performance Objective 11.D

The student determines his purpose—the effect or behavioral response he seeks to evoke from his audience.[8]

Representative Enabling Objective

The student asks questions that identify the effects he wants to produce upon his audience such as:

(1) How do I want my audience to respond?

(2) What effect do I want this piece of writing to have upon their behavior?

(3) What do I need to put into the writing to evoke the response I want in my audience?

Performance Objective 11.E

The student evaluates his available materials and knowledge in terms of its appropriateness and effectiveness for achieving his desired effects upon his audience.

Representative Enabling Objectives

a. The student asks questions that help him to choose the material most relevant to his purpose and audience. Such questions might include:

(1) How will this bit of information help me achieve my purpose? Why?

(2) How will my audience respond to this information? Why? Will that response help me to achieve my purpose?

(3) What material should I leave out? What material might detract from my purpose? Can cutting or tightening help?

b. The student asks questions that determine the completeness and clarity of his material. Such questions might include:

(1) Have I given the reader enough information about this aspect of my topic for the purpose of this paper? If not, what additional information do I need? Where can I find it?

---

[8] For one treatment of this and related points see "Reading and Writing Exposition and Argument: The Skills and Their Relationships," Morris Finder, *English Journal*, May, 1971. Finder regards *effect* as the acid test for *purpose*.

(2) Is this point perfectly clear? Will my reader interpret it the way that I mean it? What other interpretations might he give it? How can I change or augment the material to lessen the chances of misinterpretation and enhance the chances of achieving my purpose with this particular audience?

(3) Do I have the words to deal with the topic? How can I sharpen my vocabulary to deal more precisely with the subject? Will my readers understand my language? Can a thesaurus help?

c. The student will look again at the material he has left out and determine if there is anything there that ought to be included. He might ask such questions as:

Why have I left this out? Is it not important or has it been covered by some other information? If it were more complete or expressed in a different way, could it be used? Why or why not?

Performance Objective 11.F

The student seeks additional material and knowledge that is essential for producing his intended effect upon the audience. *See also* V 6.

Representative Enabling Objectives

a. While asking questions about his audience similar to those in 11.E, the student examines facts, ideas, and opinions other than his own on the subject, and uses those which are appropriate in producing the desired effect upon the reader.

b. The student uses reference books, reader's guides, books, articles, interviews, and any other appropriate source for information, interpretations, points of view, etc., that give him new and additional knowledge about his topic.

Performance Objective 11.G

The student organizes his material in order to most effectively achieve his intended effect upon his audience.

Representative Enabling Objectives

a. The student lists at least four or five possible ways of arranging the material that he has gathered.

b. The student asks questions about each possible arrangement as it relates to his purpose and audience. Such questions might include:

(1) Should I begin with my strongest points, my most obvious?

(2) Does the purpose seem to dictate a logical, chronological, or psychological approach? Does the material, the purpose, and

the audience suggest or require a different approach or a combination of approaches?

(3) Which arrangement will be the easiest for my audience to follow? Why? Will this arrangement also be the most effective in achieving the purpose? Why or why not? If not, why not? Does this mean that there is perhaps another arrangement or combination of arrangements that I ought to consider?

Performance Objective 11.H

The student adapts a written presentation of one subject for significantly different audiences. *See also* III 10.Ah; IV 23.A.

Representative Enabling Objectives

a. Given a subject (i.e., rock music, a Shakespearean play, souping a car, surfboarding), the student writes a short paper about the subject for several different people, such as:

(1) his father or mother;
(2) his grandfather or grandmother;
(3) his younger brother or sister;
(4) his teacher;
(5) a boy or girl his own age who knows little or nothing about the subject.

b. Given papers on the same subject written for three or four different audiences (as in 11.Ha), the student, orally or in writing, does such things as the following:

(1) identifies the audience for whom each paper was intended;
(2) identifies the linguistic features of each paper that contribute to its success in communicating with the particular audience;
(3) suggests changes (e.g., rendering and tightening) that would make each paper more effective in achieving its purpose, and explains why such changes would improve each paper.

Performance Objective 11.I

The student distinguishes between optional and required punctuation and other graphic conventions of writing (e.g., capitalization, paragraph indentation) to achieve clarity and ease of understanding for his audience in order that his purpose might be more effectively accomplished.

Representative Enabling Objectives

a. Given a prose passage with no paragraph indentation, no punctuation marks, and printed all in lower-case letters, the student reads it aloud to the class or members of a small group. Each person then punctuates the passage and compares his copy with others in the group.

b. Given a fully punctuated passage, the student marks out punctuation that he believes superfluous, designating that which he considers conventional, and that which he considers essential and/or useful to clarity and ease of understanding. The student orally defends his decisions.

c. Given examples of his own prose in which his punctuation causes difficulty or confusion for the reader, the student makes revisions that lead to greater clarity and achievement of his purpose. He tests his changes on a sample audience.

Performance Objective 11.J

When writing for an audience, the student uses the spelling system that would be most effective in achieving the desired response from his audience. *See also* IV 5.B, 9.A, and 17.A.

Representative Enabling Objectives

a. Given instruction in the morphemic-graphemic correspondences of English, the student demonstrates recognition of certain patterns in the English spelling system.[9]

b. After examining a large body of his own work and developing a system for classifying his own spelling errors, the student classifies his own error tendencies in a "log" and uses this information to avoid and detect spelling errors in his own work.

c. Given some representative mnemonics for words frequently misspelled (e.g., "at-ten-DANCE," "env IRON ment," "have a PIEce of PIE," etc.), the student invents (and records in his log) mnemonics of his own for spelling words that are troublesome to him. (See "Spelling," *Modern English Glossary*, Grosset, 1971.)

d. The student uses a dictionary to check and correct his own spelling.

Goal 12

The student recognizes the necessity and value of revising and rewriting and revises his own work as part of the normal writing process.

[9] The teacher may find useful in helping students with this objective, Research Report OE–32008 of the Cooperative Research Bureau, U. S. Office of Education: Paul R. Hanna *et al. Phoneme-Grapheme Correspondences as Cues to Spelling Improvement.* Washington, D. C.: U. S. Government Printing Office, 1966. "The Purdue Survey on Spelling" NCTE *Councilgram*, Nov. 1967, or *Spelling 1500*, J. N. Hook (New York: Harcourt Brace Jovanovich, 1967.)

Performance Objective 12.A

After completing a draft, the student revises it to make it more effective in achieving its purpose for its intended audience.[10] Revising systematically, he may file drafts in a folder.

Representative Enabling Objectives

a. The student reads his paper silently, looking for technical errors and asking himself if he has said what he meant to say, if what he has said is clear, if what he has said seems to achieve his purpose. He makes additions, deletions, and corrections that clarify what he has said or make it more effective or appropriate for his audience.
b. The student reads his paper aloud several times, listening carefully for punctuation errors, repetitions, poor arrangements of sentences and paragraphs, inappropriate word choices, ambiguities, etc.
c. The student reads his paper aloud to another person, preferably someone who could be a member of the audience for whom he is writing, and asks that person if the paper achieves its purpose, if it is clear, if its arrangement is useful, if the words are effective and appropriate. The student makes changes where appropriate and/or necessary.
d. The student asks a classmate or other person to read his paper and make suggestions that will help the paper to achieve its purpose more effectively. The student makes changes based on such suggestions when they are appropriate, responding especially to marginal and terminal questions.

Goal 13

The student recognizes the various factors that influence point of view, and the way point of view manifests itself in the sending and receiving of messages. *See also* II 9; III 7.C; IV 22.A and 23.A.

Performance Objective 13.A

The student analyzes how both logistic and attitudinal points of view are used in conveying messages.

Representative Enabling Objectives

a. Given two or more photographs of the same object (e.g., an automobile, a building, etc.) from two or more distinct vantage points,

---

[10] This Performance Objective and all of the Representative Enabling Objectives under it are based on the revision step in *Writing as a Process of Discovery* by Edward B. Jenkinson and Donald A. Seybold (Bloomington: Indiana University Press, 1970). *See also* Ken Macrorie, "Tightening," *Telling Writing* (N.Y.: Hayden, 1970).

the student discusses the various effects each has upon him and the various purposes each might serve.

b. Given two or more photographs of the same event, (e.g., a boxing match or other sporting event, an accident, etc.) from two or more distinct vantage points, the student discusses the various effects each has upon him and the various purposes each might serve.

c. Given several different accounts of the same event (from newspapers, magazines, speeches), the student analyzes and compares each writer's sensory emphasis, word choices, sentence structure, and inclusion and/or omission of details, and identifies those elements that indicate a particular point of view.

d. Given a set of articles, such as those in 13.Ac, the student identifies some of the influences that may have determined or influenced the point of view of the author of each article or speech.

e. Given an editorial cartoon(s), the student describes in writing the artist's point of view concerning the subject of the cartoon. Such a paper may include one or more of the following:

(1) the cartoonist's attitude toward his subject;

(2) the factors that seem significant in determining the cartoonist's point of view (political, social, geographical, etc.);

(3) a verbal statement of the cartoon's non-verbal statement or "message";

(4) the student's reaction to the problem; how it is similar to or different from the cartoonist's and why;

(5) the student's reaction to the effectiveness of the cartoon, and the reasons why he thinks it is effective or ineffective.

f. Given an art object, such as an impressionistic painting, a drawing, or a piece of sculpture, the student describes in writing his response to the object and explains the factors that seemed to influence his particular response to the object.

g. Given several varied responses to the same object, such as those in 13.Af, the student discusses the differences and identifies the factors that seem to have influenced the various points of view.

h. Given an abstract word, such as *love, hate, courage, justice, truth, wealth,* the student writes a definition of the word based on his conception of what the word means. The student compares his definition with those of other students and discusses the various sources and influences that have affected each student's extended definition of the word.[11]

---

[11] For one treatment of a writing assignment for this objective, see *Writing as a Process of Discovery* by Edward B. Jenkinson and Donald A. Seybold (Bloomington: Indiana University Press, 1970).

Performance Objective 13.B

The student writes with a clearly defined point of view.

Representative Enabling Objectives

a. Given a situation, event, or series of events in which the student was a participant, the student writes an account of that event from his point of view. His task is to make the readers see and feel what he saw and felt as he experienced the event.
b. Given an event in which at least three students were involved, the student writes an account of the event from his own point of view as well as from the point of view of both of the other participants. The student then:

(1) discusses his paper with student readers to determine his success in distinguishing among the points of view;
(2) identifies the significant factors contributing to the different points of view and the ways that the differences can be conveyed in writing.

Goal 14

The student recognizes, responds to, and is able to convey and control tone in various media. *See also* III 16.

Performance Objective 14.A

The student identifies ways in which tone is conveyed through various non-verbal media. *See also* II 8.

Representative Enabling Objectives

a. After listening to several selections of popular, and classical instrumental, music, the student discusses how and why the music conveys a certain tone or mood.
b. After looking at several photographs and/or paintings, the student discusses the tone or mood of each and describes how such things are rendered in the pictures.
c. The student views several scenes from one or more films and describes the tone or mood of each and the ways in which the effects were achieved. (Here, especially, various combinations of light, color, setting, and music might be present.)
d. The student makes a film, takes a photograph, draws or finds a picture, plays or selects some music to convey and augment the tone or mood of a poem he has written himself or has selected to present to the class.

Performance Objective 14.B

After extensive class discussion and the reading and analysis of many works of fiction and non-fiction, the student recognizes that writers convey both meaning and attitude through tone. The student demonstrates his recognition of this fact by using a specific tone to deliberately convey meaning and attitude in his own writing. *See also* V 21.J.

Representative Enabling Objectives

a. The student analyzes several editorials from various newspapers, and several letters to the editor, and describes the tone of each. He cites specific examples from the text of each editorial or letter to support his description of the tone.
b. The student writes an operational definition of tone and isolates ways in which he believes tone can be conveyed through the written language.
c. Given a writing assignment in which he is asked to respond to someone who has made him very angry, the student writes a letter in which he tells the person to whom he is writing what he thinks of him. The student edits the letter to assure appropriate tone.[12]
d. The student describes an event or a person so that the reader cannot detect the writer's attitude toward or feeling about the event or person.
e. The student describes an event or a person so that the reader responds to/detects the writer's attitude toward or feeling about the event or person.

Goal 15

Through writing documentaries, feature articles, and other pieces, the student investigates various topics of interest to him.

Performance Objective 15.A

Settling on a topic of his own choosing, the student seeks out several sources of information.

Representative Enabling Objectives

a. Given a topic of interest that he wants to write about, the student reads at least two books and six articles about the topic. (Or views

[12] For one treatment of a writing assignment for this objective, see *Writing as a Process of Discovery* by Edward B. Jenkinson and Donald A. Seybold (Bloomington: Indiana University Press, 1970).

an appropriate film or TV program.) Such sources will cover a range of opinion on the topic.

   b. The student uses the resources of local libraries.

   c. The student uses available human resources and correspondents to get information.

Performance Objective 15.B

After thought and research on a topic of interest to him the student takes a position, which he presents to an audience through writing.

Representative Enabling Objectives

   a. The student prepares a short statement of his position on a given topic and his main arguments and support.

   b. The student decides which documents he has seen or read will be used as support for his position. (He demonstrates that the authorities are being used to support his position, not that he is supporting them.)

   c. The student demonstrates an awareness of various appropriate viewpoints, opinions, ideas, and attitudes by direct and indirect reference to them whenever appropriate in his writing.

   d. The student supports his position with such devices as narrative examples, digressions, asides, or footnotes where appropriate.

   e. The student supports his position with appropriate quotations.

   f. The student takes no position except his own without documenting it according to the style sheet of the class or the publication for which he is writing.

Goal 16

The student uses writing as an outlet for his imagination.

Performance Objective 16.A

The student augments/adapts/reinterprets imaginative literature, films, and TV programs through his own imaginative writing.

Representative Enabling Objectives

   a. After reading a story or play, or watching a film, a drama, or a TV program, the student augments/adapts/reinterprets a portion of the piece or a character in it. He might do such things as rewriting the ending, adding interior monolog or exterior dialog, etc.

   b. The student rewrites a short story as a play, or film or TV script. (Or he changes a script into a short story.)

c. The student writes a fictionalized or dramatized account of an historical or biographical document he has read.

Performance Objective 16.B

The student writes imaginative stories and plays drawn directly and indirectly from his own experiences and those of others.

Representative Enabling Objectives

a. The student recalls a childhood incident that he uses as the basis for a short story or play.
b. The student writes a fairy tale or myth to explain some common experience.
c. The student writes a story projecting the present into the future.

Performance Objective 16.C

The student writes poetry when he chooses to do so and in a format that he finds comfortable.[13]

Representative Enabling Objectives

a. The student finds examples of the poetic use of language in prose writing, his own writing, advertising, speeches, etc.
b. The student keeps a journal in which he records lines he sees, hears, and writes that he considers poetic.
c. The student plays with words and combinations of words to discover new patterns, sounds, and insights.
d. The student works with the class to create a group poem.
e. The student writes lyrics for a song that he or a classmate set to music.
f. The student experiments with many conventional poetic forms, such as limericks, haiku, cinquains, sonnets, etc.

Goal 17

The student discovers himself through writing by increasing his sensitivity to, and awareness of, his own perceptions, emotions, and ideas.

Performance Objective 17.A

The student records his perceptions, emotions, and ideas accurately and clearly in his writing so that the reader interprets the

[13] For many excellent ideas on teaching poetry see *Wishes, Lies, and Dreams,* Kenneth Koch (New York: Chelsea House, 1970) and *English Through Poetry Writing,* Brian Powell (Itasca, Ill.: F. E. Peacock Publishers, 1968).

written expression in essentially the same way that the writer intended it.

Representative Enabling Objectives

a. The student describes a feeling or idea in writing and revises it until the reader can paraphrase the idea to the writer's satisfaction.
b. Given sentences from his own writing such as:

  (1) It was beautiful;
  (2) I was really scared;
  (3) The animal was huge;
  (4) The man looked suspicious;
  (5) It was a good idea;

  the student rewrites them, replacing the vague statements with concrete words and images that make the reader see and feel what the writer has described. (See "Rendering," *Modern English Glossary*, Grosset).

Performance Objective 17.B

The student frequently writes about a problem, issue, or emotion that he doesn't fully control. He uses the writing to clarify the issue, problem, or emotion in his own thinking.

Representative Enabling Objectives

a. Given a topic of his own choosing that is troublesome to him, the student writes a letter to a real or imaginary friend explaining his dilemma.
b. Given a topic that troubles him, the student writes about it as he imagines two people who have solved it in alternate ways might explain their positions.
c. Given a topic that troubles him, the student writes a short story, play, or poem about it.

Performance Objective 17.C

The student writes frequently to communicate his ideas, attitudes, and questions to others, using various techniques and forms, and for various audiences and purposes.

VII

Exploring the Mass Media

RATIONALE

For virtually all of their lives, students will rely upon the mass media for news, interpretation of news, information, and entertainment as well as for a great part of their informal education and an ever-increasing part of their formal education. Many of the decisions they will make and the opinions they will hold will be based upon what they read in the printed media (newspapers, magazines, and books) and upon what they see or hear on the electronic media (radio, television, and films). Much of what they do, say, and buy will be the result of their responses to what the mass media disseminate. Therefore, it is imperative that high school teachers of English do everything they can to help students become discriminating consumers of the mass media.

The objectives in this chapter are designed for courses in English —not solely for the introductory part of an elective course in journalism since not all students take journalism. Therefore, the objectives are not concerned with newswriting, copyediting, preparing the student newspaper and yearbook, and so forth, which are the goals of beginning and advanced courses in journalism.

The project director in charge of this section, Edward B. Jenkinson, Director of the English Curriculum Study Center and Associate Professor of Education, Indiana University, was assisted by several consultants.

205

Representative Entering Performance Objectives

Note: The designers of this section of the catalog believe a student—be he a ninth grader or a twelfth grader—should be able to complete performance objectives like these before he begins the objectives on the mass media. The developers of this section further believe that junior high school students can complete some of these objectives.

Entering Objective A.   Given a list of words like these:

run	ring
set	group
take	stand
look	stamp
game	race

the student lists as many things as he can that each word can refer to. He explains, orally or in writing, that men can give many meanings to the same word and that many of these meanings are listed in a good standard desk dictionary.

Entering Objective B.   Given sentences like these:

1. The high school *stands* on the side of a hill.
2. The *stands* were filled with partisan fans.
3. The voters challenged Senator Snort's *stands* on many issues.
4. He always *stands* on his own two feet.
5. Jack's offer still *stands* if you are ready for hard work.

the student explains, orally or in writing, how he can sometimes determine the meaning of a word by its use in a specific context.

Entering Objective C.   Given sentences written in different historical periods and sentences in which one or more familiar words seem to carry unfamiliar meanings, the student explains, orally or in writing, how words can change meaning in time as well as in context.

Entering Objective D.   Given a sentence like this:

"We will end the war," the President said.

the student substitutes five different verbs of attribution for *said* and explains how each substitution affects the message.

Entering Objective E.   Given a list of words that obviously trigger emotional responses in most people even when they see them in isolation, the student explains, orally or in writing, connotative meanings of words.

The list might include words like these:

racist	hippie
black power	yippie
white supremacy	pig
riot	death
pot	school

Entering Objective F. After listening to the same word spoken in three different sentences with slightly different intonation patterns or emphasis which seem to change the meaning of the word, the student explains, orally or in writing, how people can change the meanings of words by the way they say them.

Entering Objective G. After listening to one sentence spoken with the same intonation pattern but with different accompanying non-verbal acts of communication, the student explains, orally or in writing, how non-verbal acts of communication, such as facial expressions and gestures, can change the meaning of a verbal message.

Entering Objective H. Given a newspaper, the student demonstrates his ability to get the message off the page by giving an accurate oral summary and/or explanation of the stories on the front page or by answering questions which measure his comprehension.

Performance Objectives

Goal 1

The student considers the elements in acts of communication.

Performance Objective 1.A

The student identifies the basic elements present in any act of communication as sender, receiver, medium, and message. *See also* II 3.A; VI A.*

Representative Enabling Objective

a. Asked to examine acts of communication such as those in the list below, the student correctly identifies the sender, receiver, medium, and message.

1. a news story in a local newspaper
2. a television commercial
3. an editorial in a newspaper, in a magazine, on radio, or on television

* Roman numerals refer to chapters, Arabic numerals to goals, capital letters to performance objectives, and lower-case letters to enabling objectives.

4. the V symbol (A person raises the index finger and middle finger on one hand.)

   (The student explains how the situation affects the message. For example, he explains that the meaning of the V symbol is not the same at a peace rally as at a Scout meeting.)
5. a radio program
6. a magazine article
7. a billboard

Goal 2

The student compares individual and mass communication.

Performance Objective 2.A

The student explains, orally or in writing, the differences betwen individual and mass communication.

Representative Enabling Objectives

a. Given a personal letter and a letter to the editor of a daily newspaper, the student explains, orally or in writing, how and why the language, the use of background information, and so forth, differ and how they are similar.
b. Given a speech by any public official, such as a mayor, to a small group of people and a speech by the President to the nation over television, the student analyzes, orally or in writing, the differences between the two and also tells how they are similar.
c. Given a play to be presented in a small theater and a situation comedy to be presented on television, the student analyzes, orally or in writing, their differences and similarities.

Goal 3

The student understands why people communicate.

Performance Objective 3.A

The student identifies, orally or in writing, various purposes for both individual and mass communication.

Representative Enabling Objectives

a. Given examples of different kinds of personal communication in various contexts, the student tells, orally or in writing, the purpose of each act of communication and defends his position.
b. Given examples of different kinds of mass communication, the stu-

dent tells, orally or in writing, the purpose of each act of communication and defends his position.

Goal 4

The student distinguishes between fact and opinion. *See also* III 10.Ae; IV 22.A.

Performance Objective 4.A

The student correctly identifies the statements of fact and the statements of opinion in a news story.

Representative Enabling Objectives

a. Given sentences such as those below, the student identifies the statements of fact and the statements of opinion.

   1. John is fat.
   2. John is 5'6" tall and weighs 245 pounds.
   3. On April 20, 1970, President Nixon promised the withdrawal of 150,000 troops from Vietnam during the next twelve months.
   4. The United States was fighting an unjust war in Vietnam.
   5. The major problem in the United States is pollution.
   6. Marijuana is not habit-forming.
   7. (name of local high school) defeated (name of opponent) in basketball, (score).

b. Given a number of sentences, some of which are statements of fact, the student correctly identifies the statements of fact and explains, orally or in writing, why he would classify some statements of fact as historical, scientific, and so forth.
c. The student writes a working definition of fact.
d. After identifying ten statements of fact, the student changes them into statements of opinion by inserting a word or a phrase in each sentence to change the statement from fact to opinion.
e. The student writes a working definition of opinion.

Goal 5

The student recognizes the importance of the media's reporting the opinions of politicians, scientists, educators, and so forth.

Performance Objective 5.A

Given a news story in which the opinions of an important political figure are reported, the student identifies the statements of opinion and explains why the reporting of such statements by the printed and electronic media is of value to the citizen.

Representative Enabling Objectives

a. Given a news story in which the opinions of an important political figure are reported, the student identifies those opinions and also identifies any implied or expressed opinions of the reporter.
b. Given six direct quotations of a politician followed by the reporter's words like "he said" and "he screamed," the student identifies those verbs of attribution which reflect the reporter's opinion.

Goal 6

The student discovers what *news* is.

Performance Objective 6.A

The student identifies elements that tend to make a story newsworthy and writes his definition of news.

Representative Enabling Objectives

a. Given several items of information (some important, some unimportant, and some seemingly totally unrelated to any other statements on the list), the student decides which items he believes to be the most important, newsworthy, relevant, or interesting and tells why he thinks so.
b. The student decides which items of information in *a.* might be used on the front page of a local newspaper or on a local television news show or radio broadcast. (The items of information should range frm "the man bites dog" trivia to "the President withdraws troops from Vietnam," to "Mrs. Murphy catches flu.")
c. Given ten clippings of news stories that are approximately the same length, the student decides which of the stories are the most newsworthy, and he explains why he thinks so. The student compares his selections and reasons with those of other students, analyzing the differences of opinion.
d. The student identifies, orally or in writing, the ingredients that seem to make stories *news* stories.

Goal 7

The student discovers how news is gathered.

Performance Objective 7.A

Given several typical but different incidents or events, the student decides how he—if he were a reporter—would gather the facts of the events.

Representative Enabling Objectives

a. Given the task of reporting a meeting of a city council or other governmental group, the student explains, orally or in writing, how he would gather the facts.

b. Given the task of clarifying and expanding upon an actual announcement of a city official, the student explains, orally or in writing, how he would obtain additional information.

c. Assigned to report a speech in the school or community or on radio or television, the student explains, orally or in writing, how he would gather the information he needs to report the speech accurately. Assigned to report such a speech, he gathers the information, writes his report, and explains what he did.

d. Assigned to cover a catastrophe that just occurred and to which he was not an eyewitness, the student explains, orally or in writing, how he would gather the facts.

e. Assigned to report on a scheduled event such as a student demonstration or political rally, the student explains, orally or in writing, how he would gather the facts of the event. Assigned to report the event, he gathers the information, writes his report, and explains what he did.

f. Assigned to report on a controversial issue, the student explains, orally or in writing, how he would gather the facts of the controversy. Then he gathers information on a controversial issue, writes his story, and explains what he did.

Goal 8

The student discovers how newspapers gather information for the stories they report.

Performance Objective 8.A

The student examines a variety of newspaper stories and explains, orally or in writing, how he thinks the newspaper obtained the facts in each story. (The printed news stories should include events on the local, state, national, and international levels.)

Representative Enabling Objectives

a. Given several different local news stories (e.g., city council, accidents, achievement of local people), the student explains how he thinks the newspaper obtained the news. (Note: These representative enabling objectives could also apply to radio and television newscasting.)

b. Given several stories about news in the state (some with reporter bylines and some without them), the student explains how he thinks the newspaper obtained the news.

c. Given several stories about national and international events, the student explains how he thinks the newspaper obtained the news.

d. Given an opportunity to hear a newspaper reporter or radio or television newscaster explain how his medium gathers news on local, state, national, and international events, the student compares his speculations on how news is gathered with what the reporter or newscaster says. He notes the difference, orally or in writing.

Goal 9

The student discovers how newspapers and radio and television stations rely on wire services and syndicates for much of their news, feature stories, and columns.

Performance Objective 9.A

After examining two or three newspapers published on the same day, the student identifies the news stories, columns, features, cartoons, and so forth, that appear in all of the papers and recognizes the sources of the stories.

Performance Objective 9.B

After listening to two or three five-minute radio newscasts broadcast by different stations on the same day, the student speculates on the sources of the stories that seem to be identical. After visiting a local station, he compares his speculations with what he learns on the field trip.

Performance Objective 9.C

The student reads about the wire services and how they gather and transmit news.

Performance Objective 9.D

The student compares the treatment of an important news story transmitted by a wire service in two different newspapers and on two different radio broadcasts. He should note the differences—if any—in the wording of the story, the length, and the placement in the newspaper or in the newcast.

Goal 10

The student discovers how radio and television gather the information for the local news stories they report.

Performance Objective 10.A

The student listens to a variety of local news stories broadcast by radio and television, and he explains, orally or in writing, how he thinks the radio and television stations obtained the facts in each story.

Goal 11

The student learns how to gather information for a news story and write it for a daily newspaper; how to rewrite it for a five-minute radio broadcast; finally, how to prepare the news story for television.

Performance Objective 11.A

Given an event to report, the student, as a part of a team of reporters, gathers the information for a newspaper story, a radio newscast, and a television newscast. The student decides what facts he or another member of the reporting team would include in the newspaper story. He also decides what—if anything—should be tape recorded for the radio broadcast. Finally, he decides what portion of the event should be photographed for television.

Performance Objective 11.B

The student compares the treatment of the event for the newspaper, the radio broadcast, and the television newscast.

Performance Objective 11.C

The student explains, orally or in writing, how complete and accurate his news story was for each medium (newspaper, radio, television).

Performance Objective 11.D

If a member of the reporting team filmed the event, or portions of it, the student explains how much of the event the viewer will actually see and from whose point of view he sees it.

Performance Objective 11.E

If one member of the team tape recorded comments of actors in the event, the student decides what portion of the comments the listener will hear in the newscast and explains how accurate a record of the event the listener will have after the tape has been edited.

Goal 12

The student recognizes that headlines are frequently used to summarize the news.

Performance Objective 12.A

The student analyzes different kinds of headlines in several newspapers, and he explains, orally or in writing, (1) what headlines are, (2) what they do, (3) what limitations are placed on them, and (4) what he needs to know to become an intelligent reader of headlines.

Representative Enabling Objectives

a. The student explains how most headlines attempt to summarize the major facts in a story.
b. The student demonstrates his ability to summarize a story in no more than eight words by writing, without being given a number of rules for writing headlines, short sentences that could be used as headlines for at least five different news stories.
c. The student identifies a minimum of four headlines that do not accurately summarize the facts in news stories.
d. The student explains, orally or in writing, how headline writers can, consciously or unconsciously, distort the facts in headlines.
e. The student examines various kinds of headlines, identifying the purpose of each. He notes that not all headlines are summaries of the news, and he explains the purpose of other types of headlines.
f. The student analyzes the headlines in several daily newspapers, and he explains, orally or in writing, how newspaper editors can emphasize certain stories through selection of type faces and type sizes, as well as through the actual words in the headlines.

Goal 13

The student recognizes headline summaries of news as broadcast by the electronic media.

Performance Objective 13.A

The student analyzes several radio and television newscasts and explains, orally or in writing, how reporters for the electronic media summarize the news for their listeners and viewers.

Goal 14

The student discovers how point of view affects both the collection and presentation of facts. *See also* II 9; III 7.C; V 12; VI 13.

Performance Objective 14.A

The student explains, orally or in writing, how physical, emotional and/or experiential points of view can affect a reporter's gathering and reporting of facts.

Representative Enabling Objectives

a. Given an opportunity to watch a specific event such as a basketball game from several different vantage points, the student explains, orally or in writing, how his vantage point affects his perception of the event and his ability to report the event accurately. *See also* III 10; V 42; VI 7.

b. The student discovers how the content of a photograph or a film of an event is affected by the time when the photograph or film was taken and by the vantage point from which it was taken.

c. Assigned to report only the facts about an event such as an athletic contest in which the student has some degree of involvement because of his connection with one of the teams, he explains, orally or in writing, how his emotional involvement affected his ability to gather and report all of the facts accurately.

d. Asked to consider how well he could gather information on a subject he knows little or nothing about, the student recognizes that his lack of experience with, or knowledge about, a certain subject affects his ability to gather facts and report them completely and accurately.

Goal 15

The student learns how to distinguish among objective, subjective, and interpretative reporting. *See also* III 10 and 11; V 39.A and 42; VI 7.

Performance Objective 15.A

The student reports the same set of facts three ways: objectively, subjectively, and interpretatively.

Representative Enabling Objectives

a. Given a set of facts, the student reports the facts objectively.

b. Given a set of facts, the student reports the facts subjectively.

c. Given a set of facts about a specific event, the student writes an interpretative account so that his readers will better understand the significance of the event.

d. After completing *a*, *b*, and *c*, the student explains how his choice of words has affected his stories.

Goal 16

The student discovers the various purposes of newspaper and radio feature stories and television documentaries.

Performance Objective 16.A

The student explains, orally or in writing, the purposes of different newspaper and radio feature stories and television documentaries, and he identifies given differences between such stories and news stories.

Goal 17

The student recognizes stories in newspapers and on radio and television that convey mostly opinion—not fact.

Performance Objective 17.A

The student identifies editorials, columns, letters to the editor, and political cartoons as stories or drawings reflecting primarily the opinions of the writer, cartoonist, or newspaper. The student explains, orally or in writing, why such expressions of opinion may be important to him.

Goal 18

The student analyzes opinion for its factual base and attempts to determine the validity of the opinion.

Performance Objective 18.A

The student analyzes an editorial and identifies, orally or in writing, the factual base of the opinion(s) expressed. The student evaluates the opinion(s), explaining why he thinks the conclusions the editorial writer draws are, or are not, valid.

Goal 19

The student recognizes various kinds of propaganda. *See also* III 10.Ae; III 12.Ab, d, and m; III 13.A.

Performance Objective 19.A

Given several examples of propaganda that are not labeled as such, the student identifies them as propaganda and detects the various techniques of the propagandist. (The student can identify such propaganda techniques as card-stacking, name-calling, and so forth, but he need not use the labels.)

Goal 20

The student evaluates advertising. *See also* III 7 Cc; III 10.Af; III 11.Ad and e; III 12.Ab, c, and d; III 13.Ab.

Performance Objective 20.A

After examining a number of different kinds of advertisements, the student devises a rating system by which he can evaluate ads for such things as (1) sophistication and legitimacy of the appeal, (2) good taste, (3) logic, (4) effective use of language, and (5) factual basis for the claims made.

Goal 21

The student evaluates arguments for and against advertising.

Performance Objective 21.A

Given the summaries of at least three published arguments for, and three arguments against, advertising, the student evaluates the pros and cons of advertising.

Goal 22

The student discovers how the media are supported in the United States.

Performance Objective 22.A

Given the pros and cons of advertising, the student explains, orally or in writing, the degree to which advertising revenue supports the media in the United States.

Goal 23

The student explores the entertainment aspects of the mass media.

Performance Objective 23.A

After describing the different kinds of entertainment the mass media provide, the student arrives inductively at his own definition of "entertainment."

Goal 24

The student considers how the entertainment provided by the mass media affects him.

Performance Objective 24.A

After discussing his reactions to various forms of entertainment provided by the mass media, the student explains, orally or in writing, how different kinds of entertainment affect his life. He notes changes in attitudes, buying habits, etc.

Goal 25

The student designs his own criteria for evaluating the entertainment provided by the mass media.

Performance Objective 25.A

After exploring the entertainment function of the media, the student writes his own critical standards for various kinds of entertainment from comic strips through situation comedies to "talk shows."

Goal 26

The student considers the possibilities of photographs.

Performance Objective 26.A

After examining a number of photographs, the student explains their effect on him. He discusses their informational value and emotional impact.

Performance Objective 26.B

The student takes a number of photographs of different events, people, and places, and explains, orally or in writing, how he intended his audience to react to them.

Performance Objective 26.C

The student attempts to tell a story or create a mood through a series of photographs.

Goal 27

The student considers the possibilities of motion picture film.

Performance Objective 27.A

The student completes the same objectives for motion picture film that he did for photographs. *See also* VII 26.

Goal 28

The student evaluates movies.

Performance Objective 28.A

After viewing and discussing different kinds of movies, the student explores the potential and limitations of different kinds of films and writes his own standards of evaluation.

Goal 29

The student decides how he can influence the mass media.

Performance Objective 29.A

After discussing the responsibilities of the mass media to an individual citizen, the student explains, orally or in writing, what he can do to persuade the media to provide him with the news and information he needs to be an informed citizen. He further explains what he can do to obtain the kind of entertainment he wants.

Index

(Note: Most index items refer to chapter, goals, and objectives. Thus, V 27E means Chapter V, goal 27, objective E. The only exceptions, such as p. 32, refer to pages.)